PRI
Made

Made to Soar is for the mom who feels she needs to be everything for everyone. For the mom who puts a smile on her face pretending everything is okay when on the inside she is desperately aching for something more. For the mom who feels guilty, shameful, and alone. For the mom who feels defeated disciplining her kids and wonders if she's doing anything right. Natalie Dawn Hanson confidently and vulnerably communicates that it is time to let go of the chains and walk in freedom, peace, and joy. *Made to Soar* leads women on a journey to discover radical freedom allowing them to embrace who they are in God and to live it out boldly in ways that will have lasting and powerful impact on their children and everyone in their lives.

—Niccie Kliegl, CLC Founder of Fulfill Your Legacy and
Author of *Awakening the Living Legacy* and
Embracing the Loving Legacy

Made to Soar speaks from one mother's spirit to another. Natalie Dawn Hanson's message is balm to the weary momma's soul. Her heartfelt sharing and encouragement provide grace and truth in order to support the reader during her journey. Yes, there are struggles raising children. Yes, you will get through it. With what I would consider a manual for moms, this book is certain to become a reference to visit again and again.

—Daphne V. Smith, Speaker, Wave Maker, and Author of
*What's YOUR Scarlet Letter?: Recognize Your Hurts,
Release Your Shame, Reclaim Your Voice*

Natalie Dawn Hanson shares with a beautiful vulnerability and honesty her journey from a restless and overwhelmed mom with a heavy heart to one who discovers the magnificent key to hope, peace, and joy to which she is moved to share with others. As a mom of four young boys, Natalie reflects honestly the fear and hopelessness of feeling like she was not enough. Weaving personal, heartfelt, relatable stories; the human narrative of Scripture; and the magnificent life cycle of the Monarch butterfly; *Made to Soar* invites each of us to engage our own journey of faith. We are inspired to feel confident that in the process we, too, will find a different and lasting kind of peace, joy, purpose, and freedom as we become more aware of the amazing grace that has been given to us by this God who created us to soar.

—Katie Christensen, Gallups Certified Strengths Coach

Made to Soar is for the mom who feels she needs to be enough for everyone in her world. For the mom who feels the load from the stress and the struggles that can be associated with motherhood. For the mom who is craving to feel more happiness throughout the day. For the mom who wants to feel more present with her children. This BEAUTIFULLY written book will leave joy in your heart and calmness in your mind. And if you're like me, your soul will feel an immediate connection to the author, Natalie Dawn Hanson. You can feel her heart for Jesus and for all of us moms through her words. She connects us all in the journey of motherhood and shares how to breakthrough some of those feelings. This book will change thousands of women's lives and beyond.

—Heather Godfrey, Lifestyle & Wellness Coach, Fitness Professional, and National Speaker

There's nothing like motherhood to uncover our imperfections and make us feel like we can never measure up. Through her authenticity, Natalie Dawn Hanson helps us realize that though we are not alone in these feelings, we can find freedom and peace through God's grace to not simply endure motherhood but to enjoy it. *Made to Soar* reminds me, and every mom, how precious we are and how as beloved daughters of the Most-High God we are meant to soar to unimaginable heights.

—Renee Vidor, Speaker and Author of
Measuring Up: How to Win in a World of Comparison

In writing this labor of love, Natalie Dawn Hanson has chosen to be vulnerable, and in so doing, has encouraged her readers and brought hope and healing to all of us who are plagued by the notion that we have to be perfect. In honestly sharing her struggles as a young mom and wife, she draws the reader in as a companion on her journey and we witness her dawning realization that God's love and grace meets us where we are, with all our imperfections, but does not leave us there. Recognizing God's amazing love transforms our lives to *live freely and joyfully in our divine purpose*. Natalie teaches us how to *breathe peace* by leaning on the source of all peace. As a reader, you can take this journey with Natalie because she invites us all to recognize our part in God's story of transformation intended for all of us. We are all meant to soar, and Natalie has taken flight in sharing her story.

—Pastor Jean Ohman, Lead Pastor at
United Lutheran Church

If you feel frustrated with your life, this book is for you. If you see yourself falling into habits of self-criticism, this book is for you. If you know there has to be more to life but cannot figure out how to find that "more," this book is for you. If you want to inspire another to reach for peace, this book is for you. Natalie Dawn Hanson—wife and mother, daughter and friend—opens her heart and life so readers can learn how to build a better life, a fuller life, a blessed life. Through her experiences, Natalie truly speaks to the heart of women. Her honesty about her struggles and failures and heartbreak teach us how to cope with the hazards of life's journey. As she illustrates through the monarch butterfly, we are God's creation, and through His heart, and hers, we learn to soar.

—Susan Snyder, Teacher and Librarian Who Follows Christ
Yet is More Caterpillar than Butterfly

As a mom, if you want to find relief from the stress of motherhood, if you need a faithful, understanding friend who gets what you are feeling and is bold enough to speak transforming truths to the depths of your soul, then *Made to Soar* is a must read. Natalie Dawn Hanson invites you into her journey of motherhood while encouraging you to listen to the story God is writing in your own life through your own struggles. It is a matter of the heart and is one Natalie challenges you to lean into, to find the relief you are searching for.

—Lanelle Vasichek, Speaker and Author of
Create the Mommy Milestones

Whether you're a new momma or an experienced one, a soon-to-be momma or an empty nester, *Made to Soar* will make you feel like you're sitting with your best friend cozied on the couch with a warm blanket and a hot cup of tea. The words so delicately structured will make you feel understood and not so alone. Weaving personal, relatable stories, Scripture, and the magnificent life cycle of the Monarch butterfly, Natalie Dawn Hanson vulnerably shares her heart filled with struggles and revelations and invites you to run with her into the freedom and joy of God's grace. As a mother of four myself, I understand the struggles of motherhood and trying to be all things to all people, all the time. While reading *Made to Soar*, I found parallels to raising my own children and felt the comforting reminder we're not in this mothering journey alone.

—Lisa Moser, Speaker, Coach and Author of
*Miss Conception: 5 Step to Overcome Our Misconceptions
and Achieve Our Own Crowning Moments*

What Mommas are Saying

Made to Soar came into my life at a time when I didn't know I was needing to hear the heartfelt messages shared in this book. Natalie has a gift of writing that speaks straight to a momma's soul. She not only inspires and encourages her readers, but she also has an ability to transcend generations with her gift of understanding and insight into motherhood and the challenges we all face. Her love for the Lord, her passion, and her wisdom help take stories from the Bible we have all heard and transform them into stories that resonate with struggles we as mothers face today. This book has shown me how my journey through motherhood is more than simply being okay and surviving—it can transform into so much more!

—Chelsey Anderson, Mom of Four

My grandmother always told me, "As long as you have a book along with you, you always have a friend." Natalie has made this saying so very true for me. She has intentionally crafted this book so you truly feel like your friend has reached into the depths of your soul alongside you to bring out what you genuinely fear and long for—the types of things you didn't really want to remember or make time to talk about. She has a way of bringing topics into the light so they aren't as overwhelming. Through every chapter, she continually highlights that our Father has created us with all we need to move through motherhood and points us toward His words to guide us. Before this, I hadn't read a book that requires a box of tissues, a journal, my running shoes, and a group text to all of my girlfriends to notify them, "Natalie thinks how we think, but instead of complaining, she found a better way to move through it." If you want to stop feeling like you're sinking, slow down enough to take this in because Natalie will teach you that you were made to soar.

—Leanne Elmer, Mom of Two

From first hearing the beginning thoughts of this book being written to seeing the designs of this cover, this book has impacted me to the core. Natalie has such a way with words. You feel like you are sitting right across from her listening to her speak them. She has impeccable detail to the very challenges of motherhood and all the relatable mom failures that occurred in her incredible journey to *really* finding Jesus. You can feel her faith growing as you read her words. So much so that you will magically feel your own faith grow right alongside hers. *Made to Soar* is a beautifully written book that will have lasting impact on all of its readers, for generations to come.

—Mindy Beyer, Mom of Three

Natalie has a remarkable way of connecting Scripture to the everyday challenges of motherhood. It made me appreciate the hectic, tiring, stressful life of a mom knowing tomorrow is a whole new day and I'm not the only one feeling the struggles. When you have reached a point where your patience is at its thinnest, Natalie reminds you to add grace instead of shame, which is something I think every mom can appreciate and embrace. *Made to Soar* had me feeling like I was sitting down over a cup of coffee with Natalie, and somehow, she knew exactly what I wanted to ask. She gives advice and opened my eyes to a new perspective on finding God's grace, peace, and joy, with some ah-ha moments thrown in.

—Charlene Blume, Mom of Two

Being a mom is a gift, and also sometimes very hard. This book taught me to give myself and my kids grace. It's easy to lose sight of what is truly important. Natalie taught me that teaching my children about their Heavenly Father is, by far, the greatest gift we can ever give them.

—Julie Loken, Mom of Three

Natalie's ability to mesh the honest realities of motherhood with the wisdom of Scripture have empowered me not only as a mother but as a woman of faith. Her encouragement is palpable, leaving me feeling excited and equipped to navigate through each season of life in a thriving and joy-filled way.

—Shelli Allen, Mom of Four

As moms, we sometimes feel we're on this journey alone. Natalie is a friend, a fellow mom, who lovingly and authentically reminds us that we are all in this with and for each other— moms supporting moms! And above all, we have a heavenly Father who is our biggest supporter! No matter what stage of motherhood you are in, this book is a must read. Enjoy!

—Kaare Risbrudt, Mom of Two

In *Made to Soar*, Natalie shares both the good and the not-so-good aspects of motherhood through real-life stories to which we all can relate. As mothers, sometimes we try to appear like life is perfect. Natalie, however, doesn't shy away from addressing our real feelings of imperfection, hopelessness, or lack of purpose. She shares how God's love for us is the ONE thing that can give us peace and fill the void in our hearts, thereby helping us to find greater purpose and a new way to mother.

—Stacy Swenson, Mom of Three

Motherhood is a desired blessing filled with such joy and fulfillment, yet also surprise at the unexpected demands and feelings of exclusion. While we may feel lonely on our motherhood journey, Natalie reminds us, through beautifully illustrated personal stories and ones from Scripture, that we are never truly alone because there is power and freedom in belief. Natalie's passion for Jesus and others shines as she opens up to the honesty and truth of motherhood's struggles and triumphs.

—Mareen Biss, Mom of Three

Made to Soar is a perfectly-titled book. This is a wonderful cross between a memoir and a guide encouraging women not to lose themselves and their own identity while transitioning to the role of mom and engaging in the day-to-day battles and triumphs of raising children. A refreshing read!

—Chelsie Tatge, Mom of Two

Made to Soar

Artwork illustrated by my oldest son, Peyton James Hanson.
Thank you, my sweet boy, for this precious gift.

Made to Soar

CHRIST-CENTERED TRUTHS TO ENCOURAGE, EQUIP, AND EMPOWER MOMS

Dear Friend,

I pray you feel God's love through the stories I share and are that reminded Made to Soar! you were Breathe peace, sweetly

Natalie Dawn Hanson

Natalie Dawn Hanson

AUTHOR ACADEMY elite

Printed in the United States of America

Published by Author Academy Elite
P.O. Box 43
Powell, OH 43035
www.AuthorAcademyElite.com

Paperback ISBN: 978-1-64085-994-4
Hardcover ISBN: 978-1-64085-995-1
Ebook ISBN: 978-1-64085-996-8

Library of Congress Control Number: 2019917163

Available in paperback, hardback, e-book, and audiobook.

*To my husband, Darin, and our sons,
Peyton, Samuel, Cooper, and Parker.
You gave me the greatest gift by making me Mom.
I'm forever grateful God entrusted me with this role
that has brought such purpose and passion to my life.
I love you with all my heart.*

*To my beloved parents, Royal and Pamela Lyson.
I am who I am today because of your humble, loving guidance
and your commitment to passing on the faith.
Mom, I dedicate this book in your honor.
And Dad, I dedicate this book in your loving memory.*

Contents

Dear Friend,

I WANT YOU TO KNOW

*D*ear friend, I am so delighted you have chosen to open the pages of this book and spend a little time here with me. I don't know how these words came to be resting in your adored hands, weathered with stories of your own. Hands with years of life and memories inscribed in the creases of your palms as if documenting *your* unique journey. However it happened for you to be holding this book, I'm so grateful, for I've been praying for you.

I've been praying for mommas from the moment these words were truths etched on my heart by God Himself more than a half-decade ago. I've prayed for the courage and vulnerability to share the transforming story God has written in my life so it would glorify His name and point others to Him.

We may not know one another yet. The details of our lives may be different. We may be in opposite seasons of motherhood. Motherhood may be but a dream at this point in your life, or it may be filled with bottles, diapers, and sleepless nights. Maybe, like me, you're smack dab in the middle of raising your kids, busy running from activity to activity, or you're an empty nester loving your kids from afar as they navigate life on their own. Maybe you're not only mother anymore but have also added the roles of mother-in-law and grandma. Maybe, like me, you have four boys, or you have an only child, a houseful of kids, all girls, or a mixture of both. I've been a stay-at-home mom for years and now work independently from home. Perhaps you work full-time outside the home, or you enjoy the freedom of retirement. Like me, you may love to run, sing, and drink coffee, or you may despise running, can't sing, and only drink tea. Maybe we both grew up in a loving, nurturing, stable home, or you experienced a dysfunctional, inconsistent upbringing. There's no doubt we each have our own set of unique talents, abilities, personalities, and passions. But here's what I believe to be true: These differences don't divide us—they unite us. Despite our differences, we are moms who want the best for our kids, and that is what puts us on the same team. So in my heart, I call you friend. And now, perhaps, this is the moment where our stories intersect.

I wish we could share our stories together over coffee. Having coffee with friends is one of my favorite things. I imagine us sitting cozied up on my couch in the living room with the fireplace crackling in the background. Or maybe it's spring, and we are sitting outside on my front porch (one of my favorite places), feeling the sweet, gentle breeze upon our faces freshening the air around us. I imagine us sharing the intimate places of our hearts—trusting, encouraging, and supporting one another. And reminding one another we aren't alone in this journey of motherhood.

Your time is valuable, I know. Like you, I am a busy mom and understand there is laundry to do, bills to pay, food to cook, activities to attend, kiddos to love, bathrooms to scrub. (Yes, I mean scrub! Seriously, why can't my boys hit the target?) And like you, I have worries and fears, frustrations and struggles, hopes and dreams, situations and hardships, expectations and disappointments I'm dealing with right now.

Life could take you in a hundred different places at this very moment. In fact, you may have to go soon because life continues. It doesn't pause so you can read a book. The potential interruptions are endless.

But at this moment, can I just invite you … to breathe?

Go ahead, take that deep breath. One more. In through the nose … out through the mouth.

Doesn't that feel good? Our momma duties aren't going anywhere. But for now, I want to give you permission to just *be*. Most of us don't take time to just *be* because we are spread so thin and constantly on the go, taking care of everyone in our circle. I don't want this book to be another something on your endless to-do list. There are no expectations or responsibilities here. (None of us needs more of that.) These words are not meant to add stress but to give life. So, my friend, go on. Give it a try. Simply *be*.

I imagine you sneaking away for five minutes, reading these words in the bathroom—the only semi-private place in the house. I imagine you reading these words while sitting in a car waiting for your son or daughter to get done with practice. I imagine you reading these words in bed, exhausted from a long day, barely able to keep your eyes open. I imagine you reading while lying on a cabana on a warm, sandy beach in the tropics. (If that's you, I'm a little envious.) No matter where you are, I envision women everywhere, exactly like you and me, reading these words and feeling the intimate comfort of a sisterhood embraced by the mighty, yet gentle hands of Jesus. Now, maybe you're rockin' motherhood and loving the heck out of it and simply want to gain some insight into what God says about your role as a mom. Or maybe you are struggling because you've realized motherhood is so much more than you ever thought. Perhaps you are so overwhelmed you're simply going through the motions but not deeply connecting with your children. Or maybe you've lost the joy and delight motherhood is supposed to bring. If any of these are true for you, I trust you'll find comfort and hope in the words and stories I share.

I know you love your kids—more than words can say. No doubt. For most of us, having kids is a dream come true. I know you share amazing moments with them, ones you've dreamed about your whole life. But if you're like me, you were also surprised by motherhood. Surprised by the overwhelming work and effort it requires, the challenging behaviors, the whiny voices, the power struggles, the back talk, and so on. Because of those surprises, I'm wondering, if like me, there are times when you feel overwhelmed and insecure. When you feel alone, unloved, and scared. I'm wondering if there are times when you doubt your mothering and feel like a failure. When you are trying so hard to balance work and home life that the guilt of not being with your kids more is tearing you apart. I'm wondering if there are times when you want a do-over. When you feel unappreciated and unseen. Or times when you just need a break from it all.

I'm right there with you, friend. So, let's take another deep breath and journey together. I'm learning the more I share honestly about real life, the more freedom and relief I find. I pray the same is true for you. Therefore, I can promise you truth but not perfection. My fear of imperfection, of what others would think, of whether the book would be good enough, or if it would have any impact at all almost stopped me from writing it. Almost.

I admit, I have not arrived at some holier-than-thou place with all the answers. I'm an imperfect woman playing countless roles who is allowing God to use her broken stories as a vessel to share freedom and hope to others. I'm a work in progress. Aren't we all? I'm not successful according to the world's standards. I don't have a million followers on social media. I don't have a booming website that gets thousands of hits every day. I'm not speaking at conferences filled with thousands of people. Despite my amateur status, my lack of worldly success, my real battle with insecurity and fear, I have a heart for Jesus. A heart He is daily refining and molding. A heart so captivated by His love, I can't help but share Him with you.

And although I have stories and truths I can hardly wait to share with you, I'm not *the* expert. My words alone can't fully transform you. My hope is they challenge you and stir in you a desire to seek the One who can. God is the expert, the author of all wisdom, and the perfecter of our faith.[1] Therefore, He receives all the glory and praise, and He is the One who will do His mighty work in you. I'm simply a friend who gets to be one of His instruments of love. And for that, I am forever grateful. Let me pray for you:

Lord God, I want to thank You for this sacred moment with my new friend. I delight in the mysterious ways You intertwine our lives and am so grateful for this divine intersection. You know the delicate, fragile, broken places of her heart that need mending, Lord, just like You know mine. You know the fears, worries, struggles, hurts, and insecurities that attempt to paralyze her from living freely and joyfully. I pray these words, inspired by Your Holy presence, will speak directly into the shadowed places of her heart and bring light, hope, healing, and inspiration. I pray the stories of my life will empower her to trust in Your story for her life. I pray she will feel Your sweet presence as she journeys through transformation and begins to see Your divine workings etched into every corner of her life. Thank You for Your faithfulness, Lord, for hearing our prayer, and for being ever so present as we seek to know You more and live freely and joyfully in our divine purpose. In Jesus' precious name we pray, amen.

These words are my personal stories. They expose my weaknesses and blemishes and demonstrate God's power and grace. These words define my heart, express my purpose. A heart forever transforming. A purpose forever unfurling. Together let's discover the freedom, strength, and peace that comes from God, alone, so we can uncover and soar in the wonder and joy of our divine purpose, and confidently pass the baton of faith to our children.

Breathe peace, my friend,

The Flight of the Butterfly

One of my favorite spaces at home is the circular, dirt road, about a quarter-mile around, lined with trees and grass that lies in front of our refurbished farmhouse. It's a place where my boys know not to disturb me unless it's an emergency (By emergency, I mean bloody, physical harm. Not the "Mom, so-and-so did this, or so-and-so did that," type of kid-defined emergency). This is the place where I retreat to run.

Running has been the antidote to my bomb of emotions that builds up under the pressures and demands of motherhood. And so, this humble, little road became my refuge when my boys were little. This road provided me a loyal place to breathe, clear my mind, dream, wonder and pray—the things so hard to find time to do when we're constantly bombarded with the tedious, mundane tasks of being mom. And on those days when motherhood was too much, and I felt like I had failed yet again, this precious road absorbed my tears, soothed my anxieties, and calmed my stresses. And on those rare days when the stars aligned, kids slept through the night, and Daddy brought supper home, I'd simply do nothing but run.

On one mildly warm summer day in late August, with a hint of fall coolness in the air, I was on one of those runs on the road my feet had pounded on so many times before. The familiar sense of safety and comfort it provided was like being in the presence of a trusted friend. A friend who was willing to listen to the aches of a momma's overwhelmed, insecure, guilty heart.

My two youngest boys slept soundly in the house. A long-range baby monitor sat on the steps of the front porch so I could hear their beckoning cries when they awoke. My two big boys played outside on the playset that ornaments the center of our lawn and was known to entertain them for hours.

It was the tail-end of summer, and instead of savoring every last moment with my older two boys, I found myself counting down the days until school started. Because let's get real: Raising kids is no joke. I love them like crazy, but it's the hardest work I've ever done. My four boys have this insane ability to suck the energy right out of me.

As I ran circle after circle, one moment delighting in the way I observed my boys playing so nicely together in the sand that surrounds the playset and the next perplexed by how unexpected my motherhood journey had been, God was getting an earful from me. The mounting, self-inflicted pressure to not only to be enough today but also to live up to that expectation forever, left my heart so conflicted. I thanked

God for the gift of motherhood yet begged for His help—for answers to the confusion of my troubled heart.

JUST ANOTHER RUN ... UNTIL IT WASN'T

Without realizing it at first, now running at a comfortable, consistent pace around our dirt road, fully engaged in my dramatic prayer full of joys and sorrows, a shimmer of movement caught the corner of my eye. I slowed my pace a little, glanced to my right, and noticed a monarch butterfly accompanying me on my run. I thought nothing of it, for monarchs in Minnesota this time of year were normal. But then, it didn't leave. It kept flying right next to me.

Why is this thing following me? I wondered.

Unsuspecting of me, this beautiful butterfly captivated my attention and instantly drew me back to the aches of my heart. It felt as if everything had turned to slow motion as this sweet little butterfly and I ran around my road. And then, something unexpected happened. Something remarkable. As I concentrated on the rhythm of this butterfly's flight, I sensed a whisper from the melody of its beating wings.

"You, too, are beautiful. You, too, can feel joy. You, too, can soar freely."

I know it sounds a bit crazy. Trust me, I know. But I heard those words resounding in my mind. As if I wasn't already astounded by the presence of this monarch and the echoes of the whispers ringing in my head, I became enveloped by a flurry of monarchs—I couldn't even count them all—who seemed to be dancing to the beat of my heart and the pounding of my feet. My head was on a swivel as I tried to make sense of what was happening. A bewildered chuckle escaped my mouth as the spectacle of butterflies took my breath away causing me to stop running, mid-stride.

Standing in the middle of my dirt road—heart racing, sweat dripping—with my jaw dropped and eyes wide open, I gazed at their magnificent beauty, their joyful dance, their redeeming presence. I'm not sure how long I stood there admiring the fascinating picture being painted in front of my eyes. I couldn't help but wonder. *Why them? Why me? Why now?* I couldn't shake the feeling it was something significant.

The subtle proclamation by my oldest son, Peyton, "Mom, Parker's crying!" slowly began to shake me from my stupor.

"Huh?" I whispered back, slowly regaining awareness, not wanting to take my eyes off those monarchs.

"Parker's crying!" he yelled again as his dirt-stained hand tugged gently on my arm.

"What?" I said, turning my head in his direction, trying my best to focus on the present moment yet tempted to catch one last glimpse of the masterful dance of the butterflies.

"The baby?" he said with inflection in his voice as if saying, "What is wrong with you? You crazy or something?"

I shook my head slightly and blinked a few extra times as if I was awakening from some intense daydream. I finally glanced down at my son, consciousness now fully gained. "I'm sorry, buddy. What?"

It took a split second of seeing the odd, confused expression on his face and his dramatic full-arm point toward the house for me to know what he was trying to tell me.

"Oh, Parker!"

He giggled a little nervously. I think it's safe to say he found my behavior funny and not crazy. Thank goodness. That's all my sensitive heart needed was a son who called his momma crazy. For the record, the baby was not crying. He was babbling in that adorable baby talk that I miss so terribly. As I approached the monitor, I could even hear the sound of bubbles being blown from the gallons of baby drool that demanded several bibs a day.

I could have walked up the steps and gone directly to that sweet babe's room to retrieve him from his nap, as I had done countless times before. And although I was in the present moment, I couldn't stop thinking about *the moment*—the unexpected pause in time—that had occurred minutes ago on my dirt road.

So, I followed the urge. I felt a prompting I couldn't ignore. Instead of walking up the stairs, my feet took a hard left and walked me right into my office, where I googled *monarch butterflies*. As I waited for results, I thought to myself, *What am I doing? This is silly. I know the process of the butterfly. They lay eggs. Then, the eggs hatch into caterpillars, which form cocoons, and in a few short days, they are transformed into butterflies. What's the big deal, really?*

All I can say is something stirred in my spirit that urged me to research these magnificent creatures. It was a gut feeling I couldn't ignore. A feeling I've come to recognize as the Holy Spirit's presence within me. It's His brilliant method of communicating.

I clicked on the first link, "Monarch Butterfly Site: Life Cycle, Migration, Pictures, News, More."[2] I read through several familiar details and then fumbled upon one new fact intriguing me to read further. Monarchs migrate. I didn't know that. It didn't seem like a big deal until I learned it's not a typical migration. What I discovered is that it often takes four to five generations of monarchs to make it back home, to complete the full migratory cycle. The migration of the monarch is often called the "Relay Race of the Monarch" because it's like they are passing the baton to the next generation. Each butterfly knows its part, its purpose; therefore, they not only survive, but they also thrive. Against all odds, they endure. They fight. They never give up. They always find their way home.

Once I read those words, I instantly had images and thoughts rushing through my mind like in the movies when they show flashbacks connecting the dots to the rest of the plot. It was an image of me standing on stage with unfamiliar confidence—speaking to an audience—and in the next moment, an image of me running and passing a baton to my children. I had visions of monarchs flying all around me, similar to what I had experienced only moments before. I had this warm, comforting, peaceful feeling like there was some purpose in it all. Some message I was supposed to grasp. As I stared at the computer screen—trying to figure out what butterflies, batons, running, and speaking meant and what they had to do with me—I was flooded with a conflict of emotions from intrigue and curiosity to confusion and doubt. Was this God's way of answering the conflicting questions in my heart?

As my mind raced, I wondered, *What is the significance of the butterfly? Why the monarch?* The details we know about how a butterfly comes to be—details I'd never spent much time thinking about—are nothing but miraculous. Butterflies, as you know, go through metamorphosis—an intense physical struggle—where they are transformed from caterpillar into butterfly. This intricate, elaborate transformation is critical for the caterpillar to become all it was created to be—a beautiful butterfly. Without metamorphosis, it can never be what God created it to be.

Could the same be true for us? Does God's plan for us include going through metamorphosis—some sort of intense transformation—to realize our divine purpose and to become everything He's created us to be? If so, then our struggles mean something. They have purpose. We're not meant to be stuck in the midst of our struggles, which unfortunately is exactly where motherhood can lead us. Instead, we're meant to be transformed by them. And once transformed—like a butterfly—we have the ability to soar.

Allow me to whisper this truth, once more, directly to your heart. You, my friend, … have … the ability … to soar. Take a moment and breathe it in, right now. In through the nose … out through the mouth. Take as many deep breaths as you need so you don't rush by this moment and miss its significance. *You* were *made* to *soar*. It's not some rare gift given to a select few, rather a precious gift given to us all. When you finish this paragraph, I want you to close your eyes and let this sweet, simple truth settle on your heart. You were made to soar.

On top of that, generation after generation of monarchs inherently know what is required of them to sustain the existence of their species and significance in the world. It's like they're passing on a legacy. Could we have that same kind of inherent ability to sustain our significance and pass on a legacy—generation after generation—for some greater purpose? If so, how do we uncover it? What is the legacy we are called to pass on? And where do we find the strength, resilience, courage, and confidence to pass on a legacy when we are busy meeting the constant, daily demands of motherhood?

WHO HAS TIME TO THINK ABOUT LEGACY?

Friend, I know mothering can be rough. I know it can be overwhelming to the brink of explosion and so exhausting to the point of numbness. I know life can get so busy we lose sight of what's most important. I know we can be so focused on taking care of everyone else we forget to take care of ourselves. I know how quickly our hopes, dreams, and purposes can become buried under the daily demands of motherhood. I know life has a way of making us feel stuck, lonely, and hopeless. And, if you are like me, you've wished for life to be different but haven't had any idea how to make the change.

Girl, I understand. I hear your pain. I know your pain. The details of our lives may be different, but our hearts are so similar. I know we're told to cherish these priceless moments with our children, but sometimes, since I'm all about being real with you, my friend, I don't cherish them. I mean, come on, not all the moments with our kids are *cherishable*. They just aren't. Why, then, did I always feel so guilty if I wasn't loving motherhood every moment of every day?

Now, I'm not saying we ever lose love for our kids. That's impossible. But, perhaps, we lose love for the role of motherhood—every now and then—because we choose to bear the heavy load all on our own. Perhaps we don't fully understand the depth, significance, and purpose of our role as a mom; therefore, we don't know how to fully appreciate it nor execute it the way in which God desires. Perhaps those uncherished moments exist for a reason we have yet to understand. Maybe there are hidden, resentful places of our souls that feel cheated and lost under the umbrella of motherhood and steal the delight it is meant to bring. Could it be our sinful nature and our desire and failure to combat it on our own is causing us deep sorrow?

There is no doubt we will miss these moments when they are nothing but memories. But today, right now, let's breathe in the comfort of knowing we aren't alone, and together, we will learn how to exhale any guilt, shame, or anger that threatens to hold us captive. Countless mommas around the world are feeling what we feel. It's nothing to be ashamed of, and it's nothing to hide. It's time to unite, let go, get real, and discover a new, liberating way to live.

MADE TO SOAR

Those precious butterflies I met on my road that day were no accident. The more I learned about the butterfly, the more I realized their life journey is a comparable representation of what we experience as a mother and what's possible for us. Life is a journey filled with countless opportunities for growth and transformation. But to fully experience growth and transformation, it requires us to pay attention and make intentional choices. Transformation is not only for a select few. It's what we're all designed to go through. It's not easy, but it's absolutely worth it.

If we continue to do life on our own, out of our own strength and will, we will run dry—we will lose the joy. It traps us in a perpetual circle running around the same dirt road. We will look back and have regrets. If we continue to pretend everything is *okay* … if we continue to bear the guilt and pressure of motherhood … if we continue to neglect the ache in our hearts yearning for something more, we will miss out on the glorious gift and delight of motherhood. Our wings of beauty will never unfurl. We will never soar to the heights God has prepared for us.

It is time to uncover the answers that will release us from the pressures and inadequacies we feel. It is time to give God access to our underwhelmed hearts so the power of His love can overwhelm our souls and do its transforming work in us. It's time to claim clarity for our purpose and fuel for our passion.

It is time to give God access to our underwhelmed hearts so the power of His love can overwhelm our souls and do its transforming work in us.

Like a caterpillar goes through struggle, hardship, and change to fulfill its final destiny as a beautiful butterfly, we, too—if we choose—can relinquish control and experience transformation. We were made to soar and not to be paralyzed by life. We can unfurl our wings and fly freely and joyfully in newfound beauty and purpose despite life's circumstances. And with hearts full of courage, confidence, and trust, we can pass on the baton of lasting faith to our children. That is the legacy we are called to leave.

Because of the divine interruption (that's what I like to call it) I experienced during the pivotal run on my dirt road, the monarch butterfly has become a symbol of hope, freedom, and peace for me. Therefore, I've chosen to weave the progressive stages of its life cycle—development, struggle, metamorphosis, transformation, and migration—into the fabric of my words to illustrate profound connections to our personal, unique discovery of joy, freedom, and purpose—not only as moms—but also as daughters of the King.

As I share intimate stories of how God has transformed my life and how He's worked in the details of it, I urge you to listen to how He is working in yours. As I share the wisdom God has whispered into my heart through my struggles and triumphs, I invite you to listen to what He's whispering into yours.

I simply want to be a vessel of hope—someone who understands where you are, reminds you you're never alone, and encourages you every step of the way. I want to breathe into your delicate soul the timeless, transforming truths of God's enduring, steadfast love and His unconditional grace. It is a grace that will not only set you free, build relentless courage, and clarify your divine purpose but will also inspire authentic, grace-filled relationships with your children. Relationships with the power to organically mold their hearts to the likeness of Christ and strengthen their wings to take flight on their own journey of life-long faith.

My hope is this book will not only entertain you but will also engage you and help lead you on your path to transformation and freedom. I pray the power of the Holy Spirit will soften any hard edges of your heart, mend old wounds continuing to affect your health, and free you from any chains holding you captive. I pray the power of God's love will open your eyes to new perspectives, reveal your divine purpose as a woman and as a mom, and bring you lasting joy and peace.

Some moms do this mothering thing on their own with no spouse, no partner, no teammate. If that's you, I can only imagine the extra weight you carry, my friend. Single parenting has its own set of unique challenges, just like parenting with a spouse has its own. No matter what your reality is, God's redeeming grace and love is for every person, in any situation.

I happen to be a mom doing this parenting thing with my husband of sixteen years. My husband, Darin, is a loving, gracious, kind, witty man whose sense of humor, personality, and authenticity instantly caught my attention and has held it ever since. Without getting too mushy, I'm so grateful to still be so madly in love with that man. We're a united team with a solid, trusting, honest relationship. But nothing has strained it more than parenting our four boys. I knew when I married him, he'd be a fantastic dad. However, I had no idea how tough it would be to parent together. We don't always see every situation eye-to-eye, but there's no doubt we have the best interest of our boys at heart. It's been a wild adventure of ups and downs, trials and errors, success and failures. If it weren't for my boys, I wouldn't be here today, writing these words for you and sharing my heart with you.

Those who know me well know I love getting together with people. They know I love throwing ideas out into the world and seeing if they take flight. I love to dream big and talk about it with others. Therefore, I so wish we could be chatting face-to-face (maybe someday we will), laughing and crying, and sharing our struggles and our dreams. Since we can't (at least for now), I added some questions at the end of each chapter where we can wonder, dream, and contemplate together. Questions we would, perhaps, chat about if we were sitting face-to-face. And questions you can use to lead a small group women's book study around this message.

My hope is these questions will provide a space for you to pause, breathe, and reflect, allowing time for the messages I share to kindle your heart, bringing relevance to *your* life and *your* story. Life is so busy we rarely take time to pause and think about where we are, where we are going, and if those are, indeed, the places God *wants* us to stay and the places God *wants* us to go.

I invite you to write and journal the genuine cries and dreams of your heart. It's only when we *get real* with ourselves that true and lasting transformation can take place. And as we share the intimate places of our hearts, we will pray for God's continued grace and guidance as He moves and works in and through us to do His good works that He has already prepared, in advance, for us to do.[3]

I'm so humbly grateful you've chosen to spend some time with me. And even more delighted you are willing to let me share God's transforming truths with you. He wants us to enjoy this life on earth. Life can be so good. But life, we know, can be tough and unfair. It can be confusing and frustrating. But I'm convinced—no matter what comes our way—we, together, can release motherhood into the security of God's grace. We can trust in His design for motherhood by taking flight in the freedom and joy of newfound beauty and purpose and live inspired and confident with unfurled wings. Both you and I were made to soar, sweet friend. So, let's soar!

PART ONE

The Reality of Motherhood

THE TRAP OF THE WORLD

CHAPTER 1

The Unexpected Dream

GOD PLACES DREAMS ON YOUR HEART

I will never forget the Christmas I opened the best present ever. I had recently turned eleven—smack dab in the middle of the awkward adolescent, pre-puberty stage. It was the gift I wanted more than anything else—a karaoke machine with a double cassette player and my very own microphone. I loved to sing. But this? This took my singing to a whole new level.

This machine had all the bells and whistles a 1990s amateur karaoke machine could have. Okay, so it wasn't top-of-the-line, but it had one of the most important features: an adjustable echo system that made me sound like I was singing in a stadium filled with cheering fans. So, that's exactly what I imagined while belting out Whitney Houston's

"Greatest Love of All" in front of my mirrored closet doors for hours. And that's when my dreams of becoming a performer began to take root.

A small-town, North Dakota girl with big dreams, I dreamt of being in the spotlight—of being known and admired. I dreamt of going to New York and being a Broadway star or to L.A. and being on the big screen. I dreamt of writing music and singing on stages. Above all, I dreamt of doing what I loved, living a significant life, and making a difference. But friend, let's keep it real. Sure, I can sing. Lots of people can. But I am no Carrie Underwood.

As life would have it, my childhood dreams too quickly became tainted by the overbearing reality of adulthood. Feeling the pressure to make my own living and choose a realistic life, I laid those dreams to rest and did what everyone expected of me. I earned a college degree and found a job I had little passion for, but it paid the bills. I guess I was proud to have my first job—completely independent for the first time—yet I mourned my buried dreams.

Two years into working my first job, the ache of my abandoned dreams became so intense I began to make plans to visit a great auntie in California. However, I was already looking into one-way tickets. I kept feeling this desire for something greater, and I convinced myself I'd find it there. Despite my parents' disapproval, I was ready to take the leap and go on an adventure of a lifetime to fulfill my dreams.

Imagine my surprise when a future farmer with a tan, blond hair, blue eyes, and a smile that made my heart flutter interrupted my plans to leave North Dakota. I can still picture the way Darin looked the day he showed up at my apartment doorstep. I'm not even sure how to explain why he was the one I had invited to accompany me to an Alabama concert. Perhaps it was because I knew he loved country music. Or perhaps some other plan was unfolding I didn't yet recognize.

Timing is a peculiar thing, isn't it? You see, Darin and I had met in college a few years prior. Mutual friends had set us up on a double-date, and let's just say no sparks flew that night. In fact, I'm pretty certain both of us were intentionally trying not to impress the other. (Seriously, you should have seen the way I looked the first time we met. He still grimaces when he thinks about it.) But we became quick friends as I discovered I rather adored his witty humor and charming personality. We actually did try dating for a little while, but it went nowhere. A few months later, I graduated from college and moved three hours away. Just like that, it was done—and we lost touch.

I couldn't quite understand why, after two years, my heart felt pulled to his and his to mine, especially since we had "been-there-done-that," and it hadn't worked. All I know is six months after the never-to-be-forgotten Alabama concert, the same voice that prompted me to invite him to it was the same voice that whispered, "Say yes."

Needless to say, being swept off my feet by this man who would soon become a farmer was not in my plans at all. Marrying a farmer and moving to a small town in Minnesota? Never a part of my dreams. Don't get me wrong—for as long as I could remember, I had dreamt of love, of being a wife and mom. That was always a part of the equation, but I had personal aspirations to pursue first ... or so I thought.

I never made it to California. Perhaps my daddy's prayers had something to do with this. So much for *my* planning and *my* timing. I have since learned when it comes to future planning, it's best to trust in the One who knows and wants what's best for me.

The power of love is a strange thing. I was so captivated by this man who had interrupted my life there was no doubt in my heart he was the dream I didn't want to let go. It was this peaceful feeling that told me he was my path. The idea of performing became significantly less important. All I wanted to do was marry this man, have babies, and spend the rest of my life loving him. So less than a year later, that's exactly what I did. My dreams were coming true. And so, I suppose, that's where my story really begins.

A DREAM COME TRUE

It was an ordinary evening at home. Although scrapbooking is not my skill set, I forced myself to sit at my make-shift craft table anyway, working on our wedding scrapbook. Darin reclined on the couch with a beverage in hand and a bowl of microwave buttered popcorn on his belly, watching—on this particular night—*The Lord of the Rings* trilogy.

As I sat reminiscing about the day we said "I do,"—the day that changed the entire course of my life—I felt a settling in my abdomen. My first instinct was, yes, you guessed it. Gas. I figured my tummy was working overtime to digest the rich food we had indulged in for supper. I felt it again. And then, it was as if someone had smacked me conscious.

"Could it be? Is it really what I think it is?"

In utter excitement and a bit of disbelief, I quickly stood up, hands plastered to my belly. With bulging eyes, a racing heart, and a nervous smile, I paraded over to my husband and shyly muttered, "I think I just felt the baby move."

It took him a moment to comprehend my announcement. He was, after all, fully captivated by and committed to his evening activity of watching the dramatic tale of Frodo Baggins and his good buddy, Samwise Gamgee.

Without breaking his glance from the television, he responded, "What, hon?"

This time, with a bit more confidence, I repeated, "I think I just felt the baby move."

It was obvious he heard me this time as his eyes, too, got huge, and he scrambled for his paper towel to wipe the grease from his hands. Like most soon-to-be-first parents, we placed our hands together on my belly and waited. And waited. And waited. I sighed, thinking for a split second I had imagined it. Then, the movement came again. Our eyes met in complete awe and amazement at the fact there really was a little baby moving and growing inside me.

Three years before this, I was about to hop on a plane and fly across the country to make my dreams come true. Instead, here I was living an entirely different life as a wife and soon-to-be mom. It all happened so fast, but I trusted in this new path.

When my son was born and made me Mom, I was so madly in love with him. Nothing trumped my desire to stay home and raise him. Because of him, my dream of being a momma took root deep within my heart. All I wanted was to love him and give him the life he deserved. I know you know the feeling I'm talking about—the unexplainable desire, inspired by the most intense kind of love, to want and be the best for our kids.

My dream was unfolding so beautifully. I had a loving husband, a cozy home, and a healthy, new baby. I couldn't have been happier or more grateful.

THE DREAM THAT FELL SHORT

I was not naïve enough to assume motherhood would be a cake walk. I knew it would require a great deal of work, but I was most certainly up for the challenge because the love for my son was the fuel that inspired me to be the best I could be for him. Plus, this was my dream, so I was determined to give it my all. And dreams were meant to be enjoyed. Right? At least that's what I always thought.

Then I had another son. And another. And yet, another. Somewhere along the way as a stay-at-home mom, my dream of what motherhood would be like was overrun by the day-to-day, mundane, yet demanding tasks of taking care of my kids and managing a household. I always wanted to be a mom with a houseful of kids and a wife to a man who adored his family. But as I stood smack dab in the middle of my dream coming true, I couldn't help but feel like something was missing. I felt as if a significant piece of who I was had been buried underneath mounds of tedious chores and daily obligations. I felt like a stranger stuck in the middle of what is supposed to be *my* magnificent dream of motherhood. I was beginning to feel lost in the story of my own life. How is that possible? And how did this dream fail me? I felt cheated and trapped and wondered where God was in all of this.

What was missing? Why wasn't I more fulfilled living this dream? Did the confusion in my heart mean something

I couldn't yet recognize? Is mom the only role I will ever play? Am I meant to do something more? It was like this constant pounding on the door of my heart beckoning me to something bigger and greater than myself. A noise trying to awaken me so I could see the piece to the puzzle of why this dream was falling short.

Friend, maybe you've heard the same questions echoing in your mind. You had dreams that didn't quite end up the way you had hoped. Your role as mom surprised you and has somehow taken away a vibrant, passionate part of yourself which leaves you feeling lost and confused. You had expectations that didn't quite turn out like you imagined.

But here's what I know: God is always with you and always has been, even if you didn't feel His presence. Even when life doesn't make sense and when we feel lost and forgotten and our dreams aren't going according to *our* plan, God is not surprised by where we are or how we're feeling. We simply must trust God is working in our lives—refining our dreams—to make all things good[1] and to draw us to Him. And you and I are not the only ones whose dreams did not go exactly the way we imagined. Instead of feeling discouraged and hopeless in the midst of our dreams gone awry, we need to trust, like this woman in Scripture, God has a greater plan in store.

TRUSTING IN HIS DREAM

This woman is one of the most well-known in the Bible. Her name is Mary. When we meet her in Scripture, she is engaged to Joseph, a carpenter. We aren't given many details about her life up to this point, but we know she was a woman of deep faith and good character who lived a fairly normal, quiet life. I imagine she expected her life to remain much the same once she married Joseph. However, before that day arrived, her dreams of what her life would be like were abruptly interrupted by a message from God calling her to walk a path divergent from her chosen one. This path required her to become pregnant before her wedding with a son who wasn't her fiancé's. It was scandalous. In fact, it was a social disgrace and one which, back then, carried the penalty of death. Why on earth would she say yes to this dream that had the potential to cause her and her family so much pain and ridicule?

It's because this was not just any dream. It was *the* dream, *the* plan that would lead to the birth of a son destined to save humanity. Mary had been chosen for the greatest assignment the world had ever known. She was chosen to be the mother to the Son of God—Jesus. He would be the Savior of the World whom out of His great love for us chose to sacrifice His life on a cross so we could fully live and love the life we've been given. Although Mary didn't fully know what to expect of this detour in her dream and despite any fear or anxiety she may have felt, she trusted God completely and accepted this new path that would eventually lead to the fulfillment of God's divine plan not only for her but also for all of us. Her faith and obedience trumped her fear.

God is a good God who wants the very best for all of us. Therefore, I can't help but believe that since God had a great plan in store for Mary, He also has a great plan in store for each of us—a plan we can't imagine or accomplish on our own. Don't you suppose, then, since Mary trusted God with her unexpected dream, we, too, need to trust God with ours?

Perhaps the questions we have and the stirrings we feel which cause uncertainty and discontent are what God uses to awaken us to new, deeper revelations about who we are. These revelations can begin to clarify the confusion of our hearts and lead us down a path to realize the fullness of our dreams. God places magnificent dreams on our hearts—ones meant to have impact and make a difference in the world. They may not unfold as we anticipate or imagine, but we can't give up on our dreams. Sometimes, we need to be willing to lay aside our expectations and trust that in the midst of *our* murky, presumably failed dream, God is working to clarify and fulfill *His* dream for our lives.

> In the midst of our murky, presumably failed dream, God is working to clarify and fulfill His dream for our lives.

THE MOSAIC DESIGN

I want you to imagine the intricate mosaic design of a monarch butterfly's wings. They resemble the beauty and uniqueness of a stained-glass window, constructed by random shapes and colors of broken glass. Separately, the broken pieces are worthless junk. It's the outcome of the broken pieces—molded together out of deep intention and love—which reveal a greater beauty than before. The wings of a monarch are a perfect reminder of how God has the power to transform us by taking our brokenness and anything the world throws at us and turn it into something beautiful and magnificent. But we have to be willing to let Him do His work in us. The butterfly did not begin its life with beautiful wings. It had to go through an intense transformation to become all it was created to be and live in the beauty and design of its purpose.

And the same is true for us. It wasn't until I admitted the true condition of my life that I began to notice God taking my brokenness and putting it together—imperfect piece by imperfect piece—to help me recognize *His* dream for my life and the beauty of His original design. Therefore, I learned His plan is not contained in some perfectly ordained dream of *ours* but is unveiled through the broken pieces of our heart being molded and refined by His grace and love to reflect a dream far better than we could ever imagine.

When we choose, like Mary, to follow God's lead, God will transform our heartache and confusion into purposefully lighted pathways, guiding us toward our divine purpose. It's in Him and through Him where we'll find the significance we're searching for. But to explain how it all worked out in God's timing, and to show you how you can experience the same joy, peace, and purpose I've found, I have to go back to the beginning of when my dream began to fall apart.

God will transform our heartache and confusion into purposefully lighted pathways guiding us toward our divine purpose. It's in Him and through Him where we'll find the significance we're searching for.

Making it Matter

This section of every chapter, my friend, is for you. Some begin with stories, and others—like this one—begin with intentional questions and reminders. My purpose for this section is for you to take the time you need to allow the truths I share to absorb into your heart. I don't want this to be another book you read and throw on the shelf. I encourage you to use this as a guide to your transformation. In the space provided, I invite you to answer the questions or simply journal what's on your heart.

Have you had a dream that didn't turn out the way you expected? Are you feeling lost and confused in the midst of your unfulfilled dreams? Are you wondering how you ended up where you are? What about motherhood? Is it everything you imagined it to be? For me, motherhood was everything I dreamt it would be and so much more. It's the *more* part I struggled with and led me to a place of confusion, frustration, and sadness.

It can be easy to feel as if God has abandoned you and your dreams, especially when nothing is going your way and you have an ache in your heart for life to be different. It can be easy to feel stuck and discouraged and believe nothing will ever change. Whatever your reality is right now, I invite you to give it to God. Give Him access to your heart, and He will use whatever you are struggling with to help direct you to His divine purpose. Trust that where you are now, God will use and fit it into His greater plan—a bigger dream He's readying to unveil.

What if I reminded you God's not done with you yet? Your story is not finished. He's still writing it. This moment, right now, may not feel significant. But, let me tell you, friend, it's a part of the story He's writing for your life, none the less. Trust He's holding you in the palm of His hands. It took me thirty-four years to accept and understand how every stage of my life was and is a usable piece to His plan that is forever unfolding and how every broken part is being molded and refined to reveal greater beauty and purpose, deeper joy and peace. What if you believed that this moment—although a detour in *your* plan—is, indeed, an intentionally scheduled appointment in *God's* plan, leading you to fulfill your dreams and live out your divine purpose? How would you look at this moment differently? Your past differently? Your future differently? How would you choose to live if you believed that *the now* was a necessary step to realizing your dreams as a mother, wife, and woman? Journal your thoughts below.

_____

_____

_____

_____

_____

_____

_____

_____

_____

_____

_____

A Momma's Prayer

Lord, thank You for Your enduring presence, especially in times when we don't understand the detours of our lives. Motherhood is a beautiful gift we are so grateful for, yet often the realities don't match what we always imagined. Help us trust in You the way Mary did. To believe that Your love has the power to mold our dreams into magnificent mosaic designs of wilder beauty and deeper purpose than we ever thought possible. Remind us how right now is a significant part of the story You are writing in our lives. Help us acknowledge the unexpectedness of our life as invitations to draw closer to You. Stir in our hearts, through the power of Your presence, the knowledge of what You are calling us to fulfill and the wisdom to trust in Your timing. In Jesus' name we pray, amen.

Meaningful Truth

And at the right time he will bring everything together under the authority of Christ—everything in heaven and on earth. Furthermore, because we are united with Christ, we have received an inheritance from God, for he chose us in advance, and he makes everything work out according to his plan.

—Ephesians 1:10–11 (NLT)

CHAPTER 2

The Rise of Self-Reliance

GOD DESIRES YOUR HEART, NOT PERFECTION

I was told most babies stop crying once the car starts moving. Not my firstborn, Peyton. In fact, he proceeded to cry the entire time we were in the grocery store—our first, official outing as Mom and son. And his cry was not just a quiet whimper. It was the newborn, high-pitched, curdling cry that made every worker, shopper, and stranger stare at me with a condemning look.

"Are you going to do something about that?" or "Do you even know how to take care of your baby?" Or worse, "Are you capable of being a mother?"

You know the stares I'm talking about, right? Stares that remind me of the heat vision Superman uses to release massive amounts of energy in red, focused beams from his eyes. The stares that have the ability to shoot insecurity smack dab into the middle of our sensitive momma souls. The stares that made me think my son's unhappiness was a direct reflection of my mothering. It took every ounce of strength in me not to break down and cry right along with him while standing in the check-out line.

As new moms, none of us really knows what we're doing. We navigate foreign water and march into uncharted territory, often with little or no knowledge or experience. Here we are playing our most important roles, yet are hurled to the front lines of motherhood with a huge dose of love, several packages of diapers, and big ole "Congratulations!" Teetering on the edge of consciousness—influenced by unfamiliar exhaustion—we quickly find ourselves on the brink of battle with little training on how to successfully do motherhood let alone enjoy a life of peace and purpose.

To give in to the challenges and admit our inadequacies would be to surrender. To surrender would mean failure. So instead, we rise up. We launch into survival mode. It's really no surprise because what is a creature's primary objective upon entering uncharted territory? Survival. Not happiness. Not peace.

Take the caterpillar, for example. It hatches from an egg on a milkweed leaf, and its first response to life in this new uncharted territory is to survive. It immediately and intuitively begins to eat to survive. The same goes for new, unfamiliar experiences, like motherhood. I don't mean we *eat* to survive the stress of motherhood. (Well, maybe sometimes. I've been known to empty a bag of pistachios or white cheddar popcorn. Yum! Or dark chocolate? Ugh, can't resist.) Rather, what I mean is, as moms, we rise up and do whatever it takes to survive and be the best we can be for our families—even if it means we suffer.

The moment I got home from the grocery store and nestled my sweet babe into my breast, tears of frustration and failure rolled down my face, threatening to unravel me. Presuming I was *the* variable upon which my son's happiness and future rested, I buried and dismissed those feelings. I chose survival instead of surrender. I rose up, dried my eyes, pulled up my big girl panties, dug in my heels, and committed to trying harder to be the perfect mom my son deserved. I was determined to be everything he needed, unaware of the aftermath this confident, resilient stance would create. It was a stance for which I was all too familiar.

THE PRESSURE TO BE PERFECT

Fifth grade was the year—a critical turning point in my belief and understanding of who I needed to be—when I morphed from being a good kid into trying to be the perfect kid.

"No, I can't go to bed yet," I shouted while rolling on the floor in the living room with big sobs of fear echoing between my words.

With puffy, aching eyes, a beet red face, and a raspy voice, I declared between huge, shaky inhales, "I *have* to memorize my notes for my test tomorrow in order to get an A."

I had been studying for hours for my social studies test the next day. To get an A, I believed I *had* to memorize every single word in my notes now smudged with tears and crinkled by frustration.

"I have to get an A, or I will be a failure" was the message scrolling over and over in my mind.

My loving mother—feeling helpless and desperate to console her eleven-year-old daughter—cautiously rubbed my back and stroked my hair, assuring me everything was going to be all right. It was. I did get the A. But it was like fuel for a fire to seek perfection. It was the start of my desire and drive to be the best at everything I did. From school to sports and music to pageants, I worked so hard to succeed at it all and prove my worth. But the pressure to be perfect and maintain perfection was incredibly intense and, of course, impossible. So, when I failed, I dug deeper and tried harder.

It's no wonder this ingrained pressure of being perfect naturally seeped into my role as mom. The moment feelings of failure loomed, I chose my default. I tried harder, assuming I could—out of my own strength and will—manage and perfect this momma-hood thing on my own. And this pressure? All self-induced. Never once did my husband pressure me to be a better mom. The only message my husband ever communicated to me was how great of a mother I am to our boys. I know it hurt him to see me struggling, and I know he wished I could see what he saw in me.

Regardless of my husband's encouragement, love, and support, the pressure to be the best for my family grew more intense because it was fueled by such a profound love for my children and a desire to not mess them up and to raise them to be good, respectful kids. It was hard enough to manage the pressure to be perfect when I was responsible only for myself. It was a whole other kind of pressure when I became responsible for other human beings.

You ever felt it? The drive to be perfect? What about when you became a mom? Did you feel the weight of the world on your shoulders? That feeling of intense responsibility to be the best for everyone? And when you've fallen short, have you feared what others would think? Have you hidden your failures and acted like you've got it all together?

Imperfection terrified me, which is why I became that mother who put a smile upon my face and pretended everything was just fine, when in reality life was far from fine. I don't know if you're like this or not, but here's what I believe to be true: We don't do it intentionally to mislead ourselves or others. We are genuinely trying to be the best we can be for everyone in our lives, especially our kids, while trying to do it with a happy heart.

Sure, there are flawed and insecure parts of us we don't want to reveal to the rest of the world, but we don't hide these truths out of deceit. We hide them because it's what we think we are supposed to do—it's the "noble" thing to do. It's what "good" mommas do. We feel we would be *less than* if we dared to admit our struggles, insecurities, and flaws. And worse, we fear it would reveal we are bad moms. Plus, who has time to deal with those feelings? We have people to care for, places to be, and work to be done. So, we bury them and neglect those insecurities and fears as a way of coping and getting through the days. And instead we carry on the charade—believing it's our duty.

But tragically, we are aching inside under the pressure of trying to hold it all together on our own. But here's what I've learned, my friend: The deceit we cling to today becomes the lies we drown in tomorrow. God's chosen people, the Israelites, know more about that than anyone.

The deceit we cling to today becomes the lies we drown in tomorrow.

KINGDOM OF ME

Believing we can do life and this mothering thing out of our own strength and will is no different than the attitudes and behaviors the Israelites displayed time and time again throughout the Old Testament. Although continually opting for self-reliant and prideful hearts, they called themselves followers of God because they still went to church, gave offerings, and participated in religious practices. But they had turned their focus and their life's dependence to full reliance on themselves. Instead of relying on God, they basically lived faith on the surface. They got wrapped up in doing things *of* this world, ignoring the very One who gave them life and freedom in the first place. Listen how this Scripture exposes their complacency, their fraud, and most of all, their pride.

> You talk about God, the God-of-the-Angel-Armies, being your best friend. Well, live like it, and maybe it will happen. ...
>
> I can't stand your religious meetings. I'm fed up with your conferences and conventions. I want nothing to do with your religion projects, your pretentious slogans and

goals. I'm sick of your fund-raising schemes, your public relations and image making. I've had all I can take of your noisy ego-music.

When was the last time you sang to me?[1]

God sees right through the Israelites' superficial faith and beckons them back to Him. He's fed up with their egocentric living—their belief they can do life without Him. I have been a life-long believer and knew all about what God had done for me and the free gift of grace He offers us through Christ, yet I behaved like the Israelites who pretended they had life figured out on their own.

The most frightening reality check of all was, even though I was wrestling with an unsettled heart, I didn't think I was doing anything wrong. I thought I was being responsible for my family. I thought I was being a faithful servant. I didn't intentionally ignore God nor did I think I had superficial faith. What I've realized is I was striving for God's approval through my actions, yet it was approval I already had.

I was doing godly things. We were going to church as a family. I was leading Sunday school. We were giving offering and participating in church activities. I was praying with my children every night. I was even leading a Mothers of Preschoolers (MOPS) group at our local church. I had a genuine desire to be closely involved in a community of faith and to spread the Word of God.

But friend, please hear me when I admit I was blinded by pride, assuming *I* was the one fully responsible for creating a beautiful life for my children. For raising them to be good, kind, independent people. I assumed I had to be the best in order to give them the best. It was worldly perfection preventing me from fully understanding the meaning of the gift of grace God offers. I was not choosing nor inviting God's love and grace to do what it was meant to do for me—free me from the pressure of being perfect and doing this mothering thing on my own. I didn't have the faith God offers nor the faith He desires.

Instead, my ache for a perfection that can never be attained on this side of eternity pushed me to rise up into what I call the "Kingdom of Me" mentality. What I mean is I behaved as if my children's everything—their happiness, intelligence, faith, behavior, health—was dependent upon *my* ability as a mother. As a result, this perfect life I'd been working to attain had become my idol. I did what most of us moms do—made my children the most important thing in my life. After all, it's what good moms do, right? Well, if it was so *right*, why didn't I feel right? Why did I ache for something more? Why couldn't I be satisfied with this life? Although the answer was not clear then, it is now. I had placed my children above my relationship with God. I was missing out on the freedom, joy, and peace only He provides. It's no wonder I felt an ache in my heart.

THE MOLTING PROCESS

This Kingdom of Me mentality resembles that of a caterpillar growing. As a caterpillar grows, its skin does not grow with it. Therefore, when it gets too big for the outer layer of skin, it sheds the tight layer. This process of crawling out of its skin is called molting. Keep in mind, nothing helps the caterpillar crawl out of its old skin. The creature has to molt on its own—through its own strength.

As mommas, we constantly go through the molting process as our circumstances, moods, children, and relationships change. If you're like me, you're eager to shed what doesn't work or apply any longer so you can continue to grow, learn, and meet the needs of your kids. I have to admit, this sounds pretty wise and thoughtful. But the problem is, we too often find a new solution out of our *own* strength, which doesn't fix our heart problem and obsession with perfection. Instead, it eventually leads to more confusion, frustration, feelings of failure, and ultimately, defeat.

But there's encouraging news. Scripture reveals a reason for our desire to seek perfection. It's a truth that can help us accept our imperfections and release this Kingdom of Me mentality. This truth has the power to transform our pressure to be perfect from a debilitating stronghold into a life-giving spring of hope and purpose that can propel us from striving and surviving to thriving and living.

The pressure to be perfect can be transformed from a debilitating stronghold into a life-giving spring of hope and purpose that can propel us from striving and surviving to thriving and living.

REVEALING THE MYSTERY OF PERFECTION

Let's journey back to the beginning of time to unveil the mystery of why we feel this pressure to be perfect in the first place. Adam and Eve were the first humans created in the image of God. They lived in a beautiful garden, fell into temptation, sinned, were banished from the Garden of Eden, and separated from God. Imagine the shock and heartache of living in peace and harmony one day to living in shame and guilt the next. Have you ever paused to wonder about the significance of the occurrences before sin entered the world?

There is a verse in the creation story we tend to skim over without recognizing the transforming truth it reveals. This one verse—when accompanied with the gospel of Christ—has the power to unleash our souls from the burdens of seeking worldly perfection and the aches of not attaining. It also inspires us to see perfection from a new, godly perspective and accept its innate existence in our hearts.

"The man and his wife were both naked, and they felt no shame."[2]

Moments before the fall there existed no awareness of wrong, pain, or embarrassment. Adam and Eve felt accepted, totally and completely. They felt worthy. With nothing to prove and nothing to hide, they lived in perfect harmony with God and His creation. God looked at all He had made and saw it as good.[3] The parents of humanity walked and dwelt amid the groves of a glorious paradise. For a time, they lived in and experienced the perfection of their intentionally designed existence—a perfection of wholeness and unity with God.

But it was short lived. Scripture says as soon as they each took a bite of the forbidden fruit their eyes were opened, and they realized they were naked.[4] Furthermore, this awareness of their exposure and disobedience to God drove them to seek hiding for they instantly felt shame, guilt, and embarrassment.

Because of this one fateful choice, shame was etched into the DNA of all humankind—you and I included. It's shame—this heaviness and pain of sin and brokenness—that holds us captive, conceals the truth of our innate makeup, adds pressure that debilitates us from living our divine purpose, and steals our joy. Sin tricks us. Sin turns our desire for godly perfection into a worldly obsession involving intense pressure to perform. Sin deceives us into believing this desire for perfection is about being the best, not messing up, and being everything for everyone. In other words, the pure and wholeness of God's design for perfection becomes distorted when sin and brokenness take over our hearts and minds.

But here, my friend, is one of the most comforting revelations I've discovered. Underneath the shame of our hearts—when we peel away the brokenness and sin—God's design of perfection is still imprinted into the intricate fabrics and fibers of our souls because the human heart was created by God in the perfection of the very first man and woman—in the perfection of the first paradise. Therefore, we inherently yearn for and seek God's design of perfection because it's a part of who we are as creations of the Most High God.

Please hear me when I say this. Our desire for perfection is normal. It's not a bad thing. It's not something to be ashamed of because to be ashamed of it means we are ignoring a truth of our existence. Understanding the role sin and brokenness play in manipulating our perception of God's initial design for perfection can help us release the internal pressure of striving for worldly perfection. A pressure, when ignored, has the power to imprison and derail us from embracing our Divine purpose and experiencing joy. Seeking perfection is then simply about our heart's innate desire to push through sin and darkness and claim our unity with God again. Embrace the wholeness only He can nurture and use to transform us into who He designed us to be. However, it's a wholeness and transformation we can't attain on our own.

I love the masterful perfection of our creation, but it's only a fraction of God's creative plan for humanity. The story does not end there, thank goodness. It's only the beginning. In fact, we can't seek the true, godly perfection our hearts desire and claim unity with God without embracing the significant, eternal plan for restoration and redemption He put into motion especially for us.

BUT JESUS

Sin broke God's portrait of perfection. But Jesus—out of His great love for us—restored it—forever—by wiping the slate of sin clean[5] through His sacrificial death on the cross. You see, even before our perfection became tainted by sin, God had a restoration plan. The apostle Paul details this plan in Colossians 1:18b-22 (MSG).

> From beginning to end he's there, towering far above everything, everyone. So spacious is he, so roomy, that everything of God finds its proper place in him without

crowding. Not only that, but all the broken and dislocated pieces of the universe—people and things, animals and atoms—get properly fixed and fit together in vibrant harmonies, all because of his death, his blood that poured down from the cross.

You yourselves are a case study of what he does. At one time you all had your backs turned to God, thinking rebellious thoughts of him, giving him trouble every chance you got. But now, by giving himself completely at the Cross, actually dying for you, Christ brought you over to God's side and put your lives together, whole and holy in his presence.

As you can see, God's plan did not include us trying to do life on our own. To prove we are enough. To attain worthiness. It did not include rising after each failure with a stronger, more self-reliant posture. It did not initiate us to be in control of our lives. It did not include loneliness, insecurity, or guilt—the very debilitating feelings we mommas know all too well. These are the very strongholds that keep us in the Kingdom of Me mentality—stuck surviving and striving.

No. God is not sitting on His throne keeping score. He's not giving us check marks when we fail or rolling His eyes when we mess up. God doesn't want our worldly perfection. He wants our hearts that seek perfection through Christ. Seeking perfection in the world robs our joy, but seeking our potential through Christ produces joy. God's plan involved Him becoming one of us, in the man of Jesus, so He could repair our brokenness—the result of sin—and make us complete and perfect again through the power of His grace.

Seeking perfection in the world robs our joy, but seeking our potential through Christ produces joy.

It's in the beautiful security and comfort of God's enduring grace that comes to us through the blood of Jesus where we are molded more and more into the perfection of Christ. When God looks at us, He looks through the lens of Jesus and sees His good, beautiful creations. He doesn't see our failures and sin. It's because of Jesus, and only Jesus, that we gain the confidence and freedom to truly live and thrive with enduring hope, renewed purpose, and unwavering joy. Hebrews 10:12–14 (MSG) confirms this truth.

> Christ made a single sacrifice for sins, and that was it! Then he sat down right beside God and waited for his enemies to cave in. It was a perfect sacrifice by a perfect person to perfect some very imperfect people. By that single offering, he did everything that needed to be done for everyone who takes part in the purifying process.

Knowing this truth and living this truth are very different things. For years, I was stuck in the Kingdom of Me. As I'll share in the next chapter, it wasn't until my joy and purpose faded and became unrecognizable that I realized my radical need for Christ. The private aching of my heart could be silenced no longer. I realized I was caught up in the pressure of worldly perfection and wasn't fully accepting the grace He died to give that had the power to release me from the unnecessary pressure. It wasn't an epiphany that happened overnight. Rather, it took unexpected encounters with Jesus to help me see the life and freedom He was offering me. But this life and freedom is not exclusive to me. He's offering this life to you too. It's the start of a gradual process of refinement and transformation.

Making it Matter

"Me do it."

"Myself."

"I got it."

Ever heard those statements proclaimed in your house? My boys confidently declared these sentiments and others like it as they grew and developed their self-awareness. At a young age, they were already naturally beginning to build a deep-rooted sense of self-reliance, independence, and self-determination.

These are great qualities to nurture in our kids. But these qualities, in and of themselves, can lead to an unhealthy desire to attain perfection. They can trick us into believing we are the sole provider of happiness and success, and when that deception takes root, we believe everything is our responsibility. And when we feel like we're responsible for everything, that's when the pressures to perform and rise up with our own strength escalate.

I invite you to peer honestly into your heart as you read these questions and journal in the space below. It's a powerful way to begin taking steps toward positive change. Do you know what it's like to seek worldly perfection? What has been your response to it? Are you familiar with that pressure? Have you ever lived trapped in the Kingdom of Me mentality? The feeling of intense motivation to be everything you can be for your kids? To create a happy childhood for them? To raise them to be good, independent, successful people? To raise them to be Christ followers?

Let me emphasize, there is nothing wrong with doing our best for our children and our families. It's a normal reaction to the intense love we have for our kids. God calls us to love and to serve others. But I want you to look deeply into your heart to see if that love is prompting you to rise up, every morning, with more and more self-reliance. Where you, alone, are trying to be enough. To be perfect. To be in control. Are you treading water at a pace you can barely continue—trying with all *your* might to keep your head above water and avoid failure? If so, how is this causing you to feel? Share how you've dealt with the pressure to be perfect, as a woman, a wife, and a mom. What is holding you back from releasing that stronghold?

_____

_____

_____

_____

_____

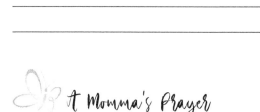 *A Momma's Prayer*

Father, we thank You for opening our eyes to the truth of our perfection. A perfection that is an inherent part of who we are. A perfection You see in us through the reflection of Christ. We are so grateful for Jesus, Lord. So grateful You manufactured a rescue plan to save us from the chains of sin. Thank You for reminding us we don't have to do this life alone nor attempt to do it perfectly because Jesus has redeemed us. Forgive us, Lord, for trying to manage and control this motherhood thing with reliance on ourselves instead of on You. Help us release the pressure to be perfect, to be enough, and instead, learn how to accept Your love and grace to cover us and free us from the pressures that tear us down, steal our joy, and diminish our purpose. Begin the refining process in us, Lord, as we rest confidently in the gentle, loving palms of Your hands. In Jesus' name we pray, amen.

Meaningful Truth

*After you have suffered a little while, the God of all grace,
who called you to His eternal glory in Christ, will Himself
perfect, confirm, strengthen, and establish you.*

—1 Peter 5:10 (NASB)

~ CHAPTER 3 ~

The Hushed Fall of Joy

GOD INVITES YOU INTO HIS PRESENCE

When my fourth baby was thirteen months old, I remember after a long, tiring day, plopping down on the rocking chair in the nursery—a chair that held years of soothing my babies to sleep and countless precious memories. Feeling the warmth and weight of his body upon mine, I snuggled and cradled Parker in my arms with his blanket in tow (the satin upon his face), rocking back and forth as the sweet, just-bathed, baby scent filled the air around us. He was my last baby, so despite my exhaustion and weary heart, which seemed to grow wearier as the demands and challenges of motherhood grew, I reminded myself to cherish these moments with him as they would soon be a distant memory. (Thinking about it now makes me wish for one more of those priceless moments.)

It was a cold, January day and snow fell lightly outside. As I sat rocking Parker in the glow of a nightlight, watching snowflakes dance outside the window and melt as they hit the glass, and singing softly some of our favorite tunes, "You Are My Sunshine" and "This Little Light of Mine," the lyrics— ones I had sung hundreds of times before—struck a chord in my being and caused silent tears to fall from my eyes.

I tried to fight them. I did. But they kept falling. The words leaving my lips stung as they vulnerably exposed the true condition of my heart. *You are my sunshine, my only sunshine. You make me happy, when skies are gray. You'll never know, dear, how much I love you. Please don't take my sunshine away.*

It seems ridiculous how a sweet lullaby could cause such a disturbing reaction. I couldn't get past the words, "You make me happy, when skies are gray." I kept repeating the phrase, over and over again as if I was willing it to be true. But the truth was, I wasn't happy. I didn't want to feel that way. I fought it for so long. Raising my four sons had quadrupled my love and joy, yet what I couldn't articulate nor understand was how that indescribable love could cohabitate with feelings of failure, guilt, doubt, fear, and discontent. How could polar opposite feelings co-exist?

Mustering, every day, all the strength and power I had, I tried, for the sake of my boys, to be a rock-star momma. To believe, *I've got this. I am in complete control. I ... am ... happy.* As I wiped the tears flooding from my eyes, I desperately yearned to embrace every precious moment I was blessed to have with my children, yet the silence and unexpected emotional release invited me to contemplate yet again:

How did I get to this place? This is the home and life I had helped build. Why am I not content?

I felt so selfish. I had a loving husband. Beautiful, healthy children. A warm, cozy home. Supportive and loving family and friends. What more did I need?

Have you ever wondered how your aches trump the joy, especially when you have so much love for your kids?

Ever questioned, "How did I go from rockin' motherhood to motherhood rockin' me?"

I know what it's like to have power struggles with our kids and feel defeated by our lack of skill and patience. I know what it's like to witness sibling scuffles which cause us to react in ways that make us feel guilty afterward. I know what it's like to be up all night with a sick kid and endure the exhaustion the next day. I know the frustration of trying to juggle the simultaneous demands from our kids, meanwhile trying to balance it all. I could go on and on about the struggles in motherhood you might be facing now, have faced, or will face in the future. Instead, I want you to pause right now and reflect on your reality so you can begin to recognize the truth and relevance in your own story.

Was there a time you remember happily breathing in the responsibilities of motherhood? Take a moment to reminisce. Over time, did you ever begin suffocating, like me, under the ongoing demands and struggles? Maybe you are now or maybe it's something you experienced in the past. Wherever you are in the process, this kind of awakening to the reality of a life we didn't expect can breed disappointment and frustration or confusion and fear. Most of the time, this awakening to our discontent happens so gradually it's hard to recognize until, one day, it's too much, and it becomes all we think about.

If you're like me, you don't give up and you don't give in to those debilitating feelings very easily. You keep waking up day after day—trying harder and harder to meet everyone's expectations—assuming if you'd only keep trying, the feelings threatening to unravel you will pass. Plus, what momma has time to think about herself and her feelings when she's constantly juggling schedules and demands from other human beings?

Here's the tragedy, my friend. If we neglect the condition of our hearts by choosing to stay in the Kingdom of Me mindset, the joy continues to fade and our hope for a better life—where dreams actually do come true—are slowly and silently destroyed.

My *fantasy* of motherhood had come to a screeching halt. What we discover is motherhood is hard. It's so hard. There's so much pressure to do it right. I was living my dream as a mom but found myself grieving for something more. It felt like I was missing something. What that was, I didn't know, but something didn't align. I wondered where I had gone wrong. As I reflected on the words of "This Little Light of Mine," I felt myself lost and trapped in some unfamiliar, uncomfortable place of my own life, unable to see and enjoy the light. If the light was nowhere to be found, how would I ever be able to shine? That is, authentically.

I think it's safe to say, for the most part, my kiddos never sensed my internal turmoil. I did a pretty good job burying those feelings, and I'm so grateful they felt my love. In fact, most people I knew had no clue as to the condition of my heart.

But that moment on the rocking chair opened my eyes to the reality and depth of my pain. It invited me to confront it, but I didn't know how. I didn't dare admit a momma who loves her children could feel this way. Instead, I silently retreated.

THE RETREAT

With little warning, one day, the caterpillar—after days of eating and growing—retreats. It moves through its final molting process, revealing a harder pupal skin, and begins to withdraw from life as it's always known. Working continuously to cover itself with a hard, outer skin, it begins to reveal an unfamiliar image and appearance.

As mommas working tirelessly to be everything for our families and continually battling new challenges and struggles, we can subconsciously experience a hushed, unanticipated retreat of the heart where we withdraw from this life we've always known. It's a silent act of defeat. We continue to do life and go through the motions, but our joy is inconsistent. Our purpose is blurred. Our hope is hidden. This retreat can cause paralyzing and hardening of our hearts, leaving us unrecognizable to ourselves.

As a caterpillar prepares for its chrysalis—the hard, outer layer of skin—it searches for a safe place for the next stage of its life development. I can't help but wonder if the hardening of *our* hearts is a sign that it's time for a new stage of development. Perhaps it's an indication we need to find a safe place to rest. And I'm not talking the Holiday Inn, although that would be lovely every now and then. Perhaps it's an invitation to find safety in the presence of our Savior.

THE PROMISE OF A RAINBOW

It was a typical evening with kids (you know the kind … loud, demanding, exhausting—at least that's what it's like with four boys) six years ago when I was huddled over a hot stove preparing supper. I was exhausted from the day home with my littles, overwhelmed by the volunteer work that awaited me once the kids were in bed, and frustrated as I paused to look around at my reality. Two hungry, tired, whiny children each demanded my attention while two wrestled in the living room with the noise level accelerating. Meanwhile, my sweet husband was trying to talk to me. And supper? Well, it was officially burning. Ever been there?

This was not an unusual situation. I'd handled it many times before with my Kingdom of Me attitude. But in that moment, I had reached my boiling point. It's as if the years of rising up again and again to manage our crazy, loud life and meet everyone's needs were like a chisel at my heart, breaking it down more and more with each obstacle or struggle I had to overcome. Over time, it had grown weak, and in this moment, my heart was ready to crumble.

Before I erupted and said things I'd clearly regret and before I even realized what I was saying, I turned to my husband and blurted, "I have to go for a run!"

I don't know if it was the look on my face that said it all or the fact that I had never demanded to leave in the middle of preparing supper and managing our evening chaos. But my sweet husband—clearly confused and perhaps a bit worried, yet having enough intuition to know I needed a break—slowly and cautiously said, "O … kay."

Instantly, it felt as if time had paused and I had been placed in a sound-proof bubble where I could only hear one voice. I know it may sound a little crazy, but I'm certain it was the voice of God beckoning me to Him. I quickly changed, ignoring all the chaos around me. Although a little confused myself by my rash behavior, I hit the road feeling this overwhelming permission to expose the aches of my heart and ask God for more than just help. I needed rescuing.

A few short moments into my run, it began to pour, without warning—no sprinkles or light rain. A downpour. Lovely timing. It certainly surprised me, but the thought of turning around never entered my mind because the rain washing over me trumped any sense of practicality as I sensed God whispering:

"That's right. Run to me. Run. Let my grace, like this rain, pour over you and renew you."

And so, I ran. Hard and furious. My feet pounding out—stride after stride—my frustrations, guilt, sadness, and insecurities. Although agitated by the atmosphere and situation I had left behind, my legs and breath—who through the years had run many miles together and had become accountable partners—quickly fell into a familiar rhythm. Naturally, I began to breathe in through my nose three strides and out through my mouth two strides. In, two, three. Out, two. In, two, three. Out, two. This natural rhythm created a steady, calming cadence that relaxed my physical body, offsetting the struggle pursuing inside.

As I concentrated on the rhythm of my breathing, the whispers came again.

"Breathe in my strength, my grace, my love, and I will give you a new, peaceful, steady cadence by which to run—a pace to your heart that will sustain you forever."

I remember the sensation of my posture—calming and relaxing—as I fell into this amazingly comfortable rhythm, confident in His presence.

Right then, a neighbor approached me in her car insisting she give me a ride home. I looked up through blinking eyes with lashes dripping wet, thanked her, but without hesitation, I graciously declined. All I can say is the deep-in-my-gut feeling that had beckoned me to the road in the first place, was so intense, I couldn't ignore it. I couldn't abandon the run now, even if it made no sense. I had a feeling this was more than just any run.

Before I continue, there is something you must know about me. I never quit a run. I never turn around early. I always, at least, run the loop, which is only a few miles. But this day—at about mile one—while the rain poured and after the lone car on the road had passed—I felt the urge to turn around. It was the same feeling or intuition I'd been sensing the entire time. Again, I've never cut a run this short. Ever. But I'd come this far. I couldn't ignore the familiar, yet unusual promptings now.

As I turned around to go home—abandoning the route I always run—the rain continued to beat hard against my body. I heard the sloshing of my shoes as each foot hit the ground beneath me and felt the splattering of mud upon my calves. I tasted the rain on my lips cascading my face from my hair that had become like a dripping faucet. I turned to run the last half mile up the hill to my house, and the downpour immediately stopped—again no warning. It's as if the universe was trying to get my attention. (By universe, yes, I mean God!)

Stunned by the abrupt halt in the rain, my eyes were drawn to the sky. It's as if some gentle, peaceful force held my gaze so I wouldn't miss what was about to come. With my eyes glued to the eastern, evening horizon, I witnessed—in humble amazement—a rainbow being painted in brilliant colors on the canvas in the sky right before my eyes. The sight of it took my breath away, gradually slowing my run to a complete stop. I impetuously fell to my knees in awe—tears instantly flowing down my cheeks—and felt an overwhelming warmth and peace.

I could feel God embracing me with His mighty, gentle arms and reminding me, "I've got you. I've always had you. Trust in Me to heal your aching heart. To show you the way to peace and joy."

We've all seen rainbows. They aren't that unusual. But this one, friend? I felt this one was hand-crafted especially for me. Not because I am more special than someone else. Not because I deserved it. Not because I asked for a sign. But because that's what God does. God makes His presence known. We simply need to open our eyes and be attentive to Him so we don't miss out on the magnificent displays of His love.

God makes His presence known. We simply need to open our eyes and be attentive to Him so we don't miss out on the magnificent displays of His love.

To make sure I was paying attention—to make sure I knew it was Him orchestrating this gorgeous display of His power, inviting me into His presence—that beautiful rainbow began to disappear as quickly as it appeared. Again, right before my eyes. It was only seconds, maybe minutes, as I watched Him paint the rainbow in the sky. And I watched Him erase it. I could have easily missed it had I made a number of different choices. But that's God! I have no doubt this was part of His rescue plan for me. My friend, God is always present. It's up to us to pay attention and seek Him. And when we do, He reveals Himself to us. Jeremiah 29:12–14 confirms this truth:

"Then you will call upon me and come and pray to me, and I will listen to you. You will seek me and find me when you seek me with all your heart. I will be found by you, declares the Lord, and will bring you back from captivity."

I intently and genuinely sought His help, and He proved faithful because I found Him. No one on earth knows me like God does; after all, He created me and knows me inside and out.[1] Therefore, I believe He knew this was the moment He could gain my full attention and demonstrate His presence and power. In addition, He knew my struggles and heartaches—exactly like He knows yours. My heart was ready to receive, fully, all He had to offer. And He knew the perfect timing for which to unveil His rescue plan and save me from more pain and despair. It was in that place of hushed, fallen joy where my vulnerable heart was finally awakened, and I could admit my struggle, lay down my pride—the Kingdom of Me mentality—seek God's face, and prepare to receive His help, joy, peace, and freedom. The time had finally come, but it required me to fall to my knees in full surrender, fix my eyes on Him, and understand the invitation He offered.

INVITED INTO HIS PRESENCE

There is a story in Scripture from the Gospel of Luke where Jesus visits two sisters, Mary and Martha. The encounter reflects similarities we as women, especially moms, still experience thousands of years later in managing the daily demands of a busy life while simultaneously feeling the ache in our heart for something more.

> As Jesus and his disciples were on their way, he came to a village where a woman named Martha opened her home to him. She had a sister called Mary, who sat at the Lord's feet listening to what he said. But Martha was distracted by all the preparations that had to be made. She came to him and asked, "Lord, don't you care that my sister has left me to do the work by myself? Tell her to help me!"
>
> "Martha, Martha," the Lord answered, "you are worried and upset about many things, but only one thing is needed. Mary has chosen what is better, and it will not be taken away from her."[2]

At first glance, it looks like Jesus is comparing these two women. It's easy to quickly presume Jesus is lovingly lecturing or reprimanding Martha about how her sister, Mary, is making a wiser choice by spending time with Him and not busying herself with household chores. This perspective, however, seems to promote guilt and one that would surely hurt Martha's feelings. I believe Martha felt she was making the right choice by obeying the law that required women to serve. She genuinely wanted to please the Lord by obeying the law. Doesn't that sound familiar? Don't we work tirelessly to please the people in our lives? To please God? To make sure everyone is taken care of? Everything is handled?

Scripture says Martha was distracted by "all the preparations that *had* to be made." So even though she wanted to show her love and appreciation to Jesus through her service, the pressure to do so perfectly had distracted her heart so much she lost the joy. This distraction turned to discouragement and frustration where she became blinded to the invitation Jesus offered her.

Serving and taking care of our family is a natural response to the love we have for them. That is until the motivation to our serving begins to change and we get caught, like Martha, in the performance trap where serving feels more like an obligation to prove something or pretend we've got it all together than a joyous privilege and humble delight.

As I dig deeper into imagining this encounter, viewing it through the lens of Jesus' compassionate nature, I don't see Him lecturing. I don't see Him purposefully making Martha feel bad for trying to make His time there perfect. Jesus' mission was not to bestow guilt but to take it away.

Therefore, I imagine Jesus intuitively understanding her heart and intention and recognizing the ache of senseless pressure written all over her face and reflected in her tone of voice. I imagine Him yearning to take it away and admiring Martha's courage to speak openly and honestly. I imagine Him looking at her with tender, endearing eyes that spoke only love and grace as He extended one hand to her, gesturing to a spot next to Him with the other, showing her the one thing she needed the most. It was not more cooking. Not more cleaning. Not more preparing. What she needed most was to sit at the feet of Jesus.

Jesus knew the remedy to her heart condition. Therefore, this was an invitation to Martha to pause and be still in His presence ... to listen to Him ... to get to know Him ... because He didn't want her to miss out on the best He had for her. He desperately wanted to mend her weary heart and have an intimate relationship with her.

And friend, the exact same invitation and remedy is available to us. Jesus is the remedy to our heart condition—the cure that mends our weary, wounded souls. Imagine with me. Will you? Imagine Jesus gazing into your eyes, fully aware of the condition of your heart, extending His hand to you with compassion and understanding, and gesturing to an open spot, specifically for you, at His feet. Will you accept His invitation? To pause? Be still? Sit in His presence? Accept the grace He offers? He doesn't want us to miss out on life with Him either.

Jesus is the remedy to our heart condition— the cure that mends our weary, wounded souls.

Like Martha, I had gotten so distracted by the busyness of daily life and so overwhelmed and discouraged by the pressures and challenges of raising four boys that, for years, I missed the invitation to be still in God's presence. I missed the gift of grace He was offering my lost, weary heart. From the outside, it looked like I had it all together. But on the inside, I was crying for help because I was realizing how incapable I was of being the perfect Christian woman, mom, and wife I had dreamed of being.

I had become far too dependent on my own ability that I neglected to recognize there is a bigger, mightier power desiring to help us, every moment of every day, in any circumstance. But because I obsessed over having and maintaining control, I clinged to the things of this world to fix my problems and the aching of my heart.

We're told to get enough sleep, eat right, be active, live out our passions. These are great additions to a healthy, happy lifestyle. However, they will not fill the void in our hearts aching to burst free from the pressure to be enough for everyone. Hearts trembling under the disappointment of unmet expectations, faulty dreams, and undefined purpose. That void is sacred. That void is intentional. That void has a private invitation of One. That void was intricately woven into the fabric of your soul as you were being formed in your mother's womb. I know this because in the third chapter of Ecclesiastes, it says so.

> He has made everything beautiful and appropriate in its time. He has also planted eternity—a sense of divine purpose—in the human heart, a mysterious longing which nothing under the sun can satisfy, except God—yet man cannot find out (comprehend, grasp) what God has done (His overall plan) from the beginning to the end.[1]

The void you're feeling was *meant* to be and can *only* be filled by God. Yes, my friend, God. We need God. We need an intimate encounter with the One who knows everything about us. The one who understands us yet desires to meet us right where we stand, today.

The void you're feeling was meant to be and can only be filled by God.

And when we do? When we seek the One who has the power to fill us with life-sustaining grace, the very thing our hearts crave? We are set free from the chains that have held us as silent prisoners and are transformed by His enduring love in ways beyond our wildest imaginations.

I have come to discover that accepting God's grace, being still in His presence, and getting to know Him is a privileged choice. It's not a duty. It's not an obligation. It's not another dreadful thing to add to the mile-long to-do list.

My "Martha turned Mary Moment"—when I turned away from all of life's distractions, sought Him, and fell to my knees on the side of the road, in the rain—was a profound step in my journey to discovering the foundational source of my joy. The cure to my aching heart. My hardened, self-reliant heart was on its way to being transformed and softened in more ways than I could ever imagine. I finally felt free to admit:

"I'm a sinner. And it's okay because I have a Savior."

I often wonder about Martha's response. Scripture doesn't tell us. Perhaps, more frustrated, she uttered excuses. Maybe—embarrassed and confused—she retreated back into the kitchen. Or perhaps—as she stood there gazing into her Savior's eyes—Martha's heart softened too. And realizing her aching soul's need for surrender, she fell to her knees and began to allow Jesus to speak truths into her heart she desperately needed. Are you ready to lay down everything and fall to your knees? Once you're ready to break free from the ways of the world and surrender to the safety of God's protective chrysalis, the transformation process begins. But first, we must ensure a solid foundation as we remember and embrace who we are and whose we are.

Making it Matter

Singing. Humming. Chanting. Yelling. Boys wrestling (by far, the loudest sound in the house). Piano playing. Blender revving. Frying pan sizzling. Dish washer running. TV blaring. You name it. Any combination of these sounds and more drown out any attempt by one of my sons to get my attention from across the house. I can often hear them call out, "Mom!" But after that, it's a bunch of rubbish I can rarely decipher.

As if their attempt to communicate isn't ridiculous enough, I find myself yelling back, "I can't hear you." (Great role model, huh? I've since learned.) The noise continues, and eventually, one of two things have to happen to make communication a success. They have to walk over to me and speak in front of my face, so I can at least read their lips. Or the distractions must be silenced. If either of those fails to occur, I will not be able to hear what my son has to say to me. I will not hear his voice.

Isn't the same true for hearing Jesus' voice? We often find ourselves in the midst of constant distractions that prevent us from hearing Him. We forget He's even there. We tend to neglect Jesus because our responsibilities take priority over intimacy with Him. It's exactly like my house, when the noise gets too loud and I'm unable to hear the beckoning calls of my sons, we are unable to decipher the freeing truths Jesus longs to speak—the very thing our hearts need to be whole and complete.

Most of us moms don't intentionally wander away from God. We don't intentionally put Him on the back burner. Sadly, that's where He often ends up, forced to call us from across the noisy room. We can so easily get wrapped up in our complex lives that are constantly influenced by the fast-paced world causing us to run ragged and leaving us no time to rest. Sometimes we don't realize what we need until another woman breaks the silence and admits her tough reality. We don't even realize there is another way to live until someone else shows us there is.

So, friend, where do you find yourself today? Are you stuck in the rat-race of life and the Kingdom of Me mentality, unable to silence the distractions long enough to hear the cries of your heart? To hear the voice of Jesus? Or, have you experienced a silent retreat of your heart where you're aching for something more that can't be filled by yourself, others, or the world? Have you reached your boiling point, like I did, where you are about to explode if something doesn't change?

Are you ready to release control and instead trust that Jesus is the answer you've been searching for? If not, what's standing in your way?

I invite you to journal your truths, right now, as I remind you wherever you are on your journey—whether you are ready to release control or whether you are still trying to do life on your own—know that Jesus is sitting right next to you, gesturing to a place at His feet for you. Friend, Jesus is the answer to your aching heart. He is working in your life, through whatever struggle, challenge, or hardship you may be experiencing, in every way possible to draw you back to Him. It may not be a rainbow, but if you open your eyes, silence the distractions, and seek Him, you will find Him. When you vulnerably and humbly turn to God and share your heart with Him, expect to be wowed. In fact, no time is like the present. Reach out to God now by journaling your heart cry to Him in the space below.

_____

_____

_____

_____

_____

_____

_____

_____

_____

A Momma's Prayer

Gracious Lord, thank You for never giving up on us. For continuing to seek us in the midst of our chaos. For inviting us to sit at Your feet. To be in Your presence. To soak up Your glory. You are our masterful creator who knows the intimate places of our hearts aching for clarity, purpose, and freedom. We're tired, Lord. We're tired of the pressure. We're tired of trying to be everything for everyone. We're tired of not soaking in all the joy and beauty surrounding us. And we know, Lord, You desire to take that stronghold from us. We know You have greater plans for us beyond our wildest dreams. You've already paid the ultimate price by dying on the cross for us. Forgive us for not walking in Your gift of freedom. For not trusting You and leaning on You. For not accepting Your extravagant love and allowing it to overwhelm us. So, today, Lord, we place our lives in Your hands. We turn the reins over to You. Take our hardened hearts and soften them. Open our eyes to Your purposes, Your plans, and Your ways. Build in us a resilient, confident spirit that chooses You, every day, so we don't stumble into a dark place again. In Jesus' name we pray, amen.

Meaningful Truth

I've tried everything and nothing helps. I'm at the end of my rope. Is there no one who can do anything for me? Isn't that the real question? The answer, thank God, is that Jesus Christ can and does. He acted to set things right in this life of contradictions where I want to serve God with all my heart and mind, but am pulled by the influence of sin to do something totally different.

—Romans 7:24–25 (MSG)

PART TWO

The Metamorphosis of
Motherhood

THE STRUGGLE TO FIND PURPOSE

CHAPTER 4

The Battle with Identity

GOD DEFINES WHO YOU ARE AND DELIGHTS IN YOU

The last day of sixth grade was a day marked with a life-altering message—a message about who I was that contradicted the truth I had always believed to be true. A truth that said, "You are amazing, just the way you are." The details, nearly thirty years later, are still vividly etched into my memory. I was a chubby kid with buck teeth, freckles, and an outgrown perm streaked with chlorine shine and texture—evidence of hours spent at swim practice. I accepted myself for who I was, for it's all I had ever known. Apart from my brothers joking and teasing me every now and then, I had no reason to doubt my value nor my beauty.

That was until a boy in my class, moments before the bell rang announcing summer vacation, squeezed my upper arm exposed by my new, neon coral tank top I was so proud to wear. The unfamiliar touch made me squirm as he wiggled it, laughed, and teased, "This is one big arm. You shouldn't be wearing shirts like this."

Confused by his abrupt comment, I remember first thinking, *What are you doing touching my arm?* And then as uncomfortable feelings set in, I silently wondered, *What do you mean?*

He must have sensed my confusion because he repeated himself. It wasn't until I witnessed other kids laughing and whispering with him that shock and humiliation overwhelmed my body. Trying with all my might not to cry, I shrugged his comment off as if it didn't bother me.

But it did. Big time. The unexpected exposure to messages about who I was that didn't match the only beliefs I had ever known—hurt. This hurt caused a wound I kept hidden for years because I was too embarrassed to tell anyone. Embarrassed because I feared he was right. It was my first glimpse through a distorted lens of reality, which caused me to silently question: *Who am I? Really?*

Although the unconditional love from my parents was the foundation that helped me endure the confusion in my heart, I felt an internal conflict take root as I began to see myself the way that boy had seen me. Little did I know at the time, my identity was slowly being hijacked by these lies.

THE COMPLIMENT THAT HIJACKED THE TRUTH

As life would have it, I matured, and my physical appearance changed significantly. Ready to enter high school, I no longer resembled that hurt twelve-year-old. Braces had straightened my teeth. Hair treatments had transformed my chlorinated hair into soft, silky locks. And puberty had taken my childhood chub and replaced it with the physique of a petite athlete. I left that awkward stage of life with newfound confidence and amazing friends who loved and accepted me and who were the source of many fun and happy memories.

Nothing, however, could top the epic party at my friend's lake cabin the summer before freshman year. It was a beautiful, hot summer day filled with everything from swimming to playing football. When the time had come to head home, an intense thunderstorm blew in out of nowhere (no smart phones with radars back then) and washed out the only road home. We were stuck there ... for the night! About fifteen teenagers—boys and girls—now having a sleepover. It was a parent's nightmare! But to a bunch of teenagers? Best ... party ... *ever*!

My friends and I were scattered everywhere throughout the night. Some were in rooms chit-chatting. Some played in the yard. Others were dancing in the garage to our favorite early nineties music. (Boys to Men all the way!) I'm pretty certain no one got much sleep that night, including the poor parents stuck there with us.

The next morning, one of the girls shared with a few of us the conversations some had in one of the rooms the night before. The girls asked the boys questions: Who do you think is the prettiest? Who do you think is the nicest? Who do you think is the best athlete? I guess you could say this is typical teenage behavior and curiosity. Little did they know the effect one answer would have on me—the answer that included my name.

The question was: Who has the best body? You'd think learning this kind of information would make any young teenage girl feel good and confident. Perhaps a bit flattered. But it did the opposite to me. Unfortunately, what was meant to be a compliment instead opened the wound inflicted on my last day of sixth grade I thought had healed. But in actuality, I had ignored it.

Doing my best to hide my true heart condition, I again pretended it was no big deal. But it turned out to be a pretty big deal. Sadly, this day—one of the most vivid memories of my young life—is also the day my real struggle with identity began. My self-inflicted pressure to attain perfection combined with my fear of ever being judged as ugly, fat, unaccepted, or worthless again jumpstarted a whirlwind of false beliefs about my identity that spiraled quickly out of control. Sadly, this led me into a ten-year battle with bulimia.

Quickly becoming obsessed with exercising and controlling what and how much I ate, the more concerned I got with what others thought of me, the more lies I believed, and the more the lies trumped the genuine truth of who I was—of who I am. I became a master at masking my insecurities and imperfections—of portraying myself as a confident, happy young woman. Meanwhile, an internal battle over my identity and worth ensued.

Like many of us, I wanted to be liked, accepted, admired, and loved. The lies within told me if I was thin, pretty, smart, and the best at everything I did, I would gain those accolades. But I already had acceptance and love from the *One* and the people who mattered most. And it had nothing to do with my appearance or performances. Yet I still got trapped in the web of lies. I began to worry so much about what others thought of me I neglected to care what it was doing to my health. The eating disorder became my way of attempting to control the pressure and fear of rejection, failure, and imperfection.

My best friends from high school—thank God for them— are the ones who had the courage to confront me and help me tell my parents, which began a long road to healing. Looking back at how well I hid my struggle from the people closest to me, I'm frightened and saddened to think how many people are going through a similar silent battle, right now.

This piece of my story stole my identity for years and one I was ashamed to speak of until God's truth overrode the twisted messages and lies and released me of the shame. But if I may be so bold, I assume you have had a similar experience that altered how you saw yourself. What comments did you receive as you were growing up that made you question your worth? What labels were you forced to live with that wrongly defined who you were? The effect of that hurt may not have led you to develop an eating disorder. But did you compress the pain and worldly pressure in other ways?

Maybe instead of an eating disorder, you turned to other forms of self-harm. Maybe you experienced depression or anxiety, which can have the overriding ability to distort the way you see yourself. Or perhaps you've been the target of bullying that caused you to doubt your value and unique beauty. Whatever it was or is that has caused you to question your identity and worth, *it's a lie*—one which every human being is confronted with at some point in time and one that must be silenced in order for you to see yourself clearly and begin to understand the truth of who you are.

WHO AM I?

For centuries, people have asked the question, "Who am I?" We answer the question based on the messages we've received throughout our lives. Our hearts and minds are like hard drives. Whatever messages we receive the most often or are the loudest, we download on our main server and those inputs become dominant beliefs. They begin to define who we believe we are and act as a virus attempting to take over our true identity.

Who have you allowed to define your identity? Maybe you grew up in a destructive home and only heard negative messages causing you to doubt your worth. Or maybe, like me, you grew up in the most loving home, yet your identity was questioned and threatened by outside influences that caused internal turmoil.

Here's what's disheartening. I grew up knowing God loved me, knowing I was special and unique. It was the message my parents expressed, in countless ways, through their love. But the deceitfulness of the world's messages and labels were so intense, consistent, and convincing it overpowered those truths. The lies of the world clouded my judgment of who I was. God's truths had become silent, hidden messages in the farthest corners of my heart, providing an opportunity for the enemy to establish a stronghold of lies and destruction within me.

And I know I'm not the only one who has ever struggled with this. I believe there is evil in the world—an enemy who threatens to hold us hostage and paralyze us from living in joy and freedom. This enemy is Satan who wants nothing more than to make us feel worthless and unloved. The wings of confidence and truth God wants to develop in us so we can soar to unimaginable heights, Satan wants to clip in an effort to prevent us from claiming our identity in Jesus and from being everything God made us to be.

But here's the truth we must embrace. God is much bigger than the enemy. And what the enemy wants to use to destroy us, God uses as a compass to lead us to Him, the only place we'll discover our true identity. Jesus is the One with the power to crush the lies and destroy the virus causing disfunction in our lives. Jesus holds the truth to our identity—a truth that will set us free. "Nothing in all creation will ever be able to separate us from the love of God which is ours through Christ Jesus our Lord."[1] I may not have recognized Jesus' presence at the time, but the internal battle was an indication He was present. He was fighting for me. And He's fighting for you too. In fact, He's fought and won for all of us and yearns to show us how beautiful and precious we are.

What the enemy wants to use to destroy us, God uses as a compass to lead us to Him, the only place we'll discover our true identity.

FULLY KNOWN AND LOVED

The lady at the well. She's nameless to us, although she's known by Jesus. She's often described as the Samaritan woman, which provides us insight into her identity and perhaps her heart condition. Samaritans were a mixed race—Jews who intermarried people of other faiths—who worshipped idols and didn't believe in God and His promise of a Messiah. The Jews, therefore, wanted nothing to do with the Samaritans.

Imagine this woman's surprise when, on her way to draw water from the well, she encounters a Jewish man sitting there as if waiting for her. Now imagine her shock as she tries to go about her business intentionally not making eye contact or having interaction of any sort with this Jewish man, when Jesus suddenly speaks to her:

"Would you give me a drink of water?" [His disciples had gone to the village to buy food for lunch.]

The Samaritan woman, taken aback, asked, "How come you, a Jew, are asking me, a Samaritan woman, for a drink? [Jews in those days wouldn't be caught dead talking to Samaritans.]

Jesus answered, "If you knew the generosity of God and who I am, you would be asking me for a drink, and I would give you fresh, living water." [2]

In this delicate moment, Jesus abandons the rules. He tears down the barriers. This Samaritan woman had everything stacked against her. Not only was she the hated race, but she was also known to be living a life filled with sin. One can assume she may have felt worthless and unaccepted. I sense a sadness in the core of her being, an ache for something more. There was a hole in her spirit she had been trying to fill in worldly ways yet remained barren. No respectable Jewish man would ever consider talking to a woman such as this.

But Jesus did. Of course He did. And He spoke with a purpose.

Recognizing the woman wasn't fully grasping what he was trying to convey, Jesus began to speak about intimate details of her personal life, touching tender, vulnerable places of her heart, slowly gaining her attention and piquing her curiosity. Jesus had a message of hope to offer this woman.

Everyone who drinks this water will get thirsty again and again. Anyone who drinks the water I give will never thirst—not ever. The water I give will be an artesian spring within, gushing fountains of endless life.[3]

He goes on to tell her that it doesn't matter what others think of her. What matters is who she is before God. I imagine her wondering:

How does this man know so much about my life?

Why is He being so kind to me, especially since He knows what I've done?

How could I be worth anything to anyone?

The woman knew about the Messiah who was proclaimed to come and save His people. But she also believed this salvation didn't include her. That is, until Jesus told her otherwise. Compelled to seek clarity for what she hoped to be true, she says to Jesus (I envision her saying this more of a question, really, than a statement):

"I know that Messiah" (called Christ) "is coming."

"When he comes, he will explain everything to us."

Then Jesus declared, "I, the one speaking to you—I am he."[4]

There are so many details I love about this story, but the one I want to emphasize now is how Jesus penetrated and healed the most hardened, hurt, misinformed places of her heart. Instead of continuing to live in the shadows of her shame, Christ's love not only renewed her identity—an identity to be found in Him—but it compelled her to share Jesus' message of hope and love to others. Because of her transforming encounter with Jesus, an entire town came to know Him. Because of Him, she found purpose, joy, and freedom. With her fear and doubt erased and her sins forgiven, she now understood what is also true for us. Our worth does not balance on what we've done nor on what others think, but on who Jesus is, what He's done, and who we are through Him. In other words, we are made new because of Him. And in Him is where we find our true identity. "Therefore,

THE BATTLE WITH IDENTITY

if anyone is in Christ, he is a new creation; the old has gone, the new has come!"[5]

Our worth does not balance on what we've done nor on what others think, but on who Jesus is, what He's done, and who we are through Him.

BEAUTY REDEFINED

We were fearfully and wonderfully[6] created in the image of God[7] with unfailing, unconditional love attached through the death and resurrection of Jesus. Therefore, Jesus sees you in the beauty and perfection in which you were first created. Your worth, your value rests, on Him, who He is, and what He's done for you on the cross—not on who the world says you are. He doesn't see you as fat or thin, ugly or awkward. He doesn't see you the way that rude boy in sixth grade saw me.

Jesus sees you in the beauty and perfection in which you were first created.

Jesus knows every intimate corner of your heart, and he loves everything he sees. He knows where you are and where you're going.[8] And He's meeting you there. He's not running away, afraid of your mess. He's waiting for you, like He did to the

87

lady at the well—mess and all—offering you what your soul desires that the world cannot give. He's offering you living water that will forever fill and quench your thirst for that *something more* and remind you of your radiant beauty and identity that comes from Him and Him alone.

The distinct visual difference between a caterpillar and a butterfly is obvious ... beauty. The creepy, crawly caterpillar pales in comparison to the beauty of a butterfly. When we look in the mirror, we tend to see the features of a caterpillar rather than the beauty of a butterfly. We struggle to see ourselves the way God sees us. I like to imagine God looks at a caterpillar and sees a beautiful butterfly because he knows what He has created is good and He sees the full beauty He's uniquely created in that creature. The same goes for us. God sees in us the beauty and potential for which He created us.

OUR IDENTIY MATTERS IN MOTHERHOOD

You may be wondering, *What does this have to do with motherhood?* Everything, actually. Without this foundational understanding and acceptance of our divine identity—of who we are to God through Christ's sacrificial act of love—we will mother from a wounded heart. And we won't ever realize and embrace the divine responsibility that accompanies this most important role.

Yes, we will try with all our might to be good, happy, rock-star mommas. But when we fall short and can't be everything to everyone, the lies and hurts of our past will surface and begin to dictate our words and actions. These words and actions—without being filtered through the knowledge of God's truth of who we are and His enduring grace and love—will be tainted with sin, frustration, and shame, gradually creating guilty hearts. And the weight of the guilt will rob us of joy and peace. And when joy and peace are absent, we lose sight of the purpose and meaning in our roles as mom, wife, and woman—and to life itself. And a vicious, desperate cycle continues. The cost, my friends, is enormous.

I know none of us want regrets or lives absent of purpose and joy, so let me remind you. Christ did not die on the cross so we'd feel trapped in our inadequacy or doubt our identity and self-worth. He didn't die so we'd carry the guilt and shame of our failures—the very aches that steal our joy and peace. Christ died to set us free so we can live a new, free life—a free life in and through Him.[9]

Understanding our identity in Christ is the first step in transforming our hearts and leading us to our divine purpose. Christ is the truth that reestablishes our heart's foundation and naturally inspires us to change the way we mother and live our lives. The sanctification process goes into effect as we become more and more like Him. And the more like Him we become, the more inspired we are to love like Him. Instead of mothering with a wounded heart, we mother with a healed heart—full of grace and forgiveness—and with a vulnerable heart—willing to admit our own weaknesses and our desperate need for Christ. Our identity in Christ inspires us to mother in ways that brings glory to God and points our kids directly to Him.

But to become more like Him takes *awareness*.

Intention.

And *desire*.

Our identity in Christ inspires us to mother in ways that brings glory to God and points our kids directly to Him.

Making it Matter

I adore the countless stages and milestones we get the privilege of witnessing our children experience. I don't mean I love everything about each stage. Potty training? I would skip that in a heartbeat. But one of the most endearing and entertaining stages is when our kids learn how to talk and put the pieces of their world together with their limited verbal abilities.

For example, I loved teaching my boys their names and the names of the people in their lives. I'd point to my son and ask, "Who are you?" Pointing to me, I'd ask, "Who am I?" Then pointing to each brother or person in the room or in a picture, I'd ask "Who is that?" They were always eagerly engaged and entertained in learning who people were. And I know we all do it. In fact, the other day during one of my son's school programs, I sat next to a mother who was asking her baby the same questions.

Here's what I find fascinating. Our kids naturally begin to learn—like we all do, very early on—that each person has a name, a role, and an identity. As we grow, we have this innate need and desire to know who we are, where we belong, and what our place and purpose is in the world. How we come to discover our identity lies in the messages we receive from the people in our world.

It's time again, friend, to grab your pen and share your heart in the space below. Have you or do you currently struggle with your identity? Thinking back to your childhood, what were the messages that defined who you were? Who were the people in your life who spoke those messages? Were they messages based on your behavior, personality, intensity, outward appearance, or circumstances of your world? How did those messages make you feel? How have they impacted who you are today? Or, were they messages filled with God's truths that, regardless of what the world said, built a solid, confident, resilient heart leading to a life of joy, peace, and purpose? How does God define you right now? Who are you to Him?

_____

_____

_____

_____

_____

_____

_____

_____

_____

_____

A Momma's Prayer

Lord, we are so grateful You know us even when we don't know or recognize ourselves. We're so grateful You love us and desire to be with us and lead us into greater purposes for Your glory. And we're so grateful You call us Your very own, especially in times when we feel lost and abandoned and manipulated by the world. Remind us, Lord, that Your love and grace for us and who You define us to be has the capacity to fill us up with confidence to pour love and grace into others. Help us, Lord, to be vessels of Your living water to people who so desperately need to hear this good news. Continue to strip away the false definitions the world throws at us about who we are. Build in us an unwavering confidence of who we are to You—a beloved, precious child with whom You are well pleased. Help us to never stray away from Your truths so we can continue to walk in freedom, joy, and peace. In Jesus' precious name, amen.

Meaningful Truth

But now the Lord Who made you, O Jacob, and
He Who made you, O Israel, says: Do not be afraid.
For I have bought you and made you free. I have called you
by name. You are Mine! … You are of great worth in my eyes.
You are honored and I love you.

—Isaiah 43: 1 & 4 (NLV)

~ CHAPTER 5 ~

The Invitation of a Lifetime

GOD LONGS FOR YOU TO SAY "YES"

My phone rang on a typical afternoon in April 2013 (three months after that winter night in the rocking chair). I had just gotten up from my desk to change the laundry when I heard it ring. Eager to have an adult conversation in the middle of my stay-at-home-momma sort of afternoon, I hustled to answer, missing the call by only seconds. Two of my boys were at school, two were napping, and I was spending the little bit of free time I had at my computer doing work for MOPS and Sunday School. But this call? This call would later turn out to be anything but typical. Little did I know at the time, but this call would be an invitation that would change the trajectory of my life.

Quickly searching my phone to see who had called, I was delighted to discover I had a voicemail message from my dear friend, Jen, which instantly brought a smile to my heart. Jen was one of the first friends I met when we moved to Minnesota. She is one of those people who contagiously exudes positivity into the world. Thinking of her now, as I write, makes me smile.

Her message was short, simple, and to the point:

"Hey, Natalie, Sara and I are signing up today. I hope you're in. I think it'd be really, really, really fun if we did this together. So ... give me a call. Bye." (It's maybe a little weird I still have this message saved on my phone, but it was *that* significant to me.)

Jen didn't spend time convincing me or begging me. She didn't even ask the question, although I knew exactly what she was referring to as it had been the topic of a few conversations in the past. In her cheery, friendly voice, she presented a clear, yet subtle invitation to join her and our friend, Sara. Sara was also one of the first friends I met shortly after we moved here and whose presence lights up a room and whose spirit I adore. These women were good for my soul. And still are. One of the things we had in common, that instantly connected us, was running. Running was the excuse we used to sneak away from the stress of home and spend some refreshing time with awesome women.

And running was, indeed, the subject of Jen's invitation. She had called to invite me to run the Twin Cities Marathon in Minneapolis/St. Paul in October. I had a choice to make. Yes. Or no.

Have you ever been asked to do something and your simple "yes" or "no" answer changed the direction of your life or offered clarity you'd been seeking? Maybe it was a question difficult to answer because it required you to put you first? Or that yes answer entailed more courage than you'd ever needed before?

This was that moment. And my answer was impulsive. I didn't think about it for weeks or weigh the pros and cons. I simply answered, "Yes."

For eight years, I'd catered to everyone else's needs above my own. It's what we mommas do, right? And I'm not complaining, but as I explained in a previous chapter, I was suffocating under the demands. I felt lost and lonely. Did I really *want* to run 26.2 miles? Did I really *want* to train for months and clock hundreds of miles? Did I have any idea what I was *really* getting into? Not necessarily. But I trusted the feeling in my heart urging me to do something for myself and step out of my comfort zone. And I didn't, at the time, even know why. I just knew I had to say "yes."

THE POWER OF "YES"

Yes. This one word instantly propelled me into months of intense, daily, physical, and mental training that not only demanded commitment, sacrifice, and discipline, but that pushed me to limits I didn't think possible. What I quickly learned was how my first yes meant I had to say, yes to that invitation again, every day, for six months. It wasn't a one-time decision. Over time, my commitment to this yes not only improved my physical ability, but the discipline it required slowly began to impact my heart in ways I never anticipated.

To some people, running a marathon is no big deal, for they have run countless races and have the gifts of athleticism. To others, a marathon is an unbelievable feat because the idea of it makes their hearts race, for running has never been a part of their lives. Although this was my first marathon, I was no stranger to running races. For me, the marathon and the training it required unexpectedly became much more than another race—more than the medal of accomplishment or the right to say, "I've run a marathon." What began as a fun opportunity to run with friends and push myself to extreme measures to reach a goal, remarkably became the yes that would lead to radical change in my life.

It's hard to explain exactly what happened. Maybe it's because I really do believe this was divine intervention and God's way of reminding me He offers a better way to live. Some may question God's part in orchestrating our lives, but all I know is in the sacred, quiet moments of those countless runs—acting like antibiotics slowly healing the wounded corners of my soul—the burden of the selfish Kingdom of Me mentality began to release and inspire me to search for something better. To say another yes. A yes to Jesus. A *real* yes to Him.

THE KINGDOM OF HIM

Like I've already shared, I've known about and loved Jesus my whole life, accepting Him as my Lord and Savior years ago. My entire existence has been grounded in faith, which led me to work at a Bible camp, in youth ministry, and inspired me to volunteer and be an active participant in our faith community. I knew about my identity in Christ, and I shared those truths with you in the last chapter. But what I finally realized is those truths didn't begin to have the impact they were designed to have until I declared a genuine, heart-cry "yes" to Jesus. Saying "yes" to Jesus means we are ready to strip me from *me* and replace me with *Him*. It's a critical step toward transformation—replacing our Kingdom of Me mentality with the *Kingdom of Him.*

Saying "yes" to Jesus means we are ready to strip me from me and replace me with Him.

Running a marathon is a conscious choice. The same is true for our choice to say "yes" to Jesus and give Him access to our hearts. We have the freedom to say "no." And many do. But many of us who do say "yes" aren't experiencing the fullness of the life He offers because we are trapped in the Kingdom of Me, striving to do life on our own, subconsciously resisting the life God has to offer. Not because we don't want that life but because we don't know how to get it. God doesn't force His love and grace upon us. He offers it to us freely, inviting us to enter into it.

Therefore, the first decision we must make that will help us mature from the Kingdom of Me to the *Kingdom of Him* is to say an intentional, heart-cry "yes" to Him. It's the first necessary step in the metamorphosis of our hearts. This yes is like a good-bye to the old way of living and a hello to the new one we are desiring to discover. It's not some magic formula that automatically cures our ache overnight, but it is the next step in the right direction. And a necessary one.

THE SURRENDER TO METAMORPHOSIS

In Genesis 1, we learn how God is the master creator of all things. The caterpillar, then, is no exception. But what's unique about the caterpillar is it's been programmed to become something completely new—a butterfly. However, for the caterpillar to become a butterfly, it must comply with the necessary stages of its development. In other words, to experience the radical change it's designed to go through, the caterpillar must surrender into the safety of its chrysalis. If it were to somehow not surrender, it would never experience metamorphosis and become all it was created to be. Surrender is a critical step toward transformation.

Like caterpillars, I believe we have been programmed with what I like to call *divine-designed DNA*. Meaning, God's intent for us is to learn, change, and grow into who He has uniquely created us to be. He wants us to become a butterfly—the fullness of the beauty He sees in us. But like a caterpillar submits to its inevitable destiny by finding a safe, quiet place to retreat and form its protective chrysalis, we, too, must say "yes" and surrender to God, allowing Him to be our protective chrysalis of love and grace. It's in our selfless surrender to God where the metamorphosis of our souls begins to take place. It's the first step in becoming more completely what God crafted us to be from the very first moment of our creation. If we neglect to surrender to Him, we miss out on reaching our full potential. We miss out on making the lasting impact He created us to have.

It's in our selfless surrender to God where the metamorphosis of our souls begins to take place. It's the first step in becoming more completely what God crafted us to be from the very first moment of our creation.

And, friend, God desperately needs us to do the work He's created us to do. He doesn't want us to remain a caterpillar, nor does He want us to remain in a chrysalis of struggle forever even though there is, indeed, purpose in the struggle. It's at the breaking point of our struggle—the intersection of doing life our way and the desperation it cultivates—where we learn to turn our eyes toward Him and say "yes" even when we have no idea where it will lead. That's faith. Jesus wants us to do what His disciples did and say "yes" to His invitation to follow Him and trust in His guidance.

THE INVITATION TO FOLLOW

At the infancy of Jesus' ministry, shortly after He was baptized by John the Baptist and tempted by Satan, He walked by the Sea of Galilee and saw two brothers, Simon and Andrew, doing what they'd done their entire lives—casting nets into the water, for they were fishermen.

I imagine Jesus strolled slowly in the sand, along the shoreline, the waves of the sea gently swooshing over his bare feet. He was in no hurry yet had a specific mission. At first sight of the two men in the distance—already knowing these were two of the first men He'd invite to join Him—a soft smile formed upon His face, and an endearing chuckle escaped as He watched them work. I even imagine He shook His head ever so slightly at the thought of how these men had no idea what they were about to experience by choosing to say "yes" to Him, but how it would be the answer that would enrich, inspire, and save their lives and cultivate significant purpose.

As Jesus approached, the men glanced up from their work, surprised by the visitor. Unafraid, yet intrigued. Recognizing Jesus—the proclaimed Lamb of God, the Messiah, the Christ whom they had met only days before—their hearts raced with eager anticipation as to why He visited them. Before small talk escaped from their mouths, before they could even wave hello, Jesus spoke: "Come, follow me, and I will make you fishers of men.'"[1] Here's what I find extraordinary. Scripture says, "At once they left their nets and followed Him."[2]

They didn't question this man they barely knew. They didn't request to make arrangements at home nor demand an explanation of where they were going. They didn't even pack a bag of food or essential items. They simply left their home, work, and family—the only life they'd ever known. Without question. I imagine the very presence of Jesus Himself calmed any fears or doubts they may have had and instead filled them with confidence, compelling them to say "yes" and follow Him.

A short time later, brothers, James and John, had the same response. Scripture says, "Jesus called them, and immediately they left the boat and their father and followed Him."[3]

I'm overcome with emotion as I write about these remarkable acts of faith. These unwavering responses of trust. Could you do what these men did? Leave everything to follow Jesus? Or would you hesitate? Would you struggle to believe in who He says He is? Would you need proof? Would you need to know the particulars of what is being asked of you? Would you need to get things in order first like a couple other men we read about in Scripture?

He said to another man, "Follow me." But the man replied, "Lord, first let me go and bury my father."

Jesus said to him, "Let the dead bury their own dead, but you go and proclaim the kingdom of God."

Still another said, "I will follow you, Lord, but first let me go back and say good-bye to my family."

Jesus replied, "No one who puts his hand to the plow and looks back is fit for service in the kingdom of God."[4]

In other words, Jesus said, "Stop procrastinating!"

"Stop putting God's kingdom on the back burner."

"Stop waiting until your life is just right to commit to following me."

"Stop getting distracted by your to-do list."

"Stop running yourself ragged for everyone else and choose me for once—really choose me."

Now, let me assure you, friend, Jesus isn't asking us to abandon our families nor to give up everything in this world. He's simply inviting us to choose Him. To put Him first. To lay aside all the stuff of the world that crowds our hearts and instead make room for Him so His grace and love can do the work it desires to do in us. He's declaring:

"Seize the day."

"Act now."

"Say, 'yes' to following me."

It sounds simple, doesn't it? "Just say, 'yes!'"

But as real life in this broken world dictates, we know it's not always that easy. The distractions are immense. Our schedules are full. Adding one more yes to our already packed lives can seem like too much. But that's the very reason to say "yes" to Jesus. Choosing to accept Him—His love and grace—and to follow Him will relieve your soul from the stress of life. It will set right your perspectives. It may not be a marathon or high-top mountain experience that gets your attention, but the Lord is calling you. The Lord is using every aspect of your life to reach you. Are you paying attention? Can you hear Him calling your name, inviting you to choose Him? How are you going to respond? I pray you're ready to say, "Yes, Jesus, yes!" And when you respond, what's next? Stay with me, friend, as we unpack how we begin to recognize God's presence and build a lasting, intimate relationship with Him.

 ## Making it Matter

Whether you are a mom in the trenches of raising kids or are now loving on grandbabies, I'm 99.9% certain you have cringed in frustration and anger at the sound of the word, "No." It's a dreadful word when articulated in countless ways by your child in resistance to your request or command to do or to stop doing something.

I led a parent coaching session the other day, and the primary frustration one father shared was hearing his child respond with a declarative "no" to his requests. I can relate. Few things get me more fired up than to hear that kind of disrespect. My internal, reactive thoughts shout, "Excuse me?"

"Did he just say what I think he said?"

"Who does he think he is that he can talk to me that way?"

"Doesn't he realize I know what's best for him?"

THE METAMORPHOSIS OF MOTHERHOOD

I have now learned to work through those intense moments with grace while at the same time nurturing my sons' hearts. More about that in a coming chapter.

These moments, however, make me consider how God feels when we consistently say "no" to Him. No to the grace and love He offers. No to the doors He opens that we slam shut because of our insecurities. No to the unique assignments He calls us to because life is too busy to recognize them. No to finding and embracing the purpose in the roles we play. I often wonder if God sits on His throne watching us ignore Him, watching us try to do life on our own and question, "Did she just say what I think she said?"

"Who does she think she is? Does she actually think she knows more than Me?"

"Doesn't she realize, that as the One who created her, I know what's best for her?"

The difference between us as mom and God as Father is that God isn't waiting in frustration for us to say "yes." He's waiting with an eager heart for us to proclaim our allegiance to Him.

Like a momma basking in the joy and delight of a compliant yes from our children (I know you've felt that too), I imagine God, too, basking in joy and delight when we say "yes" to Him.

Pause for a moment, will you?

Take a deep breath.

Now, recall the emotional high, the sensation of your heart, the physical feeling you get when your child says a delightful, obedient, "Yes, Mom!"

Amazing, right?

Hold on to that glorious feeling for a moment.

That feeling? It's but a glimpse of what our God feels when we say "yes" to Him. In fact, I imagine Him doing cartwheels in the sky and jumping with glee when one of His beloveds chooses Him and turns away from the hurts, sins, and temptations of the world. God can finally do the work He so desperately wants to do in you when you say "Yes, Jesus. Yes."

God can finally do the work He so desperately wants to do in you when you say "Yes, Jesus. Yes."

And remember, you aren't alone. Jesus is with you every step of the way. He's always working for us and in us,[5] always cultivating the seeds of faith in our hearts. Even if you don't feel He's there. Even if you've ignored Him for longer than you can remember or can't seem to make time for Him. Even if you know very little about Him or are afraid of where to begin. Jesus is with you.

Knowing my friends were showing up every Saturday for those early morning runs held me accountable to my yes. The knowledge of their presence made me eager to join them. I didn't want to miss out on time with them—time I cherished. I also didn't want to be left behind to run the long run by myself. That would have been dreadful.

The same goes for our yes to Jesus. He shows up each and every moment of our lives waiting eagerly for us to follow Him. Knowing He's there makes me not want to miss out on time with Him. And like running those long runs alone, living life without fully accepting the grace and love of Jesus would be dreadful. It was dreadful. But the good news is, we don't have to live without Him and His grace. We have the choice to choose Him.

So, say "yes," my friend. Again, the cost of *not* doing so, is too great.

If the demands of motherhood have overwhelmed your soul, leaving you yearning for more ... if you are grieving a life you thought you'd have ... if life is good, but you lack vision and direction ... if you are stuck in depression and loneliness ... if you are living an artificial life, exhausted by trying to make it all perfect ... if life's circumstances and the reality of this broken world dictate your heart condition ... if you feel unappreciated or unloved ... if you are showered with praise and adoration, yet feel an unexplainable emptiness in your soul ... if you are dissatisfied with your roles as wife and mom ... you need to say "yes" to Jesus. Your yes is the first, necessary step toward heart transformation. Trust me, you won't ever regret saying "yes" to Jesus.

What's holding you back from saying "yes" to Jesus? Fear? Doubt? Insecurities? Time? Misunderstanding? Priorities? Write them down and ask God to remove those from your thoughts and help you trust Him as you step out in faith. Are you ready to rely on Him to guide you where He's destined you to go?

Remember, friend, we are only here living this life because of Him. Don't we owe it to Him to become all that He has imagined us to be? We can only reach the potential He sees in us if we allow Him access to our hearts. Imagine the possibilities God holds for your life. Literally imagine, right now, and jot them down in the space below. He's waiting patiently to reveal them to you. Are you ready to say "yes?" If so, do it now. Mark it in pen now so as not to forget the significance of this moment.

_____

_____

_____

_____

_____

_____

_____

_____

_____

_____

_____

_____

_____

_____

_____

_____

A Momma's Prayer

Lord God, You are highly aware of the constant demands on our time, energy, and resources. You know we juggle countless responsibilities, trying hard to balance life. You know we are tired yet are doing our best. You know that to add one more thing to our already packed lives, could be the tipping point of destruction. But perhaps, we need to tip and be forced to drop the things in our life that are weighing us down. Perhaps, we need to lay everything down that is consuming our lives, and say "yes" to You first. Help us, Lord, say "yes" to You. We pray You give us the courage to trust You completely with it all. To trust You will help us pick up, piece by piece, the essential areas of our lives. Help us realize You are the answer to our ache and when we say "yes" to You, we walk toward freedom, joy, love, and peace. Make us bold like Your beloved disciples who trusted You without question. Who never looked back with regret, and who realized their divine potential and purpose. Invade our hearts with Your hope and grace, reminding us we are never walking this life alone. You are always near. Always waiting. Always present. In Jesus' name we pray, amen.

Meaningful Truth

And the God of all grace, who called you to his eternal glory in Christ, after you have suffered a little while, will himself restore you and make you strong, firm and steadfast.

—1 Peter 5:10–11 (NIV)

CHAPTER 6

The Conversion of the Heart

GOD'S GRACE CHANGES YOU

After running eighteen miles at a consistent, steady pace with exhaustion and muscle aches slowly setting in, a surprising spark of energy emerged, propelling me with new strength and ambition to run the last quarter of the marathon with everything I had left. Sensing this fresh, unfamiliar power, I glanced at my teammates who clearly recognized the increased cadence and rhythm of my strides, pulling me slightly ahead.

I'm not sure where this burst of energy came from, but the adrenaline running through my body and the look on my face clearly communicated to my teammates, my friends, that my legs wanted to run. They were no strangers to the feeling I was experiencing. As runners we have good races and bad races. And on occasion, we have great races, where we feel strong and unstoppable. They could tell this was one of those races for me, so with encouragement in their voices they both yelled, "Natalie, go! Run! If you feel it, then go."

I gave my friends one last shout of encouragement, and my legs—having received permission to run—took off, falling quickly into a new, unfamiliar pace for the last six miles of the race. Although I had this new burst of energy, my body was feeling the repercussions of having run for a few hours. My legs ached everywhere, yet surprisingly remained light and kept moving. As the miles passed, requiring me to dig deeper than ever before, my breathing became the vital component sustaining my run to the finish line.

As I turned to run the last stretch of the marathon—a gorgeous, half-mile jaunt down Summit Avenue in downtown St. Paul, MN, toward the capitol building—I awakened out of my survival zone to the unexpected roar of the crowd cheering and yelling as runner after runner sought to accomplish their goal of crossing the finish line. Completely overwhelmed by the encouraging support from the countless number of spectators lined shoulder-to-shoulder in every direction, I felt instantly transported into a bubble of slow motion with muffled sounds—like what you see in the movies to build dramatic effect for the climax of the story.

Running as fast as my legs could run those last hundred yards—more empowered and confident than ever before— and consistently gaining speed as if floating to the rhythm of cheers in the background, something in my soul—in my being—was changing. It's as if I could feel the transformation actually happening. And as I ran my last stride across the finish line, I chuckled as I recognized God's compassionate humor. His impeccable timing. His enduring faithfulness. His undeniable knowledge of me.

As I stumbled to a halt, trying to steady my steps on what felt like legs of Jell-O, I bowed my head to receive my medal of accomplishment, shuffled myself to the side, dodging a continuous stream of runners, closed my eyes, and took in the priceless awe of the moment—of how God knew how to break down my defenses. He knew how to capture my heart and turn it toward Him. As I felt the relief of finishing the marathon and stood physically sweaty, tired, and beaten—stripped of all strength and energy—an unexplainable feeling overwhelmed my chest. It felt like a huge weight was literally lifting off my heart, and I could breathe deeply again. And not only literally but also spiritually. It's so hard to explain, and because of that, there's no doubt in my mind God orchestrated it all. God had strategically used running, again, to get my attention. But this time? This time, it birthed a new heart.

THE BIG AH-HA

Looking back and putting all the pieces of my story together, there's no doubt in my mind God intricately worked to draw me closer and closer to Him and His purposes for my life. It makes me smile now thinking and writing about it.

You see, shortly after my rainbow moment that opened my heart, the same voice prompting me to leave the house and go for a run that day was the same one urging me to say "yes" to the marathon and "yes" to the daily training. Not long into my training, I heard that voice again.

This time, I felt God beckoning me to pick up the Bible and start seeking answers for my hurting, overwhelmed heart. Without realizing it at the time, I was, simultaneously, training to successfully run the race of a lifetime *and* the race of my life. Never did I imagine when I said each "yes" I would learn two significant truths that would radically change my life. Every "yes" I said seemed to be prepping my heart to discover new revelations and experience deeper growth.

As I built endurance and strength from the daily training, I also felt a lifting in my spirit—a desire that led me to read more and more about God's love for me. I can't help but think my running lifted a cloud that had been hanging over me for years, opening up space to usher in new clarity.

The first truth I slowly began to realize was the grace God offers through Jesus was not the grace I had been living. It's as if the freeing truths of His grace I had heard countless times somehow bounced off me. They hadn't penetrated my heart in the way that was necessary for my transformation. All of my attempts at being the perfect Christian mom and raising good, godly kids left me feeling overwhelmed, discouraged, frustrated, and lost because I hadn't fully received the gift of grace for myself. I finally began to see how incapable I was of being the perfect Christian mom I had always dreamed of being. It also led me to understand it was okay because I didn't have to be. The grace of God had me covered and still does to this day.

All of my attempts at being the perfect Christian mom and raising good, godly kids left me feeling overwhelmed, discouraged, frustrated, and lost because I hadn't fully received the gift of grace for myself.

For years, I had acted as if my behavior is what earned God's love, and so inadvertently, that was the message I sent to my four boys. I didn't allow God's grace to cover my imperfections and mistakes; therefore, I struggled to give God's grace to them, especially in the challenging moments.

I wonder if that is true for many of us. We know God loves us unconditionally and know He forgives us no matter what. And we have this innate desire to do right by Him. The problem is we haven't allowed His love and grace to enter our rebellious hearts and set us free to live the way He designed. To extend grace to others, we must first give grace to ourselves by accepting the grace God freely offers.

To extend grace to others, we must first give grace to ourselves by accepting the grace God freely offers.

JESUS' POWER TO CHANGE HEARTS

One of the most influential people in the Bible known for shaping the history of Christianity, apart from Jesus, and known for experiencing one of the greatest heart transformations was the apostle Paul. Long before the letters that now define his legacy, he fought intensely against the Christian faith under the name of Saul until Jesus decided to have a little personal chat with him on a dirt road—a chat that redirected the trajectory of Paul's life.

Fueled with hatred, pride, and disgust, pounding mile after mile through Israel in an anxious attempt to capture and persecute Christians, Saul felt shocked and afraid when he suddenly found himself face-to-face with Jesus. Scripture says:

"... suddenly a light from heaven flashed around him. He (Saul) fell to the ground and heard a voice say to him, "Saul, Saul, why do you persecute me?"[1]

Upon hearing those words that brought him to his knees, Saul—heart racing, palms sweating, limbs shaking, eyes squinting to see beyond the brightness of the light around him—wondered:

What is happening?

Why have I been stopped in the middle of my mission?

Can you sense the conflict in his being? *It couldn't be. Or could it?*

As if his doubtful mind and unbelieving heart were miraculously awakened by this inexpectant encounter, Saul shyly whispered, "Who are you, Lord?"[2]

Yes, indeed, Jesus chose Saul—one of the most unlikely candidates—to be a "chosen instrument to carry His name"[3] to the ends of the earth. On a desolate, dirt road, Saul's life changed forever. By the power of the Holy Spirit, God converted Saul's heart and empowered him to embark on a new mission for Christ as the apostle Paul. Talk about a 180—total heart transformation. And Paul didn't resist God's calling. Instead, he embraced the change. One quality I love and admire about Paul is his genuine heart. Although he confidently accepted God's calling, he was very honest and transparent about sharing his frustration at his inability to be perfect and overcome his sinful nature. In fact, he described in Romans 7:18–24 (MSG) the conflict many of us feel.

> I realize that I don't have what it takes. I can will it, but I can't do it. I decide to do good, but I don't really do it; I decide not to do bad, but then I do it anyway. My decisions, such as they are, don't result in actions. Something has gone wrong deep within me and gets the better of me every time.
>
> It happens so regularly that it's predictable. The moment I decide to do good, sin is there to trip me up. I truly delight in God's commands, but it's pretty obvious that not all of me joins in that delight. Parts of me covertly rebel, and just when I least expect it, they take charge.
>
> I've tried everything and nothing helps. I'm at the end of my rope. Is there no one who can do anything for me? Isn't that the real question?

Is it just me, or can you relate with what Paul experienced? I've most certainly attempted to do and be good, but sin gets in my way. The more sin gets in the way, the more overwhelmed and frustrated we become at not being able to overcome it on our own and be the godly person we want to be. That was the perpetual trap I lived in that sucked the life right out of me. But as my training and reading continued for six months, the answer to Paul's question became the very answer to my dilemma. This answer finally sunk in as I truly discovered the greatest news my heart could ever know:

> The answer, thank God, is that Jesus Christ can and does. He acted to set things right in this life of contradictions where I want to serve God with all my heart and mind, but am pulled by the influence of sin to do something totally different.
>
> With the arrival of Jesus, the Messiah, that fateful dilemma is resolved. Those who enter into Christ's being-here-for-us no longer have to live under a continuous, low-lying black cloud. A new power is in operation. The Spirit of life in Christ, like a strong wind, has magnificently cleared the air, freeing you from a fated lifetime of brutal tyranny at the hands of sin and death.[4]

Did you catch that, my friend? Jesus is the One and only One who can help lift the dark cloud of our sin and clear the air for new life to begin. That's literally what I felt happening to me as I finished the marathon. It's like a window of hope opened, and I heard God beckoning. I would never be my old self again. Romans 8:10–16 (MSG) says:

> When God lives and breathes in you (and he does, as surely as he did in Jesus), you are delivered from that dead life. With his Spirit living in you, your body will

be as alive as Christ's! So don't you see that we don't owe this old do-it-yourself-life one red cent. There's nothing in it for us, nothing at all. The best thing to do is give it a decent burial and get on with your new life. God's Spirit beckons. There are things to do and places to go! This resurrection life you received from God is not a timid, grave-tending life. It's adventurously expectant, greeting God with a child-like "What's next, Papa?"

I wanted to scream from the rooftops, "What's next, Papa?" It's like I had physically shed the remaining layer of my old life and a new one began to emerge. There's no doubt I was a different person from the one who started training six months prior.

This truth tempts me to reflect on one more part of Saul's story. You see, Saul was blind for three days after his encounter with Jesus on the road and before he was filled with the Holy Spirit. I wonder if those three days were like the six months of marathon training and struggle I endured that led me to experience the biggest shift in my life. Saul thought he knew where his life was headed. He was convinced he knew the truth. He had decided the course and purpose of his life until … Jesus intervened. Until … Jesus softened his heart and inspired him to relinquish his old, sinful ways. Until … Jesus opened his eyes to his divine purpose and provided rich clarity to the role he was to play in the story of salvation. Like Saul, I experienced an awakening to the profound truth of God's grace and was in the process of doing a 180.

But I couldn't help but wonder, *Why now?* I'd heard these truths before, so what was different this time? Apart from the mysterious workings of God and His timing, I believe my discontent and struggle in motherhood stirred a desire in my heart for something more, something better, and that desire acted as the doorway for this life-transforming truth to enter. For the first time, I was ready to acknowledge my aching heart and pursue a remedy. Really pursue. Herein lies the second truth I learned that radically changed my life and my family's and continues to be a significant part of my daily living. And it's a truth that has the power to change yours too.

THE PRICELESS LESSON

As God slowly opened the eyes of my heart, I began to understand that true, lasting freedom, peace, and joy were found in Christ and in Christ alone. But to experience them to the fullest, I had to pay attention to Him and pursue Him. Certainly, God has always been communicating with me and pursuing me, just like He's been communicating and pursuing you. But I hadn't been listening for Him or pursuing Him, at least not in the way that would bring about the change my heart so desperately needed. And then came the marathon that put it all into motion.

Coincidentally, the same principles that apply to successfully running a marathon apply to helping us figure out the life God has for us.

DESIRE

I had to *want* to get to know God, like I had to *want* to run the marathon. No one else could run it for me and no one else could get to know God for me. It's a choice—one we all have to make. If I didn't have the desire to learn about Him and seek Him, I'd lack all of the other principles necessary for discovering my purpose. A clear indication you are beginning to desire God is when your heart is aching for something more, but you don't know what. Your heart was meant to desire a relationship with God and when it's absent, it aches. Don't deny your ache any longer. Instead, open it and allow the desire of your heart to be released into the hands of God.

INTENTION

Once my desire to know and seek God took root, I naturally began to make intentional choices to get to know Him more intimately. The best way to get to know God is to read about Him in the Bible. Now, I'd certainly read Scripture throughout the years, but it was never with this amount of heart intention. And if you've never read the Bible, it's challenging to know where to begin. In fact, before I began diving into God's Word all on my own, I sought the wisdom of experienced authors to help me get started. And eventually, I started spending time reading the Word of God on my own—intentional time devoted to getting to know God's heart, truths, and hopes for my life. At the same time, I began to really share my heart with Him—to pray like I'd never prayed before. This habit is not complicated, but it requires our genuine hearts and consistency, which leads me to the next critical principle.

DISCIPLINE

Without daily discipline and commitment to my training for the marathon, I would never have been able to run 26.2 miles. My ability to run the marathon came from a compounded effort built by remaining disciplined every day to the training set before me. As a runner, you quickly learn how taking even a couple of days off can set you back in your training. In order to maintain and excel our physical capabilities and strength, daily discipline is crucial. The same is true for our minds. If we don't remain disciplined to reading and studying the Word of God on a consistent basis, our minds will stray towards the world and be tempted to believe lies meant to knock us off course and distract us from moving forward in the purposes to which God has called us to live. As God's Word daily breathed new life and truths into my heart and mind, it began to override old, debilitating thoughts and lies. I began experiencing the power of His grace as the burdens I'd been carrying and the lies I'd been believing for so long—burdens and lies that were standing in my way of being the mom I desired to be and of realizing the fullness of my dreams—were being released.

AWARENESS

Gradually, as I remained devoted to studying the Word and praying, I became inspired to pay attention to God's presence in my life and to notice, really notice, Him at work. I took intentional time to be still, to listen, and live more in the moment and in doing so became more highly aware of God's presence and work among us. He'd always been there. He'd always been attempting to communicate with me. But finally, I could hear His whispers and sense His incomprehensible presence. It was an overwhelming, unexplainable physical feeling in my gut that assured me of His presence and His work in my life.

Recognizing and surrendering to my heart's desire to know God, committing to intentionally studying the Word of God, opening my eyes and ears to be aware of His incredible presence, listening to Him in the stillness, and pouring my heart out in prayer to Him were game changers for me and were the necessary choices that led me to experience deeper wholeness. These daily, simple choices led to my heart conversion and an intimate relationship with God. The reminders of God's grace and love are what broke the chains and gave me my freedom. Acknowledging His presence cultivated supernatural joy and peace and opened my eyes to the delight and gift of motherhood. Absorbing His wisdom altered my perspective on how to do life and taught to me how to discipline and love my kids with grace. The sacred quiet time in His presence led me to discover my purpose and passions outside of motherhood—my call to write, speak, and encourage women.

Coincidentally, like my commitment to training prepared me to cross the finish line of the marathon, my commitment to diving into God's Word and praying is equipping me to run the race of my life He has uniquely prepared for me and to cross the finish line joyfully and victoriously. The way to an intimate relationship with Jesus—one rooted in His grace—and to discover your divine purpose is through His

Word and prayer. That's how God designed us to operate. In fact, King Solomon, who received God's gift of wisdom, wrote in Proverbs that to *really live,* one needs the words of God.

> Dear friends, listen well to my words;
> Tune your ears to my voice.
> Keep my message in plain view at all times.
> Concentrate! Learn it by heart!
> Those who discover these words live, really live;
> Body and soul, they're bursting with health.[5]

The way to an intimate relationship with Jesus—one rooted in His grace—and to discover your divine purpose is through His Word and prayer.

The prophet, Isaiah, concurs with King Solomon describing God's Words as "life-giving" and "life-nourishing."[6] He also explains how the Word of God is active and how when we absorb His Word, we are inspired to live our lives according to God's will, allowing the Holy Spirit to lead us "into a whole and complete life."[7] The more we learn about God's heart, the more like Christ we become. This sanctification process is ongoing as we rely more and more on His transforming power in our lives.

For as the sky soars high above earth,
so the way I work surpasses the way you work,
and the way I think is beyond the way you think.
Just as rain and snow descend from the skies
and don't go back until they've watered the earth,
Doing their work of making things grow and blossom,
producing seed for farmers and food for the hungry,
So will the words that come out of my mouth
not come back empty-handed.
They'll do the work I sent them to do,
they'll complete the assignment I gave them.
So you'll go out in joy,
you'll be led into a whole and complete life.[7]

Without the word of God as our primary source of inspiration and knowledge, we miss a critical piece of our existence as God's beloved creations and will live our lives based on worldly standards rather than heavenly ones. Not only that, but we will also miss reaching the optimal potential God created us to fulfill, because on our own, we will come up short and always feel as if something is missing. Proverbs 16:22a says, "Understanding is a fountain of life to those who have it."

You see, God's word is not simply another history book with idle words on a page. It instills wisdom. And God's wisdom is a fountain of life because it washes away the evil intentions of sin, frees and renews our hearts, and inspires us to live with intense purpose and godly, joyful perspective. This joyful perspective, this purpose, this freedom—they are within your grasp. Let me say it again: joy, purpose, and freedom are available to you if you want them. To fully emerge as the

THE METAMORPHOSIS OF MOTHERHOOD

beautiful butterflies God created us to be, we need to release the insecurities that limit our potential and take intentional action to know Him so we can grow in the knowledge and wisdom of who He is and who He says we are.

To fully emerge as the beautiful butterflies God created us to be, we need to release the insecurities that limit our potential and take intentional action to know Him so we can grow in the knowledge and wisdom of who He is and who He says we are.

THE METAMORPHOSIS OF THE HEART

God's faithful Word and the power for life-change it carries becomes the antidote to our aching hearts. God's Word is the mechanism that inspires new growth in our hearts. Given genuine time and attention, this heart transformation clears tainted views and awakens us to experience a new realm of inspiring potential and possibilities. Our transformation is synonymous with the metamorphosis a caterpillar endures while nestled in the safety of the chrysalis, where its body—the only one the caterpillar has ever known—dissolves and dormant cells, also known as imaginal cells, emerge. These are cells not quite ready or mature enough to develop until the old ones release. They transform the caterpillar into what it was always meant to be—a beautiful butterfly.

God's faithful Word and the power for life-change it carries becomes the antidote to our aching hearts.

The caterpillar was not created to remain a caterpillar, and the same is true for us. We were not created to roam the earth as a creeping caterpillar nor to remain trapped in the chrysalis of life's hardships. Through the power of God's Word and His gift of grace, our old ways can be dissolved, and we can grow into the beautiful creation God designed us to be from the moment of our conception and emerge as a beautiful butterfly, soaring freely, and with exquisite purpose.

Now, you may not be stopped on a desolate, dirt road by a blinding, bright light and the resounding voice of Jesus. But Jesus, my friend, beckons to each of us. He knows how to reach you, exactly like He knew how to reach Saul. It happened this way for me as well. He knew how to reach me through this journey from rain, to rainbow, to marathon. It was a journey involving desire, surrender, discipline, intention, and awareness.

Trust me, Jesus doesn't orchestrate these encounters for a select few. This type of life-change, heart conversion is available to everyone. You just need to seek Him through His Word and prayer, and then be bold enough to open your eyes, trusting He will make Himself known to you with a blinding, bright-light moment of your own. And when the beautiful truth of God's grace takes over your heart, your desire to love God and live your life for Him will override your desire to fall into sin. That's the mysterious power of grace. It not only melts our hearts, but it also inspires us to do the work He's called us to do in the world and embrace the roles He's called us to play.

Making it Matter

I am one of those women who had tried to read the Bible front to back but failed, time after time. I am one of those women who had great intentions to make time for daily devotions, but it never became habit. I am one of those women who ached to know God more and to sense His guiding, but I didn't do my part in building that connection. Not until, that is, my thirst became more than I could bear.

Immediately following the marathon, as my physical body recovered from the stress it had recently been exposed to, I couldn't eat or drink much. I was on an emotional high, intentionally taking in every part of this experience that had been the doorway to my transformation. It wasn't until I was on my way home, sitting comfortably in the back seat of my mom and dad's car (a 34–year-old woman feeling like a teenager again) that I recognized my intense thirst. After running 26.2 miles, my body was finally indicating to me my physical need for water.

But that wasn't the only thirst I sensed. We aren't only physical beings in need of water every day to survive, but we are also spiritual beings divinely designed to need God every day. All the yearnings and thirsts of our hearts that can't be satisfied by the things of this world can only be filled and forever quenched by the living water and Word of God.

Have you ever had an experience that has altered your life? One that has stripped you to the core, yet left you more powerful than before? How about an encounter with God you could feel to the depths of your soul? One that has led you into a more whole and complete life? And one that has forever changed you?

If not, could it be that your imaginal cells are lying dormant under the aches of your heavy heart and the struggles from this sinful, broken world—cells waiting for you to grasp the truth that will release them and transform you? Or maybe, you are waiting for that life-altering experience? Yearning for it, even? Perhaps, it's happening right now, but you haven't recognized it?

It could be something as crazy as a marathon or it could be something as lonely as a disconnection with your spouse. It could be a mountaintop experience or a mundane occurrence. Perhaps your teenage son is drifting away and making poor choices. Or your young daughter has just been diagnosed with a learning disability you have no idea how to handle. Maybe you're fed up with walking through a war zone all over the house and can't figure out where all the anger and frustration comes from. These are all possible moments where God is waiting in the chambers of your heart for you to notice Him, seek Him, and get to know Him. There is no perfect time, no special formula, no detailed instructions on how it goes. There is simply your moment etched in His perfect timing.

God is waiting in the chambers of your heart for you to notice Him, seek Him, and get to know Him. There is no perfect time, no special formula, no detailed instructions on how it goes. There is simply your moment etched in His perfect timing.

God knows infinitely more than we can imagine,[8] and He's constantly, in all things, working for the good of those who love Him,[9] even when life makes no sense, feels difficult, or seems hopeless. When you feel alone and lost, sometimes it takes a small gesture from God to help you find your way. Sometimes it takes a profound encounter with God or a rock-bottom experience to understand our need to relinquish our old, entitled, prideful ways and, instead, embrace the ways of God that are in sync and congruent with our souls—truths that will set us free and enable us to soar to heights only imaginable to God.

Once you've said "Yes" to God, your heart softens and opens to receive Him, and you make an intentional, committed effort to really get to know Him, that's when the final process of metamorphosis unfolds, relinquishing your old self so that a new, refined one may emerge. There is such confidence and courage that transpires in us when we are transformed by God, but as I'll share in the next couple of chapters, that process doesn't exempt us from the struggles and lies that are a reality of our fallen world.

In the space below, share what obstacles may be holding you back from seeking God through Scripture and prayer. Deeply reflect on moments of your life where you think God may have been beckoning you to Him. Commit to opening your eyes to how God is working in and through your life, and make note of them. Create a plan of dedicated time to seeking God and building your relationship with Him. (Check out the added resource in the back of the book, "Building a Deep Relationship with God," to give you some ideas on a plan.)

_____

_____

_____

_____

_____

_____

_____

_____

_____

_____

_____

 *A Momma's Prayer*

Gracious God, thank You for pursuing us, especially when we get so wrapped up in the rat race of life and in the temptations of the world that we neglect to pursue You ... to get to know You. Thank You for never giving up on us. Thank You for knowing each of us so intimately that You know how to reach our hearts. Thank You for being ever present in the chambers of our hearts, patiently waiting for us to drop to our knees, be blinded by Your light, and transformed by Your enduring love, Your amazing grace. Forgive us, Lord, for not giving You our whole hearts. For not giving You devoted time. We need Your help, Lord. We desire to know You. To build a relationship with You. But we need Your guidance and wisdom in how to carve out devoted time for You. Help us learn discipline when it comes to seeking You. Teach us to be committed and intentional in studying Your Word and sharing our hearts with You through prayer. Our hearts ache to know You more, Lord God. They are open and ready to pursue You so we can experience the wholeness only You can provide, and so You can do Your mighty work in us, for Your glory and for Your kingdom. In Jesus' name we pray, amen.

 Meaningful Truth

Jesus answered, "It is written: 'Man shall not live on bread alone, but on every word that comes from the mouth of God."

—Matthew 4:4 (NIV)

Since we've compiled this long and sorry record as sinners and proved that we are utterly incapable of living the glorious lives God wills for us, God did it for us. Out of sheer generosity he put us in right standing with Himself. A pure gift. He got us out of the mess we're in and restored us to where he always wanted us to be. And he did it by means of Jesus Christ.

—Romans 3:23–24 (MSG)

~ CHAPTER 7 ~

The Lies and Struggles That Hold You Hostage

GOD'S GRACE AND LOVE SET YOU FREE

*A*s I sat in my usual chair on the east side of the patio with coffee and Bible in hand, I felt the quiet, gentle breeze offering to embrace me in its comfort. It was a comfort I desperately needed yet found myself resisting. Concentrating on the warmth of the rising sun, I closed my eyes and took a deep breath, inhaling the simplicity of the moment and exhaling the confusing aches pounding upon my heart.

At the tail-end of summer, we'd enjoyed a weekend full of friends and family. One would assume my cup would be overflowing with joy and gratitude. Right? I mean, these were some of the most important people in my life, many of whom I don't get to see very often. But sadly, as I prepped to begin writing that Monday morning, I was suddenly overcome with a nasty case of the blues clouding the truths I longed to share.

Yep, I get the blues. We all have those times when we feel, well ... off ... down ... discouraged. When doubts, fears, and insecurities take over our thoughts, we can head in a downward spiral pretty fast. You ever been there? I hate it when these dark days happen because I don't *want* to feel this way. But sometimes, I can't help it. Not only do I suffer, but everyone around me also senses my struggle, especially my family.

Although I'm not certain why I woke up that morning feeling defeated, I can speculate. Summer had rocked my agenda a bit, to say the least. It had abruptly interrupted my writing flow and focus, and although my boys were my first priority all summer long, I constantly felt the weight of my writing beckoning me to the office. With only two weeks of summer left, I didn't feel I had made significant progress on my book. This book. On top of that, I had other reasons: a few disappointing friendships, some out of control hormones, and a houseful of boys who had spent a little too much time together and—whether they admitted it or not—were ready to go back to school. More accurately, I was ready for them to go back to school. However, as I sit here reflecting back, I can't help but find the timing of these blues a bit ironic as this chapter about the lies and struggles that hold us hostage lingered to be written next.

Think about it. Here I am writing a book for mommas about claiming our freedom, finding our joy, and embracing

our divine purpose—filling it with truth and encouragement—
and then, POW! In a moment of weakness, I'm hit strategically
by an arrow into the heart of my purpose and joy. In the midst
of the writing that has been so life-giving—an assignment I
agreed to out of obedience to God's calling—I began to feel
insecure, isolated, and completely unqualified to share this
message. I think it's fair to say I freaked out a bit. (Trust me,
I did. The tears flowed for days.)

*Who do I think I am writing a book? I'm no expert. I can't
do this. Who would want to read it, anyway?*

*How can I love on other moms and share with them lessons
I've learned if I'm still needing to be reminded of them myself?
If I don't feel awesome, confident, and joyful 24/7?*

I had actually contemplated giving up.

Now, I knew better. I knew God would not bring me this
far only to have me throw it all away. I knew these thoughts
were false and the feelings were ridiculous because I knew
the truth of what God thought of me, and I believed in what
He was calling me to do. I knew He wanted me to write this
book and share it with others. I also knew I was under attack,
yet I fell into the trap of lies anyway.

I never learned about spiritual attacks growing up, but I've
come to believe there's an enemy roaming the world working
against us—to discourage us from pursuing our purpose and
reaching our potential. I don't say this to frighten you. I tell
you so you are aware there is another force working to steal
you away from God's will for your life.

This awareness is the first step in our fight against the
lies. With God on our side, we have nothing to fear. But it
doesn't exempt us from the enemy's attacks. God wants us to

soar and succeed, but the enemy wants us to plummet and fail. And the enemy is sneaky. He works tirelessly to infiltrate our thoughts with lies he knows will be most effective in knocking us off the course God has planned and thus stealing our joy, hope, and peace.

Scripture says, "Your enemy the devil prowls around like a roaring lion looking for someone to devour."[1]

The enemy does not want us to say "yes" to Jesus. He doesn't want us to seek God or live freely and joyfully. He doesn't want us to embrace our gifts and use them to build up God's kingdom. He doesn't want us to trust God. He wants us to remain as a caterpillar or in the chrysalis of struggle. Never transforming. Never breaking free. Never soaring.

But here's what I want you to really hear—the vulnerable truth of my reality in that moment—because I believe it's absolutely relevant to you in your walk of faith. The knowledge and awareness *alone* of where these lies were coming from didn't make the thoughts, feelings, or pain any less real. They didn't disappear suddenly because I'm a follower of Christ. In other words, even though I'm a follower of Christ and have discovered incredible purpose through His guidance and freedom through His grace, it doesn't mean I'm exempt from pain and struggle nor shielded from the lies of the world. Just because I love and follow Jesus doesn't mean I have it all together, all the time. And it doesn't mean I'm happy all the time.

We don't simply say "yes" to God, read His Word, pray, build an intimate relationship with Him, and then everything is sunshine and roses. We don't one day arrive at some spiritual destination, close the Bible assuming we are filled to the brim with everything we need, and then, that's it. We're good and happy for life. It doesn't work like that on this side of heaven.

What I'm discovering is the closer I've moved in alignment to God's will and purposes, the stronger, more frequent, and more strategic the attacks from the enemy. He will take advantage of any struggle, and life's struggles are real. They hurt, confuse, and interrupt, leaving us vulnerable to attack. The enemy wants to use them to fill us with lies—lies that take root in our hearts and have the power to destroy, paralyze, or divide us. Lies that move us further away from God's truths if we let them.

Therefore, we are faced with a critical choice. Do we give in to the enemy's attacks on our thoughts, or do we fight for what we know is true? Do we hold on for dear life to God's eternal promises, or do we cower and give in to the weight of this broken world and allow our fears and doubts to dictate our choices? I feel this struggle came at the right time, because although it could've continued to destroy me and my confidence in pursuing writing and speaking, this dark moment instead has become a story and message of God's triumphant power and faithfulness.

Being a Christ follower is an ongoing, strategically crafted, unique journey of refinement and growth, where we must remain immoveable and steadfast in His truth, dig in our heels, and proclaim, "I will not let you [God] go unless you bless me."[2] Instead of giving into the lies and allowing them to defeat the work God planted in my heart, I used my knowledge and awareness of the enemy's attacks on my thoughts as motivation to hit the mat and wrestle. That's right. You heard me. Hit the mat!

HIT THE MAT

Wrestling is no foreign activity in my family. Well, actually, let me clarify that statement. The *sport* of wrestling is foreign in my family as we know very little about it. But the typical *boys-gone-crazy* kind of wrestling—involving body slams, headlocks, and powerbombs (whatever they are)—*that* wrestling is a daily occurrence in my household of four energetic, testosterone-filled boys. If you're a momma of boys, you know what I mean. Eventually, you get used to it and come to grips with the fact that it's part of life when you're raising boys. It doesn't mean I understand it, but I learned they need it—a physical outlet to release the bottled energy.

What is weird is I can tell when the desire to wrestle and go at it is about to happen. Their eyebrows raise. They bounce on the balls of their feet. They flash a mysterious smile. They even let out a squeal that makes the hair on my arms rise. They prance in lure of a brother to pounce on. They taunt and rile the easiest target. It's like if they don't exert this bottled energy, they will explode. As annoying as listening to their wrestling matches is, I guess I'd rather have that energy exerted on each other. The other alternative seems all too harsh (wink, wink). So, by all means, I let them wrestle.

The match often begins as a slow, quiet, innocent rumble in *my* living room, which they know is off limits. To their creative credit, they do pretend they are only loving on one another. But once I hear the crystals on the chandelier in my dining room chime, I realize I have long since surpassed the time to send them downstairs to the unfinished basement covered in three layers of carpet padding to finish their match.

(No joke, three layers of padding. And for one reason—boys wrestle.)

Now, in case you're wondering, the answer is yes. Almost always someone comes up crying, tattling, whining, or pouting. Sometimes there is a wound to mend. Sometimes it is pride put in its rightful place. And on rare occasions—when the stars align—it's nothing but absolute, unadulterated, boy *fun*!

Have you ever participated in a wrestling match? I used to when my boys were little. I soon discovered, as they grew older and stronger, it was too darn painful. Momma is way off limits now. But that doesn't mean I don't wrestle in other ways because I do. This type of wrestling I'm referring to the Lord knows all too well. Exactly like I can sense when my boys are ready to go at it, I can tell when I am spiritually heading to the mat. It often entails tears, questions, and protests of some sort. And the Lord? He's no stranger to wrestling.

There is a story in Scripture about a man named Jacob who had been chosen by God as the third link to God's plan for salvation. But Jacob was no saint. He began his life as a master manipulator by stealing his brother's inheritance and birthright. Upon discovering this deception, his brother Esau vowed to kill him, which forced Jacob to flee their home.

It wasn't until years later that Jacob returned home with the hopes of restoring peace with his brother. Terrified for his life and desperate for help, the night before their little family reunion, Jacob wrestled with God. And this wrestling stirred something within Jacob's heart because he refused—even after he was injured—to quit the match, declaring, "I will not let you go until you bless me."[2]

What began as a night of intense struggle, ended in a night of peace and hope as Jacob, one-by-one, released the sins, failures, and lies that had held him captive for years and prevented him from fulfilling his purpose. He awoke the next day no longer fearing his brother. Instead, God blessed him with the gift of renewed and strengthened faith.

And the same is true for us. God invites us to hit the mat and wrestle with Him. Now, I can barely stand to watch my boys wrestle. But when I imagine wrestling with God, it's so very different. It's this intimate picture of intense, honest interaction, including questioning, searching, wondering, crying, and exposing the full struggles of my heart. And like wrestling is necessary for my boys to do with one another to help release their energy so they feel better, wrestling is necessary for us to do with God to help us through any struggle and release the strongholds and lies attempting to hold us captive. As a result, we will not only feel better and be blessed, but we will also develop a stronger, more resilient godly character. It's an essential part in building an honest, unbreakable relationship with God and in building the confidence and courage to continue to follow God's lead.

Wrestling with God—drawing near to Him with the doubts, frustrations, shame, fears—is our best weapon against the enemy. Jesus' brother, James, a leader in the Jerusalem church and one of the beloved disciples, wrote about how to resist the enemy.

> Submit yourselves, then, to God. Resist the devil, and he will flee from you. Come near to God and he will come near to you. Wash your hands, you sinners, and purify your

hearts, you double-minded. Grieve, mourn, wail. Change your laughter to mourning and your joy to gloom. Humble yourselves before the Lord and He will lift you up.[3]

Wrestling with God—drawing near to Him with the doubts, frustrations, shame, fears— is our best weapon against the enemy.

Not only will the enemy flee when we draw near to God, but God will also use our struggles to help strengthen our resolve and faith and build up defenses for the battles yet to come. In other words, He equips us with the armor and power needed to fight the enemy's attacks, break through our chrysalis of struggle, and soar to unimaginable heights.

THE ARMOR OF DEFENSE

My boys have forever loved dress-up and pretend-play, especially a wardrobe including helmets, shields, weapons— especially swords, which come in all shapes and sizes (sticks, turkey basters, pool noodles, bats ... you name it). When I see them armored in mis-matching costumes and gear, riled up with boy-like energy and excitement, I brace myself because that means one thing and one thing only—a battle is about to ensue. Most of their battles are fun, innocent, and free from injury. But on occasion, one boy will expose a weakness in armor, opening an opportunity for the other to take advantage. And what's the result? Tears, hurt, anger, and the occasional bruise, or worse, blood. (Real life with boys.) When armor fails and weaknesses are exposed, we're left vulnerable to attack. We are susceptible to greater hurt and prone to beatings and bruising. Like my boys—in their silly battles—playfully take advantage of one another's weaknesses, so, too, does the enemy take advantage of ours. The difference is the enemy strikes with an intention to steal and destroy.

Left to myself and my own vices on that hot summer day in August—distracted by life's struggles—I had developed a momentary, thwarted internal monologue looping through my mind. It was not in line with God's truths, and it had snuck into my thoughts through moments of weakness.

We don't gain strength and weapons necessary to fight the lies by sitting on our couch, sipping wine, and watching sappy Hallmark movies. (Although I do love to do that every now and then.) The point is, we aren't left alone to fight our battles, but we are responsible for doing our part. God wants to help us fight the lies and He wants to build up our defenses, but we *must* keep wrestling with Him, trusting Him, and staying connected to His Word. God's Word is like a sword that has the ability to penetrate our thoughts, helping us discern the lies from His truths. Hebrews 4:12-13 says,

> For the word of God is alive and powerful. It is sharper than the sharpest two-edged sword, cutting between soul and spirit, between joint and marrow. It exposes our innermost thoughts and desires. Nothing in all creation is hidden from God. Everything is naked and exposed before his eyes, and He is the one to whom we are accountable. (NLT)

God's Word is like a sword that has the ability to penetrate our thoughts, helping us discern the lies from His Truths.

The more connected we are to God's Word and the closer we get to Him through prayer, the more strength we gain through the power of the Holy Spirit—power that builds up our spiritual armor. This armor includes "the belt of truth, the breastplate of righteousness, the gospel of peace, the shield of faith, the helmet of salvation, and the sword of the Spirit, which is the Word of God."[4] And this power is innate. This power is part of our divine DNA, our genetic makeup. And it's our divine defense against the enemy. It doesn't mean we won't ever waver or face a battle again. Trust me, the battles will continue to come. However, this armor means we'll have what we need to fight and win the battles.

So, in my dark moment, I wrestled with God. I cried out to Him and told Him about all the thoughts consuming me. I read His Truths and prayed for them to destroy the lies. Every moment I wrestled with God became a moment closer to victory as the divine defense in my heart strengthened.

DIVINE DEFENSE

We aren't the only ones with a divine defense. Take the delicate monarch, for example. Once the monarch breaks through the chrysalis of change and emerges as a new creation, it's vulnerable to attack from its enemy, mainly birds. The monarch can't instantly fly away and find safety because its newly formed wings need time to dry. But God, as the universe's master creator, intricately built a defense mechanism against predators within the monarch's DNA that's developed by feeding on leaves of the milkweed plant as caterpillars. Milkweed plants contain a poisonous steroid that tastes bitter to predators. Only through metamorphosis does a butterfly store these toxins to use for its protection as a new butterfly.[5]

Do you see the significant similarities here? The caterpillar, like us, has everything within its design to combat attacks from its enemies. But it is responsible for doing its part—like we are. It *must* feed on milkweed plant. Without that fuel, the emerging butterfly will not be able to withstand and survive attack. And like that butterfly, without our fuel that comes from knowing God through His Word and prayer, we will have a difficult time withstanding and surviving the attacks. These struggles may not take our physical life, but they will certainly attempt to steal our joy, peace, purpose, and hope. But even if we falter, God continually works to rebuild our strength and bring about new birth from the struggle.

THE STRUGGLE BIRTHS PURPOSE

When my boys were younger, we'd spend hours together outside playing and exploring nature in the grassland, woods, and lake that surround our home. They loved investigating insects, playing with worms, and hunting for frogs. Unknown to them, I was always on the lookout for a caterpillar—a big hungry caterpillar, just like the one described in Eric Carle's book, *The Hungry Caterpillar.* Yep, that's what I wanted to find.

And what do you know? One afternoon, while playing ball in the yard—not intentionally looking for any insects—we happened upon, yes, you guessed it. A big, hungry caterpillar! I was thrilled, to say the least. The boys ran to get their insect cage, gathered leaves and sticks to recreate its habitat, and placed the caterpillar ever so gently inside. (Side note: I know now—after doing a great deal of research on the monarch butterfly—it is best to leave them in their natural habitat.) I hoped we would get to witness the incredible transformation but secretly worried we had doomed the poor thing.

Every day, the boys ran to the garage to check for changes, and sure enough, the caterpillar began to form its chrysalis. We watched and waited, and the day finally arrived when the newly formed butterfly began to make its way out of its chrysalis. It was so exciting to witness God's creative work, first-hand.

It wasn't long after observing the butterfly struggling to free its wings from the confining protective shell that my son, Peyton—about five at the time—began to grow frustrated. He couldn't stand watching the butterfly struggle to break free. He was about to open the cage and reach in his chubby little hand to help the butterfly when I stopped him, fearing his thoughtful attempt at helping the butterfly may actually hurt the little creature.

Full confession: at the time, I had no idea what Peyton's help would have done to the butterfly. I have since learned helping the butterfly could have cost it its life. You see, before a butterfly separates from its chrysalis, it experiences intense struggle, working hard to break free. This struggle to push its way through the tiny opening of the chrysalis is imperative to its survival because it pushes the fluid out of its body and into its wings.[6] Without the struggle, the butterfly's wings would never work properly; therefore, the butterfly would never fly. Timing is everything. During this stage of development, there is an intentional breaking-free moment that must occur in its own timing for flight to be possible … for the butterfly to soar.

I've come to believe the same is true for us. The struggles we endure are imperative to our survival and are necessary in guiding us to recognize our true identity and rely fully on God. These struggles are essential in helping us unfurl our wings, soar freely, and live in the wonder and joy of our divine purpose.

The struggles we endure are imperative to our survival and are necessary in guiding us to recognize our true identity and rely fully on God.

Apart from all the potential physical challenges we bear by assuming the role of mother, that even when warned of them we gasp in horror (hemorrhoids; rock-hard, leaky breasts; chapped nipples; stretch marks; bladder issues … that's all I have to say about that), there are countless other struggles that rock our world as a mom, wife, and woman. Struggle comes in many forms and affects us all in different ways. Suffering often accompanies struggle and both are a part of life on earth because of the brokenness that exists through sin and darkness.

What I'm discovering as I continue to face new struggles is when I *choose* to wrestle with God yet rely on His strength, my perspective about struggle changes. Jesus' brother, James, whom we heard from earlier, wrote about this dichotomy and how our faith becomes real and genuine by how we choose to respond to life in this broken world. He said:

> Don't run from tests and hardships, brothers and sisters. As difficult as they are, you will ultimately find joy in them; if you embrace them, your faith will blossom under pressure and teach you true patience as you endure. And true patience brought on by endurance will equip you to complete the long journey and cross the finish line— mature, complete, and wanting nothing.[7]

Joy. Yes, you read that correctly. James said we should view our hardships as "pure joy." Does that sound like you? Do you find the joy in the midst of your struggles? Or do you find it difficult to see the good in the bad? I used to *pretend* I had joy in the midst of my struggles. As I've said before, I'd put a smile on my face and keep trying to do life on my own. I assumed struggle was simply a part of motherhood I had to silently endure and perhaps, pretend didn't even exist.

Now, by the grace of God, even in the midst of struggle, real joy—deep-down-in-my-heart joy—is present. Even if I am lured by the enemy, which as I shared at the beginning of this chapter does, indeed, still happen, I have built a deep-rooted, trusting relationship with God—one in which He has such an intense grip on my heart and one filled with unwavering peace and hope—so the enemy's lies don't hold me captive for long. I am so highly aware of what God thinks of me and what God has called me to do that I can recognize the invasion and immediately begin to go to battle, knowing I have the armor and carry the weapons God gives each of us, and trusting God is fighting for me and with me.

Friend, we choose our responses to our struggles. We can allow struggles to dictate lies in our hearts. We can complain or pass the blame. We can allow struggles to destroy our marriages, our families, our friendships—to steal our passion, joy, purpose, and dreams. We can choose to let the enemy win. Or we can see these struggles as opportunities to learn, grow, and mature as daughters of the almighty God. Paul, in his letter to the Romans, shared how our suffering does indeed have a purpose:

> But we also rejoice in our suffering, because we know that suffering produces perseverance; perseverance, character; and character, hope. And hope does not disappoint us, because God has poured out his love into our hearts by the Holy Spirit, whom he has given us.[8]

A common misconception about God, and one that leads people away from Him, is that struggle and suffering are because of God. "If God is in control of our lives, then He is to blame." That, my friend, is the enemy working, tirelessly, to make us lose hope in the very one who gives it. Struggle and suffering are *not* hand-delivered by God. He is not the one causing our pain.

Instead, God *uses* life's difficulties—a reality of living in this broken, sinful world or the enemy's sly and sneaky attacks on our hearts and minds—to build in us resilient, godly character and make us more mature and complete. God transforms our hardships filled with heartache and pain into tools of strength and confidence to help us grow as mothers and mold us into genuine followers who are more and more like Him and who grasp on to hope in all things. What the enemy intends for harm, God will use for good. Therefore, struggle and suffering are powerful vehicles with the capability to move us toward reaching the potential God sees in us. The potential He has always known exists in us.

> Struggle and suffering are powerful vehicles with the capability to move us toward reaching the potential God sees in us.

Above all, I want you to remember—in your time of struggle or fighting lies—what Jesus said to his disciples at the Last Supper, the last night he lived on earth. "In this world you will have trouble. But take heart, I have overcome the world."[9]

Jesus' death on the cross was the greatest act of genuine love in all of history. A love with the power to take our sins and hang them on the cross with Him so we are not overcome by the world and instead have the courage to claim our place in the world and soar for Him. It is a love so deep He was willing to give His life so we could live. And not *just* live. But live with freedom, joy, hope, and, purpose.

Making it Matter

A few nights into wrestling with God and combatting these lies—not feeling much like snuggling with my kids (it feels awful to admit, but I just wanted to be alone)—I found the strength to push aside these imprisoning feelings and walk upstairs to do the nightly routine. With a very quiet demeanor, I stood in the doorway of my son's room, watching him brush his teeth in the bathroom.

Samuel didn't notice me right away, but as soon as he caught my presence, a big, contagious smile adorned his sweet face. He began to brush as quickly as he could. As soon as that last spit left his mouth, he leaped over to me with that endearing look on his face and gave me a huge hug while proclaiming his enthusiastic love for me.

"Oh, Mom! I love you so much. Do you know that? I love you so, so, so much. Thank you. Thank you for coming up to say goodnight."

Samuel was well aware of the strange mood I had been in, but that didn't stop him from loving on me. It's like he knew exactly what I needed. I had been praying and reading God's Word, wrestling the turmoil ensuing in my heart. But this? No doubt God orchestrated that moment especially for me. The

Spirit of God moved in the heart of my precious boy as his great big hug destroyed the last bit of lingering lies bringing me down. I could feel both a physical and emotional release as if God, in that very moment, gently pulled an arrow from my chest. And in its place, He inserted His love and grace.

It's a beautiful mystery of God's love and the power of His Holy Spirit, isn't it? The intricate way He works in and through us and others to help draw us back to Him is nothing short of miraculous. No doubt God's Word and prayer are essential weapons against life's struggles and the lies that threaten to invade our hearts and minds. But God loves us so much and wants so badly for us to stay on course that He will use people, nature, and unexpected circumstances to demonstrate His love in ways that break through the clutter, noise, and lies to get straight to our hearts. He yearns to free us each and every day from any stronghold threatening our purpose for which He created us. We simply need to pay attention and trust He's constantly working for us.

The very next morning, the stronghold of lies had been released. Like Jacob, I felt blessed. I had clarity. That day we were leaving on a little family vacation before school started. When we got in the car, my husband looked at me and said, "It's good to have you back." Oh, let me tell you, it was good to be back. I never once doubted God would come through for me. Not only because that's what Scripture says but also because He's proved faithful before. The foundation of love and grace that has been established in my heart proved strong during this struggle. And that foundation was made even stronger.

Let's do some heart work, my friend. I really want you to take time to reflect and recognize times when you've been derailed by lies, fear, insecurities, and shame. What lies have held you captive? What was the result of your imprisonment? Did you become debilitated, unable to move forward with purpose? Did you become depressed and hopeless? Did you turn to sin? How did you overcome the lies?

I shared in chapter four about my struggle with identity, which led to a long battle with bulimia. For years, I was captive to lies that said I wasn't pretty enough. Thin enough. Good enough. On the outside, I acted confident. But on the inside, a huge battle raged. I've been asked how I overcame those lies and recovered from my eating disorder. It's a complex question to answer especially because the healing process is different for everyone experiencing this illness. I can only answer based on my personal experience: I honestly feel God healed me. I was released from the stronghold when I found out I was pregnant with my first son. It's as if something switched in my brain, and I realized my body was no longer my own. I had to protect my baby and do whatever I could to ensure his health. So, that's what I did. For the few years leading up to this point, I intentionally worked to overcome the physicality of the disease. I only attended a few therapy sessions and never took anti-depressants. Many people do need to do both as part of their path to recovery. For whatever reason, I didn't. I believe motherhood saved me. In more ways than one.

But there's one more thing I feel I need to share. Those lies about my identity that derailed me for years? They still creep into my thoughts every now and then because the enemy knows they derailed me once. Therefore, he continues to use them again and again. I just snicker when they come now and internally declare, *Bring it on!* I recognize those thoughts and know how to fight them so they no longer have power over me. That kind of strength? It only comes from God.

If there are lies right now preventing you from unfurling your wings into the beautiful butterfly God sees in you, write them down now. It's time to hit the mat with your questions and heartache. It's time to wrestle with God—absorb His Word, pray for His strength—until you are released from the stronghold and struggle. Do not give in to any thoughts that are not in line with God's heart.

In the space provided below, make a list of the people you trust to speak truth into your heart in times of struggle. Can you recall a time when God has used a person or situation to get your attention and draw you back to Him? Explain how it felt to be released from the pain.

_____

_____

_____

_____

_____

_____

_____

_____

_____

_____

A Momma's Prayer

Gracious Lord, we are so grateful You are all-knowing, all-powerful, and ever-so present. You know the lies that invade our thoughts and work to build debilitating strongholds over us. You know the doubts, fears, and insecurities that imprison our hearts and prevent us from moving forward in fulfilling the purpose You have for us and keep us from experiencing the unwavering joy and peace You freely offer. Help us recognize the joy amidst the struggles. Give us the courage to hit the mat and wrestle with You, trusting that You will bring us through the struggle with greater strength and deeper faith. Breathe in us, Lord, the power of Your wisdom and discernment to recognize the lies and replace them with Your truths. Help us put on our armor as we seek to do Your will so that we can continue to fight the good fight of faith and be a living example of Your power, love, and grace. In Jesus' name we pray, amen.

Meaningful Truth

For though we live in the world, we do not wage war as the world does. The weapons we fight with are not the weapons of the world. On the contrary, they have divine power to demolish strongholds. We demolish arguments and every pretension that sets itself up against the knowledge of God, and we take captive every thought to make it obedient to Christ.

—2 Corinthians 10:3–5 (NIV)

PART THREE

The Transformation of Motherhood

THE BIRTHING OF RENEWED PURPOSE

CHAPTER 8

The Power of His Presence

GOD NEVER ABANDONS BUT ALWAYS PURSUES

School started in a week, so we decided to squeeze in one last, little family get-away before the craziness of fall began. My son Samuel and I were in the lobby of the resort, getting coffee and breakfast for the rest of our crew to jump start our day soon to be filled with back-to-school shopping. The line was long, but coffee, to me, is always worth the wait. I watched as anxious people stood in line behind us, many trying to console hungry, tired kids. I witnessed discontented customers speak rudely to the baristas working hard to reorganize several mixed orders. I sadly observed the eyes of adults, teens, and kids alike plastered to the screens of their handheld devices, ignoring the life happening around them.

It had only been a few days since I recovered from my nasty case of the blues. Reflecting on the past week of struggle with the lies and debilitating thoughts that threatened to knock me down, I was overwhelmed with gratitude to God for helping me break through the fog so I could see life clearer again through His eyes. As I stood amidst this typical chaos of everyday life, I thought, "I'm so content. I'm so grateful."

My mind flooded with gratitude, and my heart sang for joy as I thought about how grateful I am for my children and my husband and the way we do life together ... how grateful I am for our simple life filled with amazing friends and family. Then, my thoughts lingered a bit on my loving parents and the beautiful moment I had with them before we left. I beamed with humble gratitude for them, for all of these people, for my life.

While inhaling a deep breath of internal peace, a gentle smile graced my lips as I met the eyes of a small child hiding behind her daddy's leg. As our eyes remained locked for a moment and she gifted me a smile back, I reminded myself of something very important:

Life can be tough. It can be messy and confusing. But life is good. It's so good if we just open our eyes to see the glorious happening within the mess, to see God at work everywhere, and to see life through His eyes.

Overwhelmed by that truth, I instinctively squeezed my son a little closer while we waited in the crowded coffee shop for our order to be called.

With joy in my heart and contentment in my soul, we marched back to our hotel room ready to embark on another great family day. The moment we walked through the door and I saw my husband's face, the pep in my step disappeared. My smile faded. My shoulders slouched. I noticed my phone in his hand and instantly knew something was wrong.

Noticing the look of shock and disbelief in his eyes, I asked right away:

"Is it my dad? Is he in the hospital again?"

My dad had been dealing with health issues for years, so it wasn't uncommon to get a call from my mom informing us Dad was sick again. Dad was a fighter and always pulled through. Always. But some times were worse than others. I thought perhaps he was in the hospital this time, and we may need to consider heading home early.

And then my husband came walking toward me with outstretched arms, hesitating to find the words to speak. Instantly aware of his strange behavior, my body tensed, my heart began to race, my eyes got huge. All feelings of contentment and gratitude vanished as fear overcame my body and I asked again:

"Is it my dad? Is he okay?"

My precious husband gently grabbed my shoulders and softly uttered the words he himself could hardly articulate nor believe:

"Yes, it's your dad. But, no, honey, he's … he's … gone."

It's difficult to put that moment into words. I remember losing all strength—dropping whatever was in my hands and falling to my knees. It felt like I had been sucker-punched, the air knocked right out of me. I could barely breathe. I instantly felt lost, numb, and disoriented. It felt like a part of me had been ripped out and pieces of my heart were being trampled and crushed.

My precious boys witnessed their momma, on the floor of a humble hotel room, experience real, raw, uncontrollable heartache. I could barely find the strength to comfort them as they processed this news, because in that moment, all I felt like was a little girl, aching to see her daddy one more time and longing to hold her mom.

I spent the next seven hours in the car driving to my brother's home in North Dakota where my parents had been visiting for the weekend. Flashes of memories flooded my mind as I struggled to believe this was really happening.

Although my dad's physical health had been like a roller coaster the past eight years, he seemed healthy and happy as ever the last time I saw him, two days prior. Therefore, the news of his death came as a huge shock. And although I wished it not to be true—to have just one more moment with him—I found myself thanking God for gifting him with the most peaceful death. My dad, who suffered physically, yet silently, for years, didn't have to suffer in death. He simply went to sleep and awoke in heaven.

As reality set in and we began planning the celebration of my dad's life, there is no doubt we were being held in the arms of God through family and friends who acted as His physical extensions of love and comfort. Although I could barely eat or sleep and my mind was a jumbled mess, God's supernatural strength carried me and cleared the lens of my grief so I could feel His joy, ingest His peace, and genuinely celebrate my dad's life and legacy.

There is no other explanation as to how I was able to sing a song of praise at my dad's funeral or how I was able to greet and thank countless friends and family with a smile on my face. I physically felt the comfort and peace of God's presence surrounding me like a protective bubble of strength, assuring me Dad was happy and free in the presence of Jesus.

Then, everyone left, and life went back to normal. But it wasn't *normal* for me. And I stumbled because I couldn't find *normal*. It no longer existed. As I mentioned before, my parents live right down the road from me, less than a quarter mile. I'd see them most days. I'd pop in for coffee in the morning or stop by in the afternoon with the boys for a quick chat. And now, every time I walk into their house, my daddy's chair is empty. His navy-blue zipper sweatshirt remains draped on the stool in the kitchen instead of warming his gentle frame. There is no precious greeting with a kiss and hug from him. There are no more deep conversations about life and faith. There are no more words of encouragement, love, and support uttered from his lips.

This man—from the moment I was born—loved me unconditionally. Even knowing every doubt and fear I struggled with, for I shared it all with him and my mom, he remained consistent in his unwavering support and belief in me. He never doubted my ability nor my intentions, and he never doubted my calling to write and share what God had done in my life. This man, my daddy—one of my biggest cheerleaders and encouragers—was gone, and I felt completely lost.

It's hard to comprehend how one moment we can feel so confident and inspired we're on the right road where God needs us, and the next moment we're wandering on a desolate highway with no cell signal and broken pieces of our lives scattered everywhere. Life as we know it can change in an instant.

Because I was lost and hurting—trying hard to find my footing, get through each day, and establish a new normal—I abandoned my writing. Unintentionally withdrawing from pouring my heart and energy into my dreams and my tribe of loyal online friends and followers, I lost sight of my plans and goals.

In the midst of writing this book, my dad died.

Overwhelmed by the heartache, I lost clarity and focus. But thankfully, it was only for a brief time, as eventually, I could see through the storm and focus my eyes on the only One who could save me, pick me up, and place me back exactly where He needed me. It reminds me of a story in Scripture where one of Jesus' disciples was saved by refocusing his eyes upon Christ.

HIS PRESENCE IN THE STORMS

Shortly after Jesus miraculously fed 5,000 people with only five loaves of bread and two fish, He insisted his disciples get in the boat without him and sail to the other side of the Sea of Galilee. Considering how He had been surrounded by thousands of people, I can understand why Jesus wanted some time alone to pray and recuperate.

Do you suppose the disciples questioned why Jesus sent them away, especially since He had specifically called them to follow Him, and up to this point, they hadn't left His side?

I imagine them eyeing each other thinking, *Is He serious? Is He really leaving us alone?* but no one having the courage to ask Him. The disciples, of course, obeyed and got in the boat as they watched Jesus leave them.

Already a little on edge, things worsened for the disciples. A few hours later—out of nowhere—a ferocious storm unleashed on their small boat, and they were terrified not only by the strong winds tempting to capsize their boat but because they also saw a figure walking on water. Recognizing their fear, eager to comfort them, Jesus spoke: "Take courage! It is I. Don't be afraid."[1]

Yes, you read that right. Jesus walked on water. Crazy, I know. But it gets even crazier. One brave disciple, Peter, upon learning it was Jesus walking on the water toward them, called out: "Lord, if it's you, tell me to come to you on the water."[2]

Did Peter even know what he was asking? He did realize it was impossible to walk on water, right? But Jesus, recognizing Peter's instinctive act of faith, immediately responded, "Come."[3]

Overcome with awe and wonder, perhaps a bit mesmerized by what he witnessed, I imagine Peter being overwhelmed with a supernatural confidence he did not recognize, yet he still trusted. Struggling to find his balance as the winds and waves continued to crash upon the boat, I imagine him taking a deep breath as he gazed into Jesus' eyes. Then, Peter did exactly what Jesus asked—climbed out of the boat in the middle of the storm and walked on the water toward Jesus.

What a remarkable act of faith and demonstration of God's power! But the story doesn't end there. As Peter walked toward Jesus, he became distracted by the storm raging around him. Within moments, as he began to feel the waves crashing upon his body, he realized the impossible act he was doing, became overwhelmed by fear, and began to sink. Imagine the horror he must have felt as his body began to sink deeper and deeper! As he sank, Peter frantically searched to see Jesus through the crashing waves as he cried out: "Lord, save me!" [4]

Peter had confidence in the impossible as long as he kept His eyes on Jesus. But the moment he took his eyes off Jesus and instead began to focus on the problems surrounding him, his faith wavered. The storm was going to drag him down as long as he focused on the hardship. The same goes for us, my friend. When we are overwhelmed by the difficulties life brings and neglect to seek Jesus, the waves of grief and despair swallow us. When Peter realized his own hopelessness and realigned his focus back to Jesus, he was saved.

"Immediately Jesus reached out his hand and caught him."[5]

Jesus was saying, "I'm right here. I've been here the whole time. When troubles rise, when the worries and heartaches of life wash over you, all you have to do is turn your eyes to me, and I will save you."

Just like Jesus was there immediately to save Peter the moment he called for Him, Jesus is there immediately for us when we call for Him, when we turn our focus back to Him. And even though we may not be able to see Him through the storm raging around us, He's there to grab us and save us from drowning. He never leaves us to face life's struggles alone.

Now, I know we aren't walking on water, but we certainly walk through difficult situations. And like this storm blew in quickly, life can change in an instant. Jesus never says there won't be storms. Your best friend can betray you. You or someone you love can be diagnosed with cancer. You can discover your spouse is having an affair, lose your job, have a miscarriage, or maybe, like me, one of the most beloved people in your life dies. The hurts and pains of this imperfect world can cause us to break, sink slowly into despair, and neglect our once clear purpose. But Jesus reaches out His hand and gives us the power to walk through the storm and find hope again.

BROKE BUT NOT BROKEN

Shortly after my dad's funeral, I had a conversation with a dear friend who was overcome with emotion because she was having a difficult time understanding how I didn't seem more devastated by his death. It was obvious to me the Spirit of God was stirring in her heart as she sought answers to her confusion. I didn't know how else to explain it except to say: "I broke when my dad died, but I'm not broken."

This book you now hold in your hands is evidence of that. If I had broken, I would have never gone back to writing. I would have abandoned my purpose and dreams and allowed the hurts of this world to overwhelm me and dictate my life. The truth is, there will be times in life when we will break, but that doesn't mean we are broken.

There will be times in life when we will break, but that doesn't mean we are broken.

You see, there is a difference between breaking and being broken. I miss my dad more than words can express—often moving me to tears. It absolutely breaks my heart not to be doing life with him anymore. Not feeling the softness of his hands or the gentle strength of his embrace. Not seeing his beautiful smile or hearing him say, "I love you, honey." Not having him next to me at baseball games cheering on my boys. Not seeing his golf cart come down our driveway on his way over for a little chit-chat. Not seeing him so handsomely dressed in his Sunday best for church.

I could go on and on about all the things I miss that break my heart over and over again every time I think of him. And yes, for a time, my heartbreak knocked me off what I thought was a very clear path, leaving me lost and devasted. But I wasn't broken.

When the waves of shock began to settle, and I recognized the reality of my pain, I knew I was never walking in the storm of my grief alone. When my grief overwhelms me—because it still does at times—I call out, like Peter, to Jesus, and He's always there.

I wasn't broken because the seeds of faith that had been richly cultivated into the soil of my soul over the last several years had become deeply rooted in God's Truths. The Spirit of God empowered me with the hope and promise of eternal life that comes through Christ, carrying me and giving me strength not only to endure my heartbreak but also to find my path again. Even though the path I'm on now is not quite the same as before. It never is when we experience heartbreak. But what I keep learning is God continues to use it all—our heartbreak, joys, failures, successes—to draw us closer to Him so He can keep molding us more and more into Christ's likeness.

Surprisingly, this new road I'm traveling is graced with newfound beauty, deeper purpose, and more profound passion. I feel God has gifted me with this beautiful vision cocooned in peace and hope. When I close my eyes and imagine this road I'm running on, I see a pathway illuminated by twinkling white lights ornamenting trees lined on either side whose branches hang and sway in the Spirit's gentle breeze forming a tunnel of undeniable direction.

I see my dad walking with Jesus right ahead of me, glancing back every now and then to flash me his precious, endearing smile, prodding me with a little nod to continue to run on this divinely designed road with steadfast strength and confidence.

As I mentioned earlier, my dad always had this magnificent ability to see past all my doubt, fear, and insecurity and speak honest, fatherly truth to the depths of my heart. Gifted with the ability to see directly past all the barriers I saw in my way of accomplishing my dreams, he knew my potential before I ever recognized it. It's as if he knew me better than I knew myself. Powered by his unconditional love for me, it seemed like he already saw who I would someday become.

The loss of my dad was a huge reminder of the frailty of this life—of how tomorrow is not guaranteed—and of how we only have this one life on earth to live, make a difference, become the woman, wife, mother, daughter, sister, and friend God has created us to be. Why not place our trust in the Lord and allow Him to help us become her? Why not be filled with unwavering joy and peace? Why not be courageous and live out our dreams, for crying out loud? There's no sense in shying away from our full potential, and there's no reason in doubting our calling to impact our children and the world. We should not fear the future. Even in death, my dad remains a vessel of God's love inspiring me to rise up with unwavering confidence to keep seeking God's will and keep moving forward to become the woman my dad always saw in me. And most importantly, to keep relying on God's strength to get me there.

WINGS IN NEED OF STRENGTH

Nothing can prevent heartache in our life—not reading more Scripture, saying more prayers, or building a closer relationship with God. We may try to imagine our response when life throws us a sucker punch, but we won't really know until we personally experience the blow. No matter how strong our faith is, this kind of knockout can level us, wound our hearts, weaken our resolve, make us feel instantly lost, and cause us to be overcome by the waves.

I can't help but wonder about the timing of my dad's death as this chapter was not in my original plan for the book. Because I experienced the profound, unwavering presence of God during the hardest time in my life, I felt compelled to share this message as it proves significant to our walk of faith and the incredible, unexplainable power of God.

Even when we've broken free from the chrysalis of struggle and imprisonment and know the truth of the Gospel and have been saved by Jesus ... even when we love Him and have a relationship with Him ... even when we have the wisdom to combat the enemy and soar to new heights … and even when we trust Him and seek to do His will, life can still knock us off course and lead us down unfamiliar roads. We can get lost and wounded, unable to know the next step. I don't ever want to mislead you into thinking that when you follow Jesus, life is without struggle and pain. Life is full of them. But the truth to cling to is this: When we are weak, He is strong.

Upon breaking free from its chrysalis, a delicate butterfly needs time before take-off for its wings to dry and receive the necessary blood flow and nutrients required to take flight. The same is true for us. We need time to absorb nutrients—the strength that comes only from God—before we can unfurl our wings and soar, again, on the lighted path of purpose. Every apostle and follower of Christ before us experienced heartache and unexpected set-backs as they sought to do God's will. Listen to how the apostle Paul vulnerably shares in 2 Corinthians how his weaknesses were God's opportunity to demonstrate His superpowered strength through him.

> Because of the extravagance of those revelations (truths Paul received from the Lord), and so I wouldn't get a big head, I was given the gift of a handicap to keep me in constant touch with my limitations. Satan's angel did his best to get me down; what he in fact did was push me to my knees. No danger then of walking around high and mighty! At first I didn't think of it as a gift, and begged God to remove it. Three times I did that, and then he told me,
>
> "My grace is enough; it's all you need. My strength comes into its own in your weakness."

Once I heard that, I was glad to let it happen. I quit focusing on the handicap and began appreciating the gift. It was a case of Christ's strength moving in on my weakness. Now I take limitations in stride, and with good cheer, these limitations that cut me down to size—abuse, accidents, opposition, bad breaks. I just let Christ take over! And so the weaker I get, the stronger I become.[6]

Oh friend, please not only hear this truth but also allow it to sink into the depths of your heart because it's the truth you will need when your heart breaks. And trust me, your heart will break in this lifetime if it hasn't already. This truth will be the blood that pumps again and again to revive your heart and restore it to health. Having a solid foundation of faith and having deep-rooted knowledge and understanding of God's love and grace doesn't protect us from life's hurts, but it is the *key* to nurturing hope. Christ is the key to finding light in the darkness, to seeing the good in the midst of the bad, to creating a new normal after the hurt. Christ's power and presence in us is what inspires us to keep living, keep growing, keep seeking, and keep being obedient to God's calling on our lives.

Knowing and trusting God is so powerful and essential, because when the storms of life hit and leave us feeling lost, wounded, and weak, He takes over and becomes our strength. The apostle Paul defines these handicaps as gifts! And if they're gifts, then we need to start talking more about them instead of hiding behind them in shame. Sharing with one another our truths and vulnerably opening the conversation about how our limitations, aches, bad breaks, weaknesses, insecurities, and unfortunate happenings are all gifts intended to humble us to our knees at the foot of the cross, reminding us we can't do this life on our own, inspires healing and nurtures hope in us all. Our handicaps are divine reminders that when life knocks us down, God picks us up. When we are weak, then God is strong and His power is revealed through us.

There are few greater testaments to God's presence than when His strength overcomes our weaknesses. Therefore, we need to, like Paul, learn how to look at our limitations, hardships, and difficulties with good cheer. We need to authentically "boast about our weaknesses"[7] to the people in our lives so God not only can do His mighty work in us but also receive the glory and credit, ensuring more people come to know Him.

When I answered my friend's question of why I wasn't more devasted by my dad's death, the only answer I gave was "Jesus." There's no way I could continue to live life with peace, joy, and purpose after such heartache if it weren't for Jesus. I boasted about my weakness, giving all credit and glory to God.

But sadly, we so often hide behind our handicaps and don't articulate the broken pieces of our lives. Why? What is it we fear? Shame? Embarrassment? Judgment? Do we worry we will be perceived as being less than? Maybe it's weakness itself we fear for we are so accustomed to being the strong one, all on our own.

As I mentioned in a previous chapter, I relied only on myself at one point in my life. But God put me through an intense metamorphosis, exactly like He wants to do to you. God's the one who changed my heart and reminds me often how I am an imperfect human in dire need of His perfect grace that gives strength to my every weakness. It's times when we have nothing but our faith to rely on where God's power is profoundly revealed. Only God can bring us back time and time again from the aches of this world, stronger and more driven to be His ambassadors, and more empowered to keep unfurling our wings and soaring to new heights.

I am an imperfect human in dire need of His perfect grace that gives strength to my every weakness.

When we know God, we learn to listen for His voice, sense His beckoning, and trust Him to lift us up from our darkest moments and guide us back to the light. Jesus' incredible sacrifice and the magnitude of what it means for us is what inspires me daily to give my life to Him. When we've got Jesus, we don't remain sunk, lost, or wounded. His peace, joy, love, and hope have the supernatural ability to override our sorrows and aches and help us move forward with purpose again. And the more we know Jesus, the quicker we're able to, like Peter, turn our eyes back to Him.

As we mature, most of us discover life is unpredictable. It's filled with ups and downs and unexpected turns and twists. Life pushes and pulls us in all sorts of directions, forcing us to choose how to respond. Life without Jesus leads to a dark, lonely, hopeless place. But life with Him inspires growth and revelations beyond our imaginations. And our growth is never done. We don't ever arrive at some final destination here on earth. Our final destination comes when we enter the gates of heaven and meet Jesus face to face. Therefore, while we are still living and breathing, there is work to be done and a purpose to fulfill. When we know Jesus and are disciplined to turn our eyes to Him, life's unpredictable circumstances will drive us closer and closer to our Maker, organically transforming us more and more to His likeness and nurturing in us the wisdom to confidently embrace the roles He calls us to play, including our role as moms.

 Making it Matter

Last winter, we took our first family ski trip to the mountains of Montana. All four of our boys had skied before at our little ski resort near our home, but we were ready for a little winter getaway. Keep in mind, we live in Minnesota so there's no such thing as mountains—more like really big hills. So, to graduate to a mountain was no small feat. At the time, my big boys were amateur snowboarders. To say they love it is an understatement. Although my two littles did not have much experience, they had taken lessons, so we assumed they were good to go. Key word … assumed. Lesson … never assume.

It was a gorgeous, sunny, winter day. After twelve hours in the car, everyone was eager to hit the slopes. Once everyone was geared up (no small task), we opted to bypass the bunny hill. I mean, who needs a refresher run on the bunny hill?

Not us. We were a mildly experienced family of skiers and snowboarders—or so we thought.

We made our way to the ski lift to make our first journey up the mountain. The boys were excited and amazed at the sights below. However, the moment we got off the lift and the two littles tumbled, the excitement faded and frustration set in. Big time! My husband and I spent several minutes helping them get their skis back on while the older boys had to wait (which was torture, for us and them). All they wanted to do was snowboard. But I wasn't comfortable letting them go down on their own since they weren't yet acquainted with the slopes.

I bet you can imagine how our first run went. To save time at what could be a really long story, I'll get to the point. It took us F-O-R-E-V-E-R. Forever to make our way down the hill. I'm guessing, and I may be underestimating, my littles wiped out about twenty times each—at least. My hubby and I each took one of the two little boys, and as patiently as possible, accompanied him down the hill, helping him up every time he fell.

Needless to say, they cried and whined and declared they hated skiing the entire way down (we're only here for two more days … lovely). Meanwhile, my big boys were frustrated by having to wait for us. This was our best parenting moment ever. I have to say, my husband and I both wondered if we had made a huge mistake. It turns out … yes and no. Yes, huge mistake not to put the little boys into ski school right away (which we did the minute we safely got down the mountain). And no, our trip was not a mistake. It was one of the best family vacations we've ever had. That is, once the littles learned how to ski. By the end, they were rockin' the mountain and having a blast.

Sometimes, life is like skiing down a mountain for the first time. We will fall. We may even break a bone or get lost. And this can happen even if we have the strongest faith. But like my husband and I would never leave our boys to tackle the mountain on their own, God never abandons us on the mountains of life. He's even with us on the hills, in the valleys, and through everything in between. God's watchful and present and is always right by our side, ready to pick us up, grab our skis, help us get them back on, and guide us safely down the mountain. We may fall a hundred times. We may get hurt or even complain, cry, and wish we could be transported back or forward in time to avoid pain. But God will never stop picking us up. Never. He will do whatever it takes to help us find our footing again and heal our wounds.

In fact, in Scripture God says when we trust in Him, we don't actually ever fall. We may stumble, but He always has a hold of our hands to catch our fall. And He promises to make our steps firm.[9]

And can I remind you of something? This intimate process is not without purpose. God will take our hearts that break and our aches that paralyze—He will take our falls, our stumbles, our moments of sinking in the waves—and He will nurture growth and wisdom within our souls. He will make firm our next steps. To believe in God's ability to pick us up when we fall inspires even deeper faith. He promises to take whatever we experience and turn it into good. It's up to us to trust in that and open our eyes to the blessings that come out of our aches and breaks and cling to the purposes set before us.

God will take our hearts
that break and our aches
that paralyze—He will take
our falls, our stumbles,
our moments of sinking in
the waves—and He will
nurture growth and wisdom
within our souls. He will
make firm our next steps.

I anticipate this journal time could be difficult for you, therefore I'm praying over these words as I write them, asking God to reveal His presence to you and comfort you as you remember and share, in writing, the hardships you've faced in your life. Have you ever felt confident and content about your life, and then, out of nowhere, your feet were knocked out from under you, and you were left lying on your back not knowing how to get up? Can you recall a time when you felt lost or overwhelmed by the waves of life's difficult circumstances, unsure of which step to take and in which direction? What caused you to fall, sink, or to be lost? If it's happened in the past, write how God picked you up, gave you strength to keep going, and helped you safely down the hill. Did you experience a new sense of purpose? Or, if you are lying on your back, or waves are crashing over you, or you are lost on an abandoned highway now, seek the Lord. Call to Him for help. He's there and He promises to rescue you and set you on a clear path. Write about your hopes and what you need from Him. If you are really struggling, I encourage you to reach out to a trusted friend who can help walk by your side during this difficult time. As I share in a later chapter, we were never meant to do this life alone. We're in this together. If you can't get a hold of a trusted friend of the faith, please connect with me.

_____

_____

_____

_____

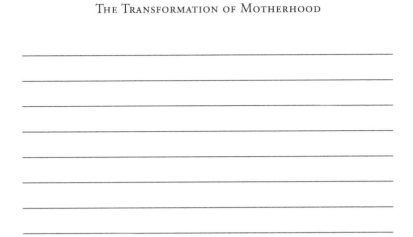

Oh, my friend. This was a difficult chapter to write, not only because it stirs the aches in my heart at the loss of my dad, but because it may also stir aches in your own. I so desire to wrap my arms around you and assure you God is holding you close no matter what you're going through right now. Remember, even when we have strong faith, we can fall and feel overwhelmed by the storm. It doesn't mean we are weak or that our faith is faulty. Hardships mean we are human experiencing the downfalls of a broken world. I know because I've experienced a great fall. The moment I learned of my dad's death, the despair overwhelmed me and I felt like I was drowning. But friend, I can't imagine that fall without God being there to reach out His hand, pick me up, and set me on my path again. Faith is so much more than believing in God. It's trusting in His divine, supernatural presence in our lives that has the power to guide us safely home, more inspired and energized to keep living, seeking, and doing good for His sake and for His kingdom.

A Momma's Prayer

Lord God, there is no doubt this life can be hard and unexpected. We can be on a good road with inspired purpose and then—out of nowhere—be knocked off course, left feeling lost and wounded. Our life can change in an instant. And that, God, is such a hard reality to recover from and accept. The aches run deep and real and have the power to knock the air right out of us. In those moments, be our breath, Lord. Be the life that sustains us in our darkest moments. Be our strength in our weakness. Help us to lean on You in times of uncertainty. Help us to trust in Your faithfulness and Your supernatural presence in times when our hearts are breaking. Heal the broken pieces of our hearts. Restore newfound purpose. Renew our confidence in what the future holds. Strengthen our hope in You as You remind us that You never abandon us and are always pursuing us. Overwhelm us with Your peace and Your comfort as we trust You to set our feet firm on a new path of purpose. In Jesus' name we pray, amen.

Meaningful Truth

This is what the Lord GOD says: I, myself, will search for my sheep and take care of them. As a shepherd takes care of his scattered flock when it is found, I will take care of my sheep. I will save them from all the places where they were scattered on a cloudy and dark day. I will feed my flock and lead them to rest, says the Lord GOD. I will search for the lost, bring back those that

*strayed away, put bandages on those that were hurt,
and make the weak strong.*

—Ezekiel 34:11–12; 15–16 (NCV)

~ CHAPTER 9 ~

The Courageous Take-Off

GOD REDEFINES YOUR ROLE AS MOM

I don't know what bedtime is like at your house, but most nights at ours, I'm upstairs for an hour or more putting boys to bed. It could be because I have four of them each needing a good portion of my time and attention. Most often, I treasure snuggling each boy on his bed because they are the most precious, sacred, meaningful moments of the day. They are the moments filled with inquisitive questions about life, conversations about struggles, updates on the latest happenings in third grade, or much-needed love and encouragement for a tough day. Filled with either laugher, crying, protests, dreams, or a combination of all, these moments build deep connections and relationships—priceless treasures for a momma's heart. Moments I will miss when they are gone. Just to keep it real, though, those moments are also filled with stinky gas, belching noises, scary boos, contagious giggles, and uncontrollable wiggles. Ah, life with boys.

One night while lying in bed next to my son Samuel chatting about his day, he said something I will never forget. I don't remember the exact content of our conversation, but I remember his response to my words of love and encouragement to him. He glanced at me with his huge blue eyes and endearing smile, sweetly sighed, and lovingly replied: "Oh, Mom, you just add God to everything."

His comment left me speechless for a moment, in awe of how God had opened my son's heart to notice how at the center of *my* heart is God and how God is the integral force dictating how I live my life. I thought my heart was about to burst out of my chest. Gathering myself so as not to alarm him with my excitement at his mature revelation, I gently responded, "You're right, buddy, I do add God to everything. I've learned it's my responsibility and privilege, as your mom, to help you become aware of God's presence, love, and power in your life."

As we continued to snuggle and soft, silent tears leaked from my eyes, I praised God for gifting me with the understanding of my primary purpose and role as mother to my four precious boys. There was a time when I thought God had made some sort of mistake giving me four boys. Not only because I always wanted a little girl, but also as I've alluded to in previous chapters, mothering was so tough I felt like a constant failure. I did not feel equipped nor qualified to juggle a newborn infant, defiant toddler, independent preschooler, and adolescent with attitude. The constant demands, high energy, whines, and cries were enough to break me.

Come to discover, it was those very struggles and challenges God creatively used to turn my eyes to Him not only to heal my aching momma heart but also to answer the longing question of my heart: *What is my purpose?* More specifically, *What is the purpose of my role as mom?*

It wasn't until my heart was intimately aligned with God's heart that I intuitively began to understand and fully embrace the priceless gift of being mom and the remarkable responsibility and joy that came with it.

The truth is, as mommas, we have countless jobs and roles to play, don't we? Many of which I never knew existed until I was thrown into the chaos of motherhood. I've been known to fill the following roles, how about you? Chauffer, chef, cheerleader, coach, coordinator, counselor, housekeeper, nurse, playmate, teammate, personal assistant, referee, teacher, and the list goes on. We choose to play these roles, because upon our children's moment of entry into the world, our hearts fall madly in love. Being a mom becomes the most important role we play, and we desire the absolute best for our children.

However, there is another role we are intended to play that is too often overlooked. And it's not because we get wrapped up in the chaotic mess of day-to-day life or because we think it's ridiculous or because we think there is no time to add one more duty to our already exhausted list. This particular role is overlooked because no one ever told us about this vital part of our role as mom. And this truth changes everything.

I know this to be true because other women in my life have told me. At a recent parenting training where I was leading and sharing this insight, one mom boldly and vulnerably declared, "I wish I would have watched a video on this before I left the hospital with my new baby. I had no idea."

She was stunned to discover the role of mom is a divine, God-ordained calling whose primary purpose is to point her children to God. In other words, God uniquely and specifically designed the role of mom with a divine purpose to shepherd her children's hearts with His love and grace so her children will come to know and love Him. God needed someone significant to help His children recognize and use their unique God-given gifts and talents to serve and love others and do so in ways that will bring glory to Him and expand His kingdom. Who better to take on this role than a mother?

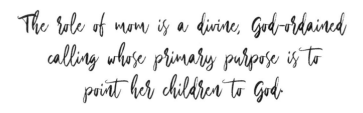

The role of mom is a divine, God-ordained calling whose primary purpose is to point her children to God.

Our role as mom, my friends, is so much bigger and more significant than simply raising good, respectful kids. Being a mom is about raising godly ones. And by that I don't mean perfect kids, rather kids who love and serve God. God Himself says so. It's a truth that encompasses eternal significance, an invaluable gift we have the privilege of bestowing to our children on behalf of Jesus Christ. We can't afford to neglect this high calling and honor.

THE DIVINE ROLE OF MOM

I've already presumed you love your kids beyond measure. But do you know how you're able to love them like that? We love because God first loved us.[1] You see, love is the very nature of God. In fact, 1 John 4:8b says, "God is love." Love is not something we initiate out of our own strength or efforts. God created us with love and out of love. Therefore, we know love. So, we do love.

The ability to love—without conditions—is a divine gift inserted into the masterful design of our DNA. And it's the supernatural love of God ingrained in our being that makes us "Godlike"—reflecting the very nature of God. The book of Genesis confirms we were not only created to reflect God's very nature of love but also to continue His legacy of humanity. In other words, we were called to produce more children who will also reflect His nature.

> God spoke: "Let us make human beings in our image,
> make them reflecting our nature …
> God created human beings;
> he created them godlike,
> Reflecting God's nature.
> He created them male and female.
> God blessed them. "Prosper! Reproduce! Fill Earth!
> Take charge![2]

The ability to love—
without conditions—is a divine
gift inserted into the masterful
design of our DNA. And it's
the supernatural love of God
ingrained in our being that
makes us "Godlike"—reflecting
the very nature of God.

Okay, so I realize creating offspring is not a huge surprise to you. It's what God had planned for humanity. He wanted us to be fruitful and multiply. But that's not all. Check out what God says in the book of Malachi about the type of children He is seeking.

"Has He not made you and your wife one? You belong to Him, body and spirit. And what does He seek from such a union? Godly children."[3]

Godly children. Godly. God's entire plan for humanity was, yes, to increase in number, but it was so much more. There was a significant condition added to His plan. His whole plan was wrapped in *love* so His children and their children and their children's children would grow to know, love, and serve Him. He desires a world filled with godly people—people who are so inspired by His love and truth that they can't help but live their lives in ways that honor Him, bring glory to His kingdom, and point others to Him. The world God designed didn't include simply "good" people. The "good" comes as a result of the "godly." And there's more.

The whole reason God desires us to live a godly life and pass on that culture to our children is because it's in living a godly life where we receive the fullness of His love and grace and experience the unique, soulful abundance and prosperity God provides which far exceeds that of the world. It's in living *godly* where we build an intimate relationship with God which leads to lasting joy, peace, hope, and love. I desire that life for myself, and I desire that life for my children.

God is no fool. He knows what types of struggles and challenges we are up against in this broken world, and He knows raising kids is no easy task. Therefore, the good news is He doesn't abandon us to do this mothering thing alone. That was never His intention nor His hope. However, the world has a way of interfering and, sadly, so many women end up feeling alone, overwhelmed, frustrated, angry, and discouraged. These debilitating feelings cause them to miss out on the incredible joy motherhood is meant to be.

God witnessed countless people throughout the centuries turn away from Him, time and time again. With heaviness in His heart, He watched as parents neglected to teach their kids about Him. Sadly, He observed children wandering aimlessly with no direction and no sense of purpose. The bonds of love created by His power He saw break and be forgotten. His dreams of parents passing on the legacy of faith to their children was shattered as He watched batons of faith fall, never to be picked up again. I can't imagine how much His heart aches to see families ignore His presence, neglect His significance, and forget His promises.

Recognizing His people needed to learn what His expectations were for them and how they were to live, God spoke through the prophet Moses. Moses not only was God's instrument for setting the Israelites—God's chosen people— free from slavery in Egypt, but he was also a messenger of truths His people needed to hear. These are the same truths we need to hear today.

> This is the commandment, the rules and regulations, that GOD, your God, commanded me to teach you ... This is so that you'll live in deep reverence before GOD lifelong, observing all his rules and regulations that

188

I'm commanding you, you and your children and your
grandchildren, living good long lives.

Listen obediently, Israel. Do what you're told so that
you'll have a good life, a life of abundance and bounty,
just as God promised, in a land abounding in milk and
honey ...

Love God, your God, with your whole heart: love
Him with all that's in you, love Him with all you've got!

Write these commandments that I've given you today
on your hearts. Get them inside of you and then get them
inside your children. Talk about them wherever you are,
sitting at home or walking in the street; talk about them
from the time you get up in the morning to when you fall
into bed at night.[4]

"Love God ... love Him with all that's in you." And
then, teach your children to do it—all day, every day. In any
opportunity or situation, insert God. That's what God is
calling us mommas to do. Now I realize this can be a daunting
revelation, especially for those of you raised in a home with
no faith or if your only model of faith appeared once a week
at church. But instead of cowering away from this calling, I
invite you to lean into it because it's that important.

I want you to notice the urgency Moses places on this
role. It's an urgency the world and all its distractions and
temptations have stripped from our consciousness. It's as if the
culture of faith in the family has become lazy or surface-level,
side-tracked from its original design and purpose.

"When Moses had finished saying all these words to all
Israel, he said, 'Take to heart all these words to which I give

witness today and urgently command your children to put them into practice, every single word of this Revelation. Yes. This is no small matter for you; it's your life.'"[5]

"This is no small matter ... it's your life." In other words, take this instruction seriously because God is the only answer to a good, rich, meaningful life. The role of mom comes with a divine purpose not to be taken lightly.

Now, you may wonder, *How in the world do I add God to everything else I'm already doing? I don't even know where to begin.*

Or, *I know this is important, but I don't have the knowledge or the understanding to explain faith to my kids.*

Or, *I have the knowledge, but I don't know how to connect organically with my children in ways that directly impact their faith.*

It can be rather intimidating and uncomfortable for many moms to talk about faith or God with their children. Sadly, too often, kids enter this world and are given no faith foundation. Some may get a little church once a week or vacation Bible school in the summer, but they aren't witnessing and experiencing Christlike attitudes and behaviors in their homes from the people they love and admire most. Too many parents are unaware of their unique and divine calling and responsibility to point their kids to Christ because the parents never had that model of faith to follow themselves.

The ties of faith have been damaged generation after generation, creating a culture in homes filled with surface-level faith or no faith at all. Do you now see why God was so adamant about us passing on the baton of faith to our kids? If we don't, the world will swallow them up, and faith in an all-powerful, all-mighty, all-loving God will be lost for generations. These are generations who will never fully experience the joy and purpose to which they were created in the first place.

Allow me to pause for a moment to reassure you that all is not gloom and doom. As long as we are living and breathing, there is hope to restore faith in our families. I only meant to demonstrate the urgency and responsibility we have to pass on faith to our children, and there's good news: it doesn't require a degree in theology or some special talent. It doesn't even require you to go to church every Sunday or do daily devotions. The requirement is simple—a heart with desire and intention to seek Christ, to grow in His wisdom, and to develop an authentic spirit full of God's love and grace. And God? God is waiting and God wants to cultivate that desire in your heart and nurture it in ways that will have lasting impact on you and your children for generations to come.

RESEARCH SPEAKS LOUDLY

I believe you are the greatest, most significant influencer in your child's life. *You* are who they love the most and who they aspire to become. Your children watch what you do and how you react to life. They listen to the words you speak and how you speak them. Your children notice how you cope with joys and struggles, and they mimic your beliefs, including faith.

The National Study of Youth and Religion reports that "parents are the greatest influence on teenage faith."[6] The study also concludes that parents are the "hidden curriculum." Meaning, parents have the most power to instill lifelong faith in their children. Church, Sunday school, family devotions, youth group, and Bible studies—although great supplements to building faith—don't hold a candle to the impact parents have on the faith of their children. But sadly, the study also reveals that "teenagers have ho-hum feelings about religion."[7] That leads me to presume most parents aren't accepting the responsibility God gave us to raise godly children. In fact, the study suggests most parents "sport lackluster faith,"[8] leading Kendra Creasy Dean, theologian and youth minister, "to describe the situation of youth and the American church as 'almost Christian.'"[9]

I don't know about you, but I think this information can do one of two things: sadden us or empower us. For me, I've been empowered, which is why I wrote this book. We are the *key*, my friend, to creating a powerful shift in our generation of families. A shift that declares: We accept the responsibility to raise godly children. That's empowering. When we make that commitment, we hold onto the hope that we will pass on the faith not only into the hearts of our children but also into the hearts of our grandchildren and their children. Let's never underestimate the incredible impact intentionally passing on the faith can have in the world for generations.

Now, before you go and be all independent as if your child's happiness and faith is all up to you and you begin to feel mounting pressure to do everything right, I want you to pause and remember you're not in this alone. It's not solely up to you. God is walking with you every step of the way. He wants your child's heart more than you want your child's heart to want and know God. Therefore, instilling faith in our children becomes a dance of doing *our part* and then trusting and allowing God to do *His part* in capturing and molding their hearts. In fact, as I'll detail more in a later chapter, when we own and admit our weaknesses and inadequacies to our children, they learn perfection is not a requirement but an invitation to place their dependence on God.

Instilling faith in our children becomes a dance of doing our part and then trusting and allowing God to do His part in capturing and molding their hearts.

TIME TO TAKE FLIGHT

The previous chapters have laid the foundation for you to be ready to embark on embracing the divine nature of your role as mom. It's a very personal journey, and one I pray you have begun. I pray you're embracing your identity in Christ, allowing His grace to set you free from any guilt or lies, getting to know God's heart, and being transformed by His love. It's essential you do the personal, heart work so your words and actions prove genuine and so you can experience the joy and peace that transpires despite the struggles that continue to come.

If you're not quite ready, I encourage you to go back to those chapters and do the *heart* work. Dive into Scripture. Spend time in prayer. Seek God with all your heart. Do all these things intentionally every day. In His timing, He will move in you, and you will be inspired to do His work in your home. Believe that His faithfulness will breathe new life and renewed purpose into the veins of your being.

When we mommas become aligned with God's will and His heart, when we've gone through the struggle of metamorphosis and are transformed into the beauty God sees in us, we will have the ready, confident hearts to learn, embrace, execute, and enjoy the divine role of motherhood. By the grace and wisdom of God, we intuitively know how to soar in this newly discovered role.

Listen to how Jesus describes having insight into God's kingdom is a gift. This is what we've been given, my friend: insight and understanding; however, insight comes only when our hearts are willing to receive it. If you haven't received it already, prepare to receive it, my friend. Prepare and receive it.

> The disciples came up and asked, "Why do you tell stories?
>
> He (Jesus) replied, "You've been given insight into God's kingdom. You know how it works. Not everybody has this gift, this insight; it hasn't been given to them [unbelievers]. Whenever someone has a ready heart for this, the insights and understandings flow freely. But if there is no readiness, any trace of receptivity soon disappears. That's why I tell stories: to create readiness, to nudge the people toward receptive insight.[10]

When we have ready hearts that absorb the redeeming truths of God's love and grace, we are prepared to take flight with newfound purpose, just like a monarch butterfly whose wings have dried and strengthened and whose refined identity has an unwavering confidence of its new existence. Life ahead for the monarch butterfly is brand new. As a caterpillar, it only ever lived on one plant. Now, as a butterfly, it's unleashed to explore the world. Intuitively, because of the divine plan of its creation, the new monarch knows where to go and what to do.

When we have ready hearts that absorb the redeeming truths of God's love and grace, we are prepared to take flight with newfound purpose.

Making it Matter

Few things are worse than your child having the stomach flu on Christmas Eve. Some festivities and celebrations are put on hold, others go on without him. My poor Cooper experienced this one year. As the rest of the family left for Christmas Eve service all dolled up in their Sunday best, he and I snuggled on the couch surrounded by buckets, tissues, towels, and washcloths. In the stillness of our home, among the subtle moans of my sick child, I quietly sang, "Silent Night." I gently rubbed his back assuring him everything was going to be alright.

With the little energy he could muster, he slowly lifted his hands from beneath his blanket, clasped them together, lifted his eyelids enough to catch my glance. Without a word spoken, he communicated to me: "Mom, will you pray for me?"

I immediately knew what he was asking and replied, "Yes, of course, sweet boy. Yes, I will pray for you."

I can't help but wonder if my son's response to turn to prayer in his time of need was because he'd witnessed his momma go to prayer for him and with him countless times before. I have no doubt God is working to capture his heart, but God is also working in mine and using me as His instrument to do His work in my home.

Here's what I'm learning, friend. The more I seek God, the closer I grow in relationship to Him and the more my life reflects His nature. Influenced then by God's heart and presence, the more organically I point my children to Him. As a result, the more I discipline, teach, and nurture with the love and grace of Christ, and the more I witness the fruits of my hopes for them growing. In other words, the character qualities I desperately desire to develop in my kids are the beautiful, organic result of a heart in love with God.

We have been gifted the role of showing our children the way to Him. And since our hearts desire the absolute best for our children, then we have no choice but to point them to God because without God they won't ever get the best this life on earth has to offer. Oh, and don't worry, the how-to is coming.

But first I want you to take a moment and write down how you would define *your* current role as mom. Is faith-nurturer part of your description? Do you talk about faith in your home? If not, why don't you? Do you walk the walk of a heart freed by Christ and in love with God? If not, what's holding you back? Uncertainty? Fear? Confusion? After reading this chapter, has your view of your role as mom changed? If so, explain below in what way. Are you ready to embrace the divine character of your role? Share how you feel about embarking on the next stage of your journey as mom by embracing the divine character accompanying this role. Write about any doubts, fears, insecurities. And then write about the hopes and dreams you have as you seek to fully accept the divine responsibility of your role as mom.

_____

_____

_____

_____

_____

_____

_____

_____

_____

_____

_____

_____

_____

A Momma's Prayer

Gracious God, thank You for entrusting Your precious children into our care. Thank You for creating us in Your image, thereby gifting us with the supernatural ability to love them unconditionally. Loving our children is the biggest joy of our lives. But Lord, we ask You to teach us how to love them even better, to love them how You would have us love them. Refine our hearts in ways that are in tune with Your desires, not the world's, so that we can reflect You in our homes. Lord, we accept the precious responsibility You give us to teach our kids about You. But, God, we need Your help. We can't do it on our own. Mold us into Your instruments of love and grace so that Your power, love, and presence is made known in our homes. Help us recognize opportunities in the midst of our busy, chaotic days to speak Your name, to make You relevant, to communicate Your presence and significance in our lives. In Jesus' name we pray, amen.

Meaningful Truth

Train up a child in the way he should go; even when he is old, he will not depart from it.

—Proverbs 22:6 (ESV)

~ CHAPTER 10 ~

The Unselfish Choice

GOD PROVIDES FOR YOUR WHOLENESS

A couple years ago right before my twenty-year class reunion, I couldn't help but reflect on my life since high school. This self-analysis may have been slightly influenced by the stigma that often accompanies class reunions—the place and time where you want to be impressive and show the world you've arrived. This is your time to prove to others that you've achieved success and reached your potential. In other words, you must have an answer to the question: "What have you done with your life?"

Talk about pressure. Anxiety built inside me as I pondered, *What will I tell people? What have I achieved? What success can I talk about?*

Sure, I had gone to college and earned an undergraduate degree in mass communications, but I had friends who had high-level degrees, prestigious jobs, and owned their own successful businesses. Impressive!

Me? Well, let's see. I had birthed four sons. I was a housewife, stay-at-home mom, and professional volunteer. I had mastered the art of changing diapers, building forts, playing make-believe, and drawing dinosaurs. I could recite several story books by heart and engineer a mean train track. I mean, *mean* train track. Sometimes my greatest success and feeling of relevance for the day came in the creative ways I placed those train tracks together, piece-by-piece.

Then, I realized I was being tempted by my age-old fear of what others thought—displaced comparison—and my desire to attain a higher level of achievement and worldly success. I admit it—I felt a little self-induced pressure to recite my resume of awesomeness, meanwhile fearing I had nothing awesome to share.

But I knew better than to get caught up in that lie threatening to discredit the value and significance of *choosing* to stay home and raise my sons. It's the best, most important work I will ever do in my life. I have determined I will never again feel less-than for choosing this path—one that's led me to discovering deeper purpose and passion and my life's work. So, I took those lies captive and transferred my focus to what God was inviting me to consider.

Although this reflection on my life was influenced by a pressure to impress classmates from twenty years ago, it turned out to be my next step in becoming more complete and closer to the person God created me to be. If we pay attention, God, when we least expect it, summons us to deeper greatness. It is a greatness that will further equip us to do the work He's called us to do.

CHOOSING ME

The truth is, I had plenty of things to share about my life. Life was good. Really good. I had newfound purpose in my role as mom, and gratefully, I had discovered a beautiful way to do life with my kids—a priceless treasure. The love, support, and encouragement I had from my husband, family, and friends was out of this world. To top it off, I had started my own parent-coaching/training business with plans to launch a speaking career. (At the time, I didn't know I'd be writing a book.) What more could I ask for? What more did I need?

Having grown in my relationship with God—knowing He's never, ever done refining us—I soon recognized the unsettled stirring in my heart could very well be God's way of getting my attention. I knew what I had to do.

"What is it, Lord?" I asked. "What are you trying to tell me this time?"

A few days later, I found myself in 1 Corinthians. It was when I read the following verse, that I felt my question was being answered.

"Do you not know that your bodies are temples of the Holy Spirit, who is in you, whom you have received from God? You are not your own; you were bought at a price. Therefore, honor God with your bodies."[1]

"Honor God with your bodies."

Much to my surprise, this hit me hard. For years, I had not honored God with my body. My struggle with bulimia led me to treat His beautiful creation with cruelty and rejection. Here I was going back to the place where it had begun—high school. Coincidence? I think not.

As I boldly peeled back the layers of why I had felt nervous and insecure at the thought of going back to my hometown, I realized, subconsciously, I was being sucked into old pressures and lies. The mind has a sneaky way of remembering trauma, and I believe this was God's way of intercepting those lies and using my past to promote further growth.

After a bit of soul searching and time with God, I realized I had not made my physical health a priority. Motherhood had engulfed me so much I wasn't being intentional in taking care of myself. I lacked energy. I struggled to maintain focus and clarity. My tummy rarely felt good. Although I've always been active, I knew I wasn't fueling my body with the best nutrition, and without that key component, not only were my physical systems an absolute mess, but I was not experiencing the optimal benefits of my fitness efforts.

Sensing a confident assurance, this was indeed the source of my heart's stirring, I decided to choose me right then and there. I contacted a dear friend in the fitness/nutrition industry and began to make significant changes to my diet and fitness regimen. I began meal planning and prepping and being intentional in what I put into my body. My mindset around food completely changed as I began to view it as fuel to sustain, strengthen, and equip this beautiful body God gave me. It made all the difference in the world, and more than two years later, I'm still making my health a priority and committed to taking optimal care of it.

You might be thinking, *What in the world does this have to do with motherhood?*

A lot, actually, because it was the chaos of motherhood that had blinded me from seeing what *I* needed to be the best for me and everyone else.

Think about how quickly life can get away from us. Our calendars can get so full—so fast—with everyone else's stuff that we accidentally become prisoners to our schedules, leaving little to no room for ourselves. In the chaos of juggling countless responsibilities, working tirelessly to balance work, kids, and home, we neglect to keep tabs on ourselves. The thought of finding time, let alone making time, for *just us* can seem impossible. Setting goals to better ourselves? Focusing on our health and our needs? Scheduling time to explore our passions and have fun? Forget it! Who has time for that? This voice beckoning my attention had been continuously muffled by the craziness and distractions of life that naturally accompany motherhood.

The dilemma is caused by our divine instinct to love and care for our families—to put their needs above our own. It's this love that inspires us to put everyone else first and sacrifice our needs for theirs. God calls us to love and serve, and so we do, but are we sacrificing too much? At what point does putting everyone else before ourselves become destructive and ineffective?

We moms who tend to carry a majority of the family responsibility have a tendency to sacrifice everything for their sake—our health, passions, fun, and dreams. Nowhere in Scripture does it say, "Mothers, in order to best care for your children and family, you must neglect your own needs and desires and run yourselves ragged."

Why then, do so many of us act like there is such a verse? I'm here to tell you there is a verse in Scripture that gives us incredible insight on how to care for others, but it's quite the contrary.

LOVING ME

How would you respond if I told you God commands you to take care of yourself? Would you be inspired to consider it or tempted to evaluate your life and recognize the needs you've neglected? God does, indeed, give such a command. The gift of being a mother was never meant to be at the expense of robbing us of vital necessities that help us reach the wholeness God has for us—a wholeness which empowers us to thrive in our roles as wife, mom, and woman.

Here is crucial truth we must embrace from the mouth of Jesus that is too often overlooked yet is the very truth that gives us permission to choose ourselves. Here Jesus answers the question, "Which is the most important commandment?"

"The most important one," answered Jesus, "is this: ... Love the Lord your God with all your heart and with all your soul and with all your mind and with all your strength. The second is this: Love your neighbor as yourself. There is no commandment greater than these."[2]

The gift of being mother
was never meant to be
at the expense of robbing
us of vital necessities
that help us reach the
wholeness God has for us—
a wholeness which empowers
us to thrive in our roles
as wife, mom, and woman.

"Love God and love others" are the greatest commandments—the most important ones. Jesus says if we keep these commandments, we keep them all. And by keeping commandments, we live a full, prosperous life. However, there are two words often ignored but are just as significant a part of this command. "Love your neighbor *as yourself*." As yourself. As I see it, it's not two commands, but three Jesus gives. Love God. Love others. Love yourself. That's right … love yourself.

It's not two commands, but three Jesus gives. Love God. Love others. Love yourself. That's right … love yourself.

Now, I want you to take a moment to think about all the love you have for your spouse, kiddos, and significant others—and how that love inspires you to daily, unendingly, give and give and give to them and take care of their every need. It's a huge amount of love, isn't it? Well, that kind of love … that's the kind of love Jesus commands us to give ourselves. He's not calling it selfish. He's defining it as necessary.

This love is more than accepting who we are in Christ. It requires us to dive deeper and make some sacrifices. This love calls us to take care of our body, mind, and soul—one that takes care of our own needs for the purpose of continued growth and transformation.

Think about it. What if we woke up every morning and took care of ourselves—before we even tried to care for others—and released the guilt that often accompanies putting ourselves first? What if we vulnerably and courageously admitted our *need* to care for ourselves? And what if that was something to be admired instead of condemned? What if we chose to move, fuel, rest, and nourish our body, mind, and, soul with deep intention and focus so that our physical, mental, emotional, and spiritual needs were met? Or we intentionally connected with friends who would enrich our lives? Or made time to do the things we love and pursue the dreams impressed upon our hearts? What would be the payoff? Would the discipline, commitment, and intentionality it requires be worth it?

Absolutely! As long as our hearts and intentions are in the right place. Please understand this. When I realized I needed to begin taking better care of my physical health, it wasn't about putting *me* first for *my* sake. It was about putting *me* first for *God's* sake. Did I reap personal benefits? Of course, but the central message for my motivation was NOT: *How can I improve myself so that I can be better for my sake?*

Instead, the central message was: *What areas of my life are in need of attention and growth so that God can continue to use me for His purposes and for His sake?* Do you recognize the heart difference I'm talking about here?

He calls us to love ourselves, but at this point in my life, He instructed me to take better care of my physical body so I'd be equipped and ready—at any time—to do the work He needs me to do. Feeling sluggish and blah certainly weren't helping me be effective at any role. And as I began to put myself first, God continued to strengthen me with more confidence and ability to live out His will for my life in all the roles I play, especially as a mom.

GOD MAKES US WHOLE

What's even more encouraging than taking my word for it is hearing God declare not only His ability to make us whole and holy but His promise to do so. The apostle Paul left the people of Thessalonica with this final blessing—a blessing which holds true for us today.

> May God Himself, the God who makes everything holy and whole, make you holy and whole, put you together— spirit, soul, and body—and keep you fit for the coming of our Master, Jesus Christ. The One who called you is completely dependable. If He said it, He'll do it![3]

God's primary purpose and desire is for all of us to become more and more like Christ. He wants the best for us, and He knows that drawing us closer to Christ will transform us into the best version of ourselves. But we must consciously choose to submit our body, mind, and soul to God for the Holy Spirit to do its transforming work in us, which continues until the day we meet Jesus face-to-face.

This process of growth—of sanctification—looks different for each and every one of us for He knows us intimately. He knows what will work to get your attention and what will work to get mine. God didn't impress upon my heart this desire to improve my physical health until specific places of my heart were ready to receive and embrace this next step of growth. He's that all-knowing, creative, and patient with each and every one of us. My life was great before, but God molded and refined me so I could continue to grow, prosper, and develop. But that doesn't mean the process is easy.

Although God doesn't ask for more than we are able to give—for He knows our situations and capabilities—quite often what He's calling us to be (all in an effort to make us more holy and whole) will require courage to step outside our comfort zone. It will most likely involve sacrifice, and it will most certainly require our attention. It's at the intersection of our attentive surrender and God's presence where growth happens. He knows the desires of our hearts for He created them, and He knows when the times are right to push us into deeper growth, even though the timing may feel off to us. That's when faith steps in and trusts in His perfect timing. He progressively makes us fit—ready or prepared—for what's to come. Life is about transformation, and the more we listen to God and respond with action, the more fit in body, mind, and spirit we become, moving us to greater wholeness.

It's at the intersection of our attentive surrender and God's presence where growth happens.

THE EXHILERATING TAKE-OFF

I want you to imagine for a moment a brand-new monarch butterfly hanging ever so delicately on the edge of her chrysalis.

Her wings are dried. Her veins are filled with the blood needed to give her strength for what's to come. She can sense the world beckoning her, needing her. The struggle, the hurt, the submission, the obedience, the transformation has all led her to this moment. Yet she finds herself teetering back and forth. She's both excited to explore the world inviting her to newfound purpose yet drawn to reflect on the intense, sensational transformation she just endured.

With great courage and confidence, she begins to flutter her wings—feeling the gentle breeze whooshing beneath them. She leans forward—hearing the sound of her heart beating rapidly in her chest.

She senses a whisper: "It's time for the release. It's time."

Trusting her intuition and renewed heart, she lifts her feet and falls, instantly overcome by exhilarating freedom lifting her to new heights. A smile graces her face as she realizes ... she's soaring.

Her innate wisdom draws her to a source of nourishment. Her first priority in fulfilling her purpose is to fuel her body. To take care of herself. She doesn't give precedence to reproduction, offspring, or motherhood, which is most certainly a part of her purpose. She simply cares for herself first.

Now, imagine you are that monarch. All your struggles, aches, submission, obedience, and transformation have led you to this moment. You've claimed your identity in Christ. You've been set free by the grace of God. You've embraced the divine calling of your role as mom. And here you are—wings unfurled, teetering on a leaf—building the courage to let go and live your purpose. Trusting in your renewed heart, you take a deep breath, lean ever so gently forward, release your grip, and fall. The exhilaration takes your breath away, but your extended wings catch the breeze, steadying your descent. You can't help but smile as you lift your eyes toward the heavens and realize you are soaring in the beauty in which you were divinely created. You're inspired—like never before—to get to work.

But like the butterfly, for you to do what you've been called to do, you must first take care of yourself. To endure and enjoy the journey, your body, mind, and soul need proper nourishment and care.

So, friend, I'm here to encourage you to choose you. By now, you know I don't mean in some selfish, prideful way. I mean, choose *you* because God *needs* you to. He commands you to. No matter what the world says, it's not selfish to put *you* first. Because in choosing you, God will inspire obedience and discipline and reveal to you more and more of His plans for your life—and you will soar to unimaginable heights.

But let me caution you. Distractions will come every day. They will seek your attention and try to keep you running to manage your busy life. Distractions prevent us from pausing to take note of our current life status, thereby hindering us from recognizing areas of our life in need of attention. These areas when left unattended for too long can paralyze us from taking action and seeking necessary change. When paralysis occurs, excuses take root and hopelessness grows, making change seem unattainable.

When change seems unattainable, we feel stuck, unable to move forward in purpose and intention. Distractions interfere in our relationship with Jesus and stunt our growth to a more complete life. If we allow the countless distractions of this life to divert our attention away from the areas of our lives in need of nourishment, we will miss out on the fullness of the life God offers.

Distractions interfere in our relationship with Jesus and stunt our growth to a more complete life.

Thankfully, Jesus doesn't leave us alone in the chaos of our lives. Ever. It's not His nature. Never has been. Never will be. We simply need to turn our eyes to Him and see Him, ready and willing with outstretched hands, to help and guide us toward freedom, joy, and peace.

Will there be countless times when we still put others first, especially our children? Absolutely. It's part of the job description. But we don't have to sacrifice one for the other. The two can co-exist. And here's what's even more beautiful. There's a priceless payoff worth all the discipline, time, energy, and intentionality. There's a gift that comes from being faithful to ourselves. When we choose to focus on ourselves and what we need to be our best selves, our precious loved ones reap the benefits. I'm a better wife, mom, and woman when I take care of myself. In other words, I am more capable, better equipped, and increasingly confident in giving my family what they need. And then before long, I see the fruits of my faithfulness blossom and ripen right before my eyes.

When we choose to focus on ourselves and what we need to be our best selves, our precious loved ones reap the benefits.

My high school class reunion was the tool God used to prompt me to take inventory of my life—an exploration which revealed necessities in my life I had been lacking. In addition to becoming aware of my need to take better care of my health, I also realized I was missing time with my friends.

God built us to have connections, and I had allowed the busyness of motherhood to interfere with my heart's desire to nurture my friendships. When I started to take intentional action in addressing my needs, I not only experienced more joy, but it also propelled me to my next level of growth and maturity as a child of God.

The Master Transformer—God Himself—has rich, significant work He wants to do in each and every one of us, right now. It will require us, however, to *choose us* so that our cups overflow with the power we need to do His work and make an impact for His sake.

Truth is, I'm a better me when I love myself first—when I seek to fuel and nourish my body, mind, and soul before I give of myself to the loves and purposes of my life. Fuel and nourishment come in many forms and although they may look a little different for each of us, I feel there are universal needs we all share. For me, I need time with God through prayer, worship and His Word; a healthy diet and regular fitness routine; quality time with family and friends; and time to pursue the passions God has ignited in my heart.

If permission to focus on you is what you've needed, consider your permission granted. God is waiting eagerly to nurture your growth and lead you to a more complete life.

This journey toward becoming more and more like Christ is guaranteed to bring you lasting joy, hope, and peace—the very feelings that will fuel your ability, desire, and resilience not only to be God's vessels of love and grace to your children no matter what circumstances, behaviors, or attitudes come your way but also to pass on the heritage of faith.

Making it Matter

Several years ago, we renovated an old, two-story farmhouse. If you've ever experienced a home remodel or built a home from scratch, you know about the countless decisions from wall texture to paint color, light fixtures to faucets, counters to flooring. It's overwhelming, to say the least. The one choice I was certain of, from the beginning, was my flooring. I wanted my main living, dining, and kitchen areas to be covered in rich, distressed, mahogany floors.

Yep, I wanted dark floors. You do know what that means, right? They show *everything*—every crumb, speck of dust, dry flake of skin, blond piece of dog hair, and every random, unknown particle present in your home that you never knew existed before. It's laying right out in the open for the whole world to see. There's no camouflage. Just dirty imperfection staring up at me snickering, "I told you so."

Even knowing this drawback to be true when I decided on these gorgeous floors, I'll admit, the obvious mess drives me crazy at times. However, I'm pretty sure it drives my husband, Darin, even crazier. A dirty toilet? He doesn't seem to mind. But a floor I haven't swept in several days means he takes initiative. He'll grab my dusting mop and sweep until his little ole' heart is content.

Awesome, right? I'll take it every time! But it never failed. I'd walk around the corner in our dining room a day or two later to find the dust-mop leaning up against the wall with a huge mound of dust, crumbs, hair and who knows what else lying beneath it. It would take everything in me not to, you know what. Give him the how to … the not to … the what to. I so badly wanted to lecture him about finishing the job, cleaning up the mess, and following through. I think it's fair to say I never fully freaked out, yet I did—clouded with frustration—sneak some snarky comments in under my breath. (I've since learned to focus on the positive—he swept the floor, for Pete's sake.)

I'm pretty certain the mound of dust he had collected would sit there in that quiet corner forever unless I chose to deal with it or I reminded him to finish the job. This "filthy" memory got me thinking: That mound of dust is like the things in our lives we always think about doing but never do. We push these things into a corner, promising we'll get to them someday—like growing an intimate relationship with God, getting healthy, pursuing our dreams and passions, or making quality time for friends. We dream about these actions, but our dreams are somehow interrupted by the realities of our lives—hectic schedules, work, kids. So, we let the mound of dust sit. The longer we let it sit in the corner, the more apt we are to forget about it. Until one day we walk by and see the mess and are reminded of all the things we want to do. Then, the cycle continues, and frustration and guilt build.

Unless, of course, we make a different choice and sweep up the mess. Instead of neglecting those things we've pushed into the corner, perhaps it's time we give them attention, value, and relevance. If they are things you think about, but don't do, it's time to silence the excuses, choose you, and take action. Because if a positive change is on your heart and mind, it could very well be God prompting you to growth, which will move you to deeper wholeness.

Perhaps what we all need is what my husband found to be the solution to our minor floor problem. Our favorite buddy we've named, Robo, aka, the Roomba (an autonomous robotic vacuum). All I have to say is … game changer! Maybe we all need someone—like an accountability partner—to automatically sweep through the realities of our lives with the intention to open our eyes to our deep needs and help hold us accountable to putting those needs first. If you pay attention, God will reveal the corners in need of dusting.

It's time to get real and honest, my friend. Do you get distracted by the realities of life? Do you get swallowed up by the waves of constant demands where you seem to keep running on cruise control never slowing down to consider the choices and priorities you really want to make? What are the dreams on your heart? What are those things you think about doing, but never do? Write them down. Give them a voice. Give them merit. Do you think about getting healthier or pursuing a passion you've ignored for years? Perhaps you wish to find time to read Scripture and pray? Maybe you think about gathering friends at your home or connecting with family? Now consider and journal why you aren't giving them the attention and priority they need. Excuses? Lack of resources or support? Fear? Uncertainty? Pray about the things on your heart and then define a plan on how to move forward with intentional change.

No matter where you are, Jesus is near, offering His hand. Turn your eyes to Him. Call to Him and trust He will provide the clarity and confidence you need to choose you. Because by choosing you, you unlock even greater potential, freedom, and joy that leads you to becoming all He's created you to be.

_____

_____

_____

_____

_____

_____

_____

_____

_____

_____

_____

_____

_____

_____

A Momma's Prayer

Lord God, You know what we need in order to experience optimal living. You know the areas of our lives we push to the corners, not because we don't think they're important, but because our schedules are full. It's hard to make time for everything and everyone, especially ourselves. Knowing You want the best for us, help us focus our eyes on You in the midst of the chaos, trusting You will reveal to us the areas in which we need to start giving time and attention. And then help us choose ourselves. Help us develop the habit of loving ourselves—filling our cup daily with all we need, so we have the strength, endurance, and passion to love our people and do Your work in the world. Thank You for being a faithful God. We are so grateful to be Your daughters. In Jesus' name we pray, amen.

Meaningful Truths

Let us hold unswervingly to the hope we profess,
for He who promised is faithful.

—Hebrews 10:23 (NIV)

Blessed is the one who trusts in the Lord,
whose confidence is in Him.

—Jeremiah 17:7 (NIV)

PART FOUR

The Migration of Motherhood

THE JOURNEY TO LEAVING A LEGACY OF FAITH

CHAPTER 11

The Innate Gift

GOD GIVES YOU EVERYTHING YOU NEED

*C*arrying a baby in your belly for the first time is amazing but also a bit frightening. Nothing can quite prepare a woman for the crazy, miraculous way her body morphs into a life-giving vessel. God's intricate blueprint for how life is created within the womb will forever wow me. What blows me away even more than the physicality and mechanics of birth is the emotional and spiritual intentions weaved into life's divinely sophisticated design.

A few days overdue with my first son, Peyton, the anticipation and uncertainty of how the birth would go made me so nervous. On top of that, the awkwardness of my front-heavy body (although I loved being pregnant) had gotten to be a bit much. After tossing and turning in and out of sleep, I was startled awake by a big bursting sound. I didn't realize what it was until I stood up and felt the gush. My water had broken. It was *go* time. However, I was under the impression—from all the books I had read—that I'd have plenty of time to get to the hospital. Imagine our surprise when the contractions came fast and furious.

At the risk of boring you with birthing details, I'll jump ahead an hour or so later to the moment I heard the doctor say, "Ok, one last push."

This was it. There was no going back. This was a defining moment. It's a moment that changes everything. As I felt my baby leave the comfort of my womb and enter the security of my embrace the thoughts of worry, uncertainty, and fear were instantly trumped by the biggest, most inexplainable and extravagant kind of love I had ever felt before in my life. It took my breath away. If you're a momma, I know you know what I mean.

Think about the first moment you laid eyes on your precious baby … felt her heartbeat against yours … heard the sound of her sweet, newborn cry. We all have unique stories about how we became Mom. But we share one undeniable truth:

Our hearts burst with indescribable love for our children.

My heart fluttered at a speed that paralyzed the words I had desperately longed to whisper, leaving them stranded on the tip of my tongue. Awestruck by the miraculous moment of birthing life, my heart ached to declare, "Oh, sweet baby. I'm your momma. Momma loves you."

In the moments following Peyton's first breath of life, I savored the warmth and weight of his little body upon my chest. Inhaling the peaceful presence that warmly surrounded us, I memorized every detail of his sweet, round face and the intricate design of his tiny fingers and toes. He was an absolute miracle—like every child—yet a complete mystery, for I knew nothing about him. Except that he was mine. And I loved him more than I ever thought possible, with a love I had never felt before.

My love for him miraculously existed. There was nothing he had to do to earn my love. He already had it. And there was nothing he could do to lose my love. I loved him because he was my son, and I was his momma. That simple. That certain. That significant. What a priceless treasure it is to be gifted the ability to love like that—to love merely based on the blessed reality of this divinely designed, precious existence. I believe it's the moment we come closest to experiencing the kind of love God has for us.

I know we've chatted briefly about this before, but it's so important that I feel it's okay I mention it again. The love we have for our kids? God loves us like that—with no conditions. And He is the One who enables us to love like He loves. It's an innate gift. Love is woven into the foundational chains of our DNA, and it's *the very thing* which inspires us to parent our kids the way God desires and which feels right with our souls.

Love is woven into the foundational chains of our DNA and it's the very thing which inspires us to parent our kids the way God desires and which feels right with our souls.

No matter what your relationship status is with God—whether you've been in touch with God lately or you haven't, whether you're delighted with Him or mad at Him, whether you know Him well or only just met, whether you've been obedient to Him or turned your back on Him—He loves you, and your innate ability to love comes only through Him. The certainty of God's love does not rest on the ability of what we can do but on the reality of whose we are. Period. And that truth will never change, but believing that truth changes everything. That truth helps us become God's instruments of love and grace, which organically has the power to infuse faith into the center of our children's lives.

As moms living life in the real world, we know it's not always easy to express ourselves in loving ways to our kids, especially when they confront us with challenging behaviors and attitudes—ones that can lead us to question: *Do I have what it takes? Is my love enough?*

The certainty of God's love does not rest on the ability of what we can do but on the reality of whose we are.

LOVE IS ENOUGH

Think about the love you felt that first moment you held your baby in your arms. Is that love enough to raise your kids the way God commands? Is that love enough to inspire them to live up to their godly potential? Is that love enough to give you joy and meaning amid the challenges and behaviors that accompany raising kids?

I'm fully aware we may be in different seasons and challenges of motherhood. You might be dealing with toddler tantrums. Maybe your tween is having a hard time in school. Or you've learned she's having suicidal thoughts. Perhaps your teenage son has been suspended for fighting. Or you've discovered he's vaping and experimenting with other drugs. Maybe your teenage daughter is rebelling against your rules and expectations. Or you've recently discovered she's having sex with a nineteen-year-old. Maybe you have a child so angry the only way he communicates with you is by yelling cruel language. Maybe you're an empty nester and your adult children can't hold a job, stay out of prison, or stop abusing alcohol. Maybe you're a grandma who is having a hard time connecting with her intense grandchild.

No doubt, parenting is hard work. And it's not always fun. When the challenges arise and we're faced head-on with nasty behaviors and attitudes and every attempt at parenting with reason and a calm demeanor fails, we can feel guilty, inadequate, and hopeless, wondering, *Where did I go wrong? Is my love enough?*

We begin to doubt our ability to raise our kids to be good people. And when we doubt ourselves, we tend to go down a very negative, depressing road that leads to a dead end filled with frustration, fear, and anger. Sadly, when we get to that place, we are unable to recognize the delight motherhood is supposed to be.

But I have good news. *Love* is not the issue. Lack of love is not the cause of the challenges we face with our children. The issue is: Our love has a competitor. Knowing about this competitor can transform our perspective about our children's behaviors and can empower us to nurture with Christlike love and grace.

Our competitor?

Rebellion.

In *our* hearts and in our *children's*.

It's a rebellion we were born into. This rebellion has been present since Adam and Eve took the bite of the forbidden fruit introducing sin into the world, and it works to fight against the very beautiful, loving nature in which we were created. It's our rebellion—as sinful, broken humans—that contaminates our acts of love.

The acts of rebellion from my kids and me were discouraging—led me to throwing my hands up in defeat. It left me crying in my bed at night frustrated by their behaviors and upset about the way I responded. I found myself entangled in power struggles that would seep negativity into the center of our home. Perhaps you can relate.

Rebellion will always exist (that is until Jesus comes back to banish it forever). It will always work to counteract the good and love our hearts yearn to give. But there is hope. It's not a question of whether love is enough. It's a question of whether we know how to tap into our *source* of love that combats our rebellion and empowers our ability to love—no matter the circumstance or situation—in ways that will kindle joy, build connection, ignite greatness, nurture goodness, and inspire lasting faith in the hearts of our children.

It's not a question of whether love is enough. It's a question of whether we know how to tap into our source of love that combats our rebellion and empowers our ability to love.

OUR SOURCE OF LOVE

Our *source* of love, my friend, is a gift Jesus left to all believers. The entirety of His purpose was rooted in love. Because of His great love for us, Jesus chose to die on the cross to restore wholeness, freedom, and beauty to His beloved children.

Jesus is the only answer to fighting the rebellion that threatens to take over our hearts. Because we can't have Jesus in the flesh and because He didn't want to leave us alone without guidance, He gifted us an "advocate"[1]—a counselor, comforter, and friend—to take His place in leading us in truth, guiding us in grace, and directing us in love.

This advocate is a power that provides glorious inner strength,[2] wisdom, and revelation.[3] It's a power that's incomparably great for us who believe.[4] This same mighty power and strength raised Christ from the dead and seated Him in the heavenly realms.[5] It is the very presence of God Himself in our hearts.

The Holy Spirit.

Attempting to wrap your human brain around this mysterious concept can be rather difficult. It's a supernatural kind of force—one we can't see with our eyes or touch with our hands. And although it's a mystery to me, I've learned it's a power and presence we can sense and feel with our heart and soul.

The Holy Spirit—our *source* of love—is a power we come to recognize the closer we draw to Jesus. The closer we draw to Jesus, the more we get to know Him, the more like Him we are inspired to become. Consequently, the more like Him we become, the more we absorb His wisdom, truth, strength, and understanding—the very powers that help us combat our rebellion.

When we can combat our rebellion through the power of the Holy Spirit, we are then empowered to mother with the heart of Christ. And when we mother with a heart of Christ, it changes everything. It did for me. That's when Christ becomes the center of our homes, and that's when joy, peace, and hope become deeply rooted into the fabric of our lives.

There's a story in Scripture where Jesus so beautifully exemplifies the heart posture we must take when confronted with rebellion and the posture we are called to embrace to be Christ to our children and point them to Him.

THE HEART POSTURE OF CHRIST

"We've got you now," they yelled as they yanked her out of bed and dragged her out of the house toward the center of town. With barely an opportunity to cover her body, the woman cowered from the accusing glares and insults as the priests boastfully paraded her through the streets, forcing her to endure the walk of shame as the screams of judgment and scornful stares from the townspeople grew like a wave moving through the ocean.

"Shame on you."

"Who do you think you are?"

"What's wrong with you?"

"You know better."

As if this hadn't been punishment enough for her, the priests abruptly interrupted Jesus' teaching and pushed her into the middle of the crowd.

> At dawn Jesus appeared in the temple courts again, and soon all the people gathered around to listen to his words, so He sat down and taught them. Then in the middle of His teaching, the religious scholars and the Pharisees broke through the crowd and brought a woman who had been caught in the act of adultery and made her stand in the middle of everyone.
>
> Then they said to Jesus, "Teacher, we caught this woman in the very act of adultery. Doesn't Moses' law command us to stone to death a woman like this? Tell us, what do you say we should do with her?"[6]

Within moments, the city of Jerusalem had become a jury, gripping rocks in hands, ready to condemn this woman for her sin. She was fully exposed and had nowhere to go. No escape plans. No lawyer defending her. No one to speak on her behalf.

Or so she thought.

Someone did stand up for her. Actually He bent down for her. "Jesus didn't answer them. Instead He bent down and wrote in the dust with His finger."[7]

Have you ever wondered why, amid this highly intense moment, Jesus bent down to write in the dirt? Perhaps it was to buy Himself some time as He contemplated what He'd say. But I don't think Jesus needed time. He already knew what He'd say. Maybe He was trying to distract the accusers from looking at the woman, but I wonder if it was more than that.

I wonder if Jesus ran His fingers through the dirt because He was remembering when Adam was created from the dust of the earth. And as His fingers traced back and forth in the soft soil, perhaps He was reminded about the truth of humanity and how all people are prone to sin—the very reason for Jesus' existence. I imagine Him taking a deep breath and feeling a surge of compassion rise in His heart as He reflected on the divine purpose to which He was sent to fulfill.

The priests and crowd grew impatient and angry, insisting Jesus answer them.

As Jesus stood to speak on behalf of this frightened, sinful, desperate woman, I imagine Him stepping in front of the woman to protect her from the angry mob as he said, "Let's have the man who has never had a sinful desire throw the first stone at her."[8]

That was it. He didn't give a long lecture—He only spoke the simple truth. And as Jesus bent down again to trace His fingers in the dust, He heard the sound of rocks falling to the ground, one-by-one, and the trampling of feet as the accusers abandoned the scene carrying conviction in their heart, realizing they, too, were sinners.

But it doesn't end there.

Jesus was left alone with the woman still standing there in front of Him. So He stood back up and said to her, "Dear woman, where are your accusers? Is there no one here to condemn you?"

Looking around, she replied, "I see no one, Lord."

Jesus said, "Then I certainly don't condemn you either. Go, and from now on, be free from a life of sin."[9]

In this compelling story, Jesus made it crystal clear how we are all sinners who fight rebellion in our hearts. That's true for us and our children. And because of that truth, we have no right to condemn or punish others for their sins. Furthermore, Scripture says there is "no condemnation for those who are in Christ Jesus."[10] Jesus doesn't condemn us. He liberates us. So, in the face of sin, Jesus models the posture we are to take with one another when confronting sin. This posture does not yell nor shame. It does not demean nor judge. It does not get angry nor criticize.

The heart posture of Christ, that as moms we are called to embrace when we confront our own sin and the sin of our children, is one of compassion, understanding, mercy, grace, and forgiveness.

Believe me, I do realize it's easier said than done. How do we practically take on that posture when life and challenges get really hard? How do we utilize the power of the Holy Spirit to help us make positive change in our homes? How do we show understanding when our child is being disrespectful? How do we point our kids to Christ when their behaviors are out of control? Before I share some strategies that have drastically improved life for me and my family, it's imperative to establish the mindset necessary to effectively experience the life change that comes from mothering with the heart posture of Christ.

But can we quickly linger one more moment? In the courtyard now abandoned? In a place one woman will never forget? Rocks lay strewn about the ground. A hush of silence fills the air. The dust slowly settles from the accusers' hasty retreat upon the scribbles where Jesus knelt. We don't know the words Jesus wrote, but I can't help but wonder. Perhaps they read something like this:

> *You are the reason I am here. I love you. I came to set you free from your sin so you can live in joy and peace. Watch what I do and pass it on to others.*

CHRIST-CENTERED MINDSET

Mindset is a choice, and your mindset dictates your actions, reactions, words, gestures, thinking, and beliefs. Many people tend to coast through life without giving much attention to their mindset. Therefore, they become stuck in a worldly mindset often tainted with pride, frustration, guilt, inadequacy, cynicism, and fear—a belief system that counteracts God's.

If you've stayed with me this long, my friend, and absorbed the truths I've shared up to this point, then you are ready to not only take flight into your newfound understanding of the role of mom—to point your kids to Christ—but to organically execute your role by intentionally infusing Christ-like grace and love into the center of your lives.

A critical element that leads you toward transformation in your mothering and in your relationships with your children is dedicating time to knowing Christ more intimately and absorbing the love and grace He freely gives. When we accept His truths for ourselves, that's when we are more naturally able to extend those very truths to our kids. That's why the first several chapters—focused on personal growth in Christ—are essential foundation blocks that set the stage for this next step: Mothering with the heart posture of Christ.

I want to quickly remind you: God has given you everything you need to mother your kids the way your heart desires. Remember, you are on your journey to becoming the beautiful butterfly God created you to be. After a newly birthed butterfly emerges from her chrysalis, breaks free, soars, and takes care of her needs, she's fueled and ready to innately do what she's been designed to do. She understands her role. For the butterfly, she reproduces. For us, we point our children back to their creator.

It can sound like an overwhelming task, especially if you are a new believer or haven't spent much time with Jesus. If motherhood has been a struggle, I can understand if it's difficult to muster hope for something better. If you are learning for the first time God's purpose for mothers, moving forward with new intentions can be a challenge. If you currently have a negative tone and culture in your home, I can understand if you're skeptical that change is possible. If you feel it's too late and your children are grown, let me assure you, it's never too late. And friend, nothing is impossible with God. If you are feeling nervous or insecure about moving forward with powerful intention, now is when you need to trust that God *will* help you through your fears and insecurities. Trust God to be your source of strength and power that will fuel, nurture, and awaken your innate ability to know exactly how to love and nurture your kids.

Before we go on, can you promise me something? Don't, for one moment, feel guilty for the past. If you're like me, you've wasted precious time feeling guilty for not being enough ... for not loving bigger and better ... for losing your cool ... or for not connecting better. The list goes on. But remember, Jesus came to set you free from that guilt. He knows, and I believe you've been doing your best with the knowledge and strategies you've had. So, release the guilt and trust in Jesus to continue to mold and refine you.

The power of Christ in you nurtures a Christ-centered mindset—one that's inspired to extend Christ's love and grace to others in all circumstances and one that helps a momma vulnerably admit her weaknesses and flaws and deep need for grace itself. A Christ-centered mindset is the overflow of Christ's love from your heart into the hearts of others. And this love we're talking about is selfless and extravagant. The apostle Paul explained so beautifully in Ephesians 5:1–2 (MSG) how we are to love.

> Watch what God does, and then you do it, like children who learn proper behavior from their parents. Mostly what God does is love you. Keep company with Him and learn a life of love. Observe how Christ loved us. His love was not cautious but extravagant. He didn't love in

order to get something from us but to give everything of Himself to us. Love like that.

A Christ-centered mindset is the overflow of Christ's love from your heart into the hearts of others.

A Christ-centered mindset within the realm of mothering, although naturally fueled and inspired by the Holy Spirit, invites us to embrace the following six beliefs that set the stage for executing the extravagant love of Christ.

BELIEF ONE—BURDENS OF OUR PAST REQUIRE HEALING

He heals the brokenhearted and binds up their wounds.[11]

We all have wounds from our past. It's a reality of living in this broken world. However, if these wounds are not properly cared for, they become heavy burdens that negatively impact our ability to mother with the heart posture of Christ. Thankfully, we have a God who heals wounds—the broken, burdened, aching places of our hearts—and restores us to new life. Because of Christ's great love for us and His sacrifice on the cross, we don't have to carry our burdens with us forever. He's come to take them away.

But if we don't allow God to heal the places of our heart in desperate need of healing, we will end up mothering from a wounded heart. In other words, if there are any insecurities, fears, hurts, or lies we hold on to from our past, they will seep into our mothering and become insecurities, fears, hurts, and lies our children absorb and carry with them, forming a perpetual cycle of brokenness and despair. No mother wants their child to grow up wounded. Seeking God to heal the broken, wounded places of our hearts not only sets us free, but it protects our children from suffering the same wounds. God breaks the cycle. He restores wholeness. And our faith produces fruit.

BELIEF TWO—BOTH SINNERS IN NEED OF A SAVIOR

...for all have sinned and fall short of the glory of God, and are justified freely by his grace through the redemption that came by Christ Jesus.[12]

As the parent, we automatically take on an authoritative role. We dictate expectations and responsibilities. We issue consequences and correction. We do our best to keep order, set boundaries and limits, and establish respect. It's part of our job to lead and guide our children into understanding life and expected behavior and actions. But to lead with a Christ-centered mindset means we must remember we, too, are sinners in need of a Savior.

In other words, we are more like our children than we are different. Embracing this truth—acknowledging our own sin and rebellion—gives us greater compassion and understanding for our children who battle the same sin and rebellion. Let's not put ourselves on a pedestal as if we are better than they. We may be older, more mature, and thus wiser, but we never outgrow our rebellious hearts. Instead, let's humble ourselves and remember Jesus' message to the angry crowd ready to stone the woman caught in sin—no one is without sin. By internalizing this belief, you will naturally view your child's sins through the lens of Christ, thereby building greater ability to parent with extravagant love and grace.

BELIEF THREE—BOSS OF THE NARRATIVE

But you are the ones chosen by God, chosen for the high calling of priestly work, chosen to be a holy people, God's instruments to do his work and speak out for Him, to tell others of the night-and-day difference he made for you—from nothing to something, from rejected to accepted.[13]

Even though we don't have ultimate control of our kids' choices and hearts, we do have incredible power through our words, actions, reactions, gestures, emotions, and perspectives, to have lasting, positive impact on their lives.

Based on our choices, we control the narrative our children internalize—the story that tells them the truth of who they are and how they are called to act in the world. We are their primary examples. What we believe will dictate what they believe. How we act will dictate how they act. What we say will dictate what they say.

We can be an example that builds up or tears down, ignites greatness or ignores it, kindles inner strength and confidence or extinguishes the light. We have the power to inspire our kids to greatness beyond our wildest dreams. Therefore, believing we control the narrative creates in us a great deal of intention, discipline, presence, and consistency. It forces us to consider the part we play in the overall atmosphere of our home.

The power to establish the culture we want to nurture and cultivate in our home is in our hands. What culture are you creating in your home? Is it one filled with love, grace, forgiveness, and understanding? Or is it one tainted with anger, shame, pressure, fear, and disappointment? Maybe it's one filled with mixed messages, a roller coaster of emotions? No matter what your current culture looks like—the good news is—you have the power to change it or enhance it. Making this positive change is never too late.

BELIEF FOUR—BLAME IS NOT OURS TO BEAR

Therefore, my dear brothers, stand firm. Let nothing move you. Always give yourselves fully to the work of the Lord, because you know that your labor in the Lord is not in vain.[14]

How many times have you blamed yourself for your children's behavior? It's tempting to interpret their behaviors through our lens of insecurities, fears, and doubts and then internalize them as:

I'm a bad mom.

I don't know how to parent my child.

If I don't get this behavior under control, my child is going to grow up to be a disrespectful, irresponsible adult.

I've been there. And the guilt? Oh, the guilt. It can fester like an unattended wound and rob us of the joy and delight motherhood is meant to bring.

As difficult as it is to accept, we can't *really* make our kids do anything. Every choice is theirs. Therefore, the blame is not ours to bear. Did you hear that, friend? You aren't to blame for your children's poor behaviors. We can have incredible influence on their behavior, but we don't get to claim it—the good or the bad. It's time to release the guilt and adopt this belief. It's time to embrace the belief that our children's behavior is not a direct reflection of our mothering and trust the work we are doing will have positive impact.

BELIEF FIVE—BEHAVIOR IS A GIFT

Let us draw near with true hearts full of faith, with hearts rinsed clean of any evil conscience, and with bodies cleansed with pure water. Let us hold strong to the confession of our hope, never wavering, since the One who promised it to us is faithful. Let us consider how to inspire each other to greater love and righteous deeds.[15]

I'm talking of every behavior as a gift. The good, the bad, and the ugly. It's the ugly, however, that gets us really fired up. Yes? It comes in so many forms—the disrespectful back-talk, fighting with siblings, screaming and shoving, snotty remarks laced with entitlement. It can make our blood boil and cause us to lose all control. Trust me, I've been there. You may be wondering how in the world that type of behavior can be considered a gift. But what I've learned is that by genuinely internalizing behavior as a gift, we establish the foundational perspective needed to love our children bigger and better.

Believe it or not, when your kids misbehave, they aren't out to get you. They don't misbehave to make your life miserable, no matter what they say. Their misbehaviors are a result of the rebellion in their hearts. It's a truth of their humanity and a natural tendency they exert. Therefore, we need to expect misbehavior, instead of being surprised by it. We need to view their misbehavior as a gift, rather than an action to be feared. Misbehavior is a gift, because when it's exposed to us, we get to be a part of the rescue plan. Misbehavior is a priceless opportunity to instill faith-centered values.

As moms, we get to take an active role in being God's instruments of love and grace to our children so we can guide them and spur them on to good deeds before the rebellion takes control of their impressionable hearts. Viewing misbehavior as a gift rather than some act of cruelty toward us or others that we need to control, manage, or punish helps alleviate the fear of where this behavior may lead and the feeling that their behavior is a personal attack on us. Accepting this belief, therefore, lessens our instinctive reactions of anger, frustration, disappointment, and shame.

BELIEF SIX—BUILDING DESIRES IS GOD'S JOB

Saving is all his idea, and all his work. All we do is trust Him enough to let Him do it. It's God's gift from start to finish! We don't play the major role. If we did, we'd probably go around bragging that we'd done the whole thing! No, we neither make nor save ourselves. God does both the making and saving. He creates each of us by Christ Jesus to join Him in the work He does, the good work He has gotten ready for us to do, work we had better be doing.[16]

As a momma in love with Jesus and one who's been transformed by Him, I desire for my kids to experience the same. More than anything, I want them to love Jesus. I want them to have an intimate relationship with Him. I want them to be set free from the burdens of this world. I want them to understand and recognize their unique purpose that comes through Him. I want them to use their gifts, talents, and passions to love others and pass the baton of faith on to their children.

These desires fuel my intentions to teach my children about the God who loves them and made them and to show them Christ-like love and grace. However, I can only do so much. There comes a point where we must accept our inability to create desires in our child's heart. Building desires—ones that seek God and His ways—in the hearts of our children is ultimately God's job, not ours. Understanding this truth requires us to trust in God's greater desire to capture the hearts of our children.

CHRIST-CENTERED ACTION

Once these beliefs become ingrained in us and the power of the Holy Spirit begins to do its work, these new beliefs begin to override the old. They reign in our hearts and inspire us to demonstrate godly action.

The brilliant Sir Isaac Newton learned in his discovery of the law of motion that every action creates a reaction. In other words, our actions and our words breed results or consequences. It's a similar concept Paul described in Galatians 6:7b-10.

A man reaps what he sows. The one who sows to please his sinful nature, from that nature will reap destruction; the one who sows to please the Spirit, from the Spirit will reap eternal life. Let us not become weary in doing good, for at the proper time we will reap a harvest if we do not give up. Therefore, as we have opportunity, let us do good to all people, especially to those who belong to the family of believers.

Our words and actions impact the spiritual, mental, and emotional development of our children. If we sow a little, we'll reap a little. If we sow a lot, we'll reap a lot.[17] But it matters *what* we sow. The content of what we sow determines the content of what we reap. Therefore, it's essential our intention be to sow good fruit into our children so we will reap good fruit. Let's use our words to empower rather than cripple, to build up rather than tear down, to relieve the pressure to perform rather than intensify it. Let's communicate a message that says:

"I love you no matter what."

"You are valuable and precious."

"I forgive you and will always offer you second chances."

I've identified six actions or ways to organically infuse faith—sow the seeds—into everyday life with our children in hopes of reaping a harvest of godly hearts who follow in His ways and will pass on the baton of faith. Many of the intentional strategies and tactical tools I share within these actions have been inspired by my training in the Nurtured Heart Approach® created by Howard Glasser. Although the Approach® was not developed based on Christian values, its overall purpose of igniting greatness, building Inner Wealth™, and celebrating the spirit that is alive in our children mirrors God's expectations of who we are in Christ and how we are called to be in community with one another as children of God. Therefore, I've combined faith with the Approach® to create an undeniably powerful way to do life with our kids that will do everything the Approach® is meant to do while building faith in our children.

When we know Christ and have accepted His grace and love to cover us completely, Christ's grace and love become the underlying message and theme in all we do and say, even when we mess up. In fact, especially when we mess up.

ACTION ONE—AIM TO CONNECT BEFORE WE CORRECT

Our kids have so much to learn. As moms, we want to instill in our kids a sense of responsibility, integrity, hard work, commitment, honesty, generosity. The list goes on. And as Christian moms, we want to instill faith in our kids. Because we want so badly for our kids to attain these valuable, life-sustaining characteristics, criticism for not showing these qualities—even if our intentions are good—can be an easy response. However, a critical response is not the best method because it can instantly shut our kids down and sever connection, which is the last thing we want. Without connection, we have no relationship. Without relationship, we have little chance of having an impact and an even lesser chance at instilling faith and leading them to Jesus. Constant criticism leads to shame and can affect the way children view themselves. If all they ever hear is how they are doing things wrong and how they can do things better, they will begin to believe an internal dialogue that says:

I'm not good enough.

I'll never measure up.

I'm worthless.

I'm a loser.

I know that's not the message we want to give to our kids. Without having a strong intention to connect first before we offer correction—an intention that comes with applying grace instead of shame—the correction we wish to give will generate more negative consequences than good ones and push our kids further away.

As parents, we absolutely must correct our children— teach them right from wrong. But there's no need to do it in a critical manner. Instead, let's aim to connect with our child before we correct. In other words, acknowledge the good you see your child doing before you offer any correction. The truth is, there is *always* something positive to recognize, even if it seems like everything is going wrong because there could always be something more going wrong. For example:

"I can see you're angry, and that's okay. Therefore, I'm going to give you some time to cool down and then we can talk about what happened. But I appreciate that even though you're upset, you are not hitting or throwing things. I also appreciate you are no longer yelling at me. That shows incredible self-control and power. Let me know when you're ready to talk calmly."

As you can imagine, aiming to connect first rather than correct requires us to be in a calm state of mind, filled with grace. When we choose to connect first, our children are more willing to accept our correction and more willing to walk with us toward Jesus and into His Word. This positive exchange naturally cultivates mutual trust and respect, which nurtures and builds a deeper relationship.

ACTION TWO—ADMIT OUR OWN FLAWS

We've all done it. We've lost our cool. We've criticized. We've yelled. We've said things and done things we don't mean and later regret. Yes? Oh, friend, I sure hope you're with me on this because messing up is not only a given, but it also invites the most powerful message of faith we can ever give our kids.

To ask for forgiveness and admit when we are wrong—when we've misspoken or reacted poorly—not only gives our children an incredible opportunity to offer us Christ-like love and grace, but it demonstrates to our children our inability to attain perfection and our desperate need for a Savior.

Therefore, when you mess up, admit your mistake. Be vulnerable with your flaws. For example:

"I was mad, and I apologize for yelling at you. You don't deserve to be treated like that. I lost my temper. Just like you, I'm not perfect. I mess up. I'm a sinner. It's the whole reason Jesus came and why we need Him so desperately. Jesus gives us grace, and loves us regardless of our mistakes. And He asks us to do the same. Will you forgive me?"

Admitting our imperfections automatically gives our children permission to mess up without fearing harsh punishment, shame, or condemnation. Our transparency conveys the message that it's okay to be a sinner, which is why we need Christ every day to forgive us and renew us. It's also a message that says:

"I can never and will never be enough for you. But Jesus is."

They will learn perfection is not a requirement and their imperfection is continually covered by the love, grace, and perfection of Christ.

ACTION THREE—APPLY GRACE INSTEAD OF SHAME

Let's be honest, there are misbehaviors that make us mad. So mad we want to yell, punish, and shame.

"How could you?"

"You know better than that!"

"What were you thinking?"

Remember when we last heard these questions? That's right—when the crowd was condemning the woman caught in adultery. We're all rebellious at times, but, friend, we're all worthy of grace. And our kids need it more than ever as they seek to learn right from wrong and understand the ways of God versus the ways of the world.

We will get angry. Anger is okay. It expresses when something has gone wrong. But that doesn't mean we have to act out in anger. I know it's challenging to intentionally apply grace instead of shame when our children's misbehaviors generate intense anger and disappointment. Believe me, I know. But it's those very moments that are *the* most invaluable moments to demonstrate the power of God's grace and lead our kids to Jesus.

The last thing we want to do is give big, negative energy to our kids' big, negative behavior. This is a beautiful truth I learned from Howard Glasser and one he teaches in the Nurtured Heart Approach®. Not only does it send the wrong message and inadvertently communicate to our kids that they get more of us when things are going wrong, but acting out in anger also only makes things worse and has a tendency to escalate the problem or the behavior. As a result, it causes us to say things we regret, leading to hurt feelings and injured hearts. We may gain some compliance out of fear, for a time, but we will lose connection and relationship.

Applying grace instead of shame is congruent with Christ's heart, and grace takes a great deal of self-control, intention, and desire—everything a heart in line with Christ's is absolutely capable of doing. You are capable of applying grace. So, the next time your child does something to upset or disappoint you—before you react—pause and breathe. That's right, breathe. Big breaths. In through the nose and out through the mouth. It sounds elementary, I know, but trust me. Purposeful breathing will automatically help calm your heightened energy.

While you're breathing, say a little prayer. Ask for God's supernatural power to give you the patience, self-control, and understanding you need. Remember all the beliefs you know to be true, especially how behavior is a gift—your opportunity to lead your kids to Jesus and to love and correct with the grace of God. Remember who your children are in Christ (precious, beloved, saved, and forgiven). Remember how Christ—out of His great love for them—died to save them from their rebellion and set them free to live joyfully and in His presence.

Lastly, visualize the cross between you and your child and imagine how Jesus would respond to his/her actions. Choosing to turn our attention to God, first, is a helpful tool in resetting our energy, calming our hearts, and realigning our intentions. Then and only then are we best able to communicate with grace. For example:

> When your child acts out in negative behavior, take a deep breath, pray, visualize the cross, and as calmly as possible, say, "I'm going to give you time to cool down." (In my house, I use the phrase taught in the Nurtured Heart Approach®, "I need you to reset." This indicates to my kids they need to cool down before I give them any of my time and attention and before I address the behavior.) This also gives you and me time to cool down. Once everyone is in a calmer state of mind, I then recognize the successes in the moment instead of focusing on the negative behaviors of the past and say, "I see you are calmer and no longer yelling. I also see you are no longer [insert negative behavior—ex. hitting your brother]. You could have chosen to continue, but you stopped. That shows powerful self-control and maturity. It also shows me respect and kindness."

I then bring them with me to Jesus. I communicate with them the reason for their sin and how it's not because they are bad, disrespectful kids. This is critical because many kids associate their poor behaviors with an internal belief that says, "I'm a bad kid." And that's when shame takes root. For example, I might say:

> "It's hard to do the right thing all the time, isn't it? It's just part of being human. We have rebellion in our hearts that leads us into making poor choices. But the good news is Jesus died on the cross so our mistakes—our sins—could be forgiven and so we could have the opportunity to try again. That's called grace. And it's why we need Jesus. As children of God who are so deeply loved by Jesus, we have the Holy Spirit living in our hearts helping us fight our urges to sin. I can see the Holy Spirit working in you right now, helping you make a kinder, more loving choice."

Making kids feel badly for their behaviors won't inspire them to better behavior and will certainly not ignite greatness nor help them understand the grace of God. Marriage and family therapist, Howard Glasser, creator of the Nurtured Heart Approach®, said, "Children do not awaken by the fear of punishment, they awaken to their greatness."[18] And greatness is the innate truth of who they are as precious, beloved children of God. I don't, in any way, want to crush the greatness living inside my children. I want to ignite it. And God agrees:

"Don't you realize how patient he (God) is being with you? Or don't you care? Can't you see that he has been waiting all this time without punishing you, to give you time to turn from your sin? His kindness is meant to lead you to repentance."[19]

God's kindness is a firm type of kindness, one rooted in grace. It is a kindness meant to turn our hearts away from sin. The Spirit of God is already at work in our children's hearts, convicting them of their wrongdoing and indicating to them their innate desire to act in love and kindness. If we give them enough time to ponder their actions, they will naturally feel remorse and be drawn to repentance. Therefore, acknowledge that and invite reconciliation. But never force reconciliation because then it's ingenuine. Reconciliation must come from the heart. For example:

> "Now that you've reset and understand your behavior hurt your brother, is there anything you feel you want to say or need to make right? If you need support or help, please let me know. I'm here for you."

Apologies may not happen right away, but eventually, things are made right. Be sure to notice and acknowledge when you see reconciliation take place. The truth is, the more grace we give, the more our children want to give it back and the more inspired they are to choose better behavior. And when we see the softening occurring in their hearts—softening which inspires apologies or admitting of wrongs—we need to be ready to recognize and articulate—with detail and specificity—the fruits of the Spirit[20] we witness growing in them. It's through intentional, first-hand recognition where they will begin to understand the power of the Spirit living inside of them, helping and inspiring them to live out the characteristics of Christ.

ACTION FOUR—ACTIVATE GREATNESS

What percentage of the time are your children behaving well? Doing what's expected of them? Living within the boundaries and rules? I think it's safe to assume … most of the time. And how often do we neglect to acknowledge their amazing choices and behavior? Not because we don't appreciate it, but because, well, it's what we expect. Plus, when things are going well with our kids, we busy ourselves with other things.

The tragedy is we miss incredible opportunities to awaken our kids to the innate greatness growing inside of them. Not only that, but we also miss a priceless, eternal opportunity to show them Jesus. What a gift it is to our children to slow down, be present, connect, appreciate, recognize, and acknowledge the divine greatness we see in them. I'm referring to *all* the good moments, the big and the little.

It's natural for us to praise the big, awesome choices our kids make. But what about the everyday choices they make that we ignore? For example, getting out of bed, brushing teeth, packing backpacks, being nice to siblings, doing chores without complaints. What a perfect opportunity, every day, to recognize the responsibility, maturity, and independence you see growing in your child. The opportunities to recognize our kids and ignite the greatness we see in them are endless. We simply need to stop and pay attention. For example:

> "Hey, boys, I want you to know I'm noticing how you both are playing the game without fighting or arguing. It shows me you care about one another and that warms my

heart. Thank you for being kind, respectful, caring kids. I can see God's greatness growing in you."

When we articulate—with intention and specificity—to our children what we see them doing right and what that tells us about who they are, they begin to live out those qualities more and more. We get the pleasure of watching the fruits of the Spirit[19] grow in them and the privilege of reminding them the source of those fruits. The more we acknowledge the power of the Holy Spirit working in their lives, the more they come to understand His power and presence. And over time, through intentionality and consistency, their faith takes deep root and grows all on its own.

ACTION FIVE—ADHERE TO PRAYER

By prayer, I don't mean the memorized prayers we mechanically say and give little or no thought to as we recite them. You know the ones I'm talking about, right? "Now I lay me down to sleep ..." or "Come Lord Jesus be our guest ..." Now please, don't misinterpret me. I'm not, in any way, saying these prayers are bad or wrong. If these are the only prayers you're doing, it's a start. But if you want to point your kids to a real, intimate God in powerful, meaningful ways, then personal, heartfelt prayers are the answer.

The thought of saying an unscripted prayer with and for your kids terrifies some mommas, I know, especially if you've never really prayed on your own. However, saying prayers together with your children not only deepens your relationship with them and God, but it also nurtures in their hearts a greater understanding as to the presence and power of God. It shows our kids God is accessible to us. Plus, the more we pray with our kids and the more they hear our prayers for them, the more comfortable they feel to pray on their own and out loud in front of others.

I can't begin to tell you how powerful prayer is in enriching and sustaining the faith life of our children. Few things warm this momma's heart more than to hear my sons say, "Mom, will you pray for me?" Or to feel my son grab my hand, lean his head into my chest, and say, "Mom, I'll pray for you." It's precious and it's praise worthy. That's when I know God is moving and working in their hearts through the practices and intentions I'm establishing and committing to in our home.

ACTION SIX—AFFIRM ROUTINES AND TRADITIONS

I used to get so frustrated when I'd attempt to do family devotions, but I laugh at the absurdity of it now. More or less, I'd force my boys to sit quietly with their hands to themselves in the living room. That picture? All wrong! Brothers sitting? Doesn't happen. Quietly, so I could read and teach? No way. Hands to themselves? Impossible. And my demeanor? Let's just say it wasn't filled with grace and love.

Oh, we've come so far. I used to think family devotions were the key to instilling faith. I thought going to church or having a sensational Sunday school or youth group for my kids to attend was how they were going to find faith. Don't get me wrong, these are all great additions and routines for reinforcing faith in our kids. However, I've come to learn these aren't the most impactful ways to introduce God to our kids and nurture a lifelong faith. *We* are.

Although our daily, genuine interactions with our kids are most pivotal in instilling faith, there are routines and habits I've established that have become sacred moments that force us to pause and remember who we are and whose we are. The routines we have in our home don't add stress or much time. They are natural and an ingrained way of life for us that all my boys have come to accept and expect. For example:

> I place my hand upon their heads and bless them with the same message every night and every morning, reminding them of how precious, loved, and known they are by a God who is so available to them. It's a practice so embedded, they remind me if I forget. Nothing's sweeter than when they choose to give the blessing back to me. (See the resource, Blessings to Pray Over Your Children, in the back of the book.)

We pray together—before school, at supper time, and at bedtime. I try to stay as consistent as I can to do individual devotions with them at night and quick ones in the morning before school. Each family is different, so find what works for you, but don't underestimate the value of establishing routines and traditions in your home because these will be the ones they take with them and pass on to their own families.

Remember, there is no need for perfection in this. My family knows first-hand all the ways I fall short of perfection. I do my best at weaving authentic, Christ-like grace and love into every part of my interactions with my boys—even the ones where I mess up—because the Lord's inspired me to do so. It's what we've been called to do as moms, and it's what makes faith real, enticing, and tangible for our kids, sparking a desire in them to grow a deeper faith.

There's no greater message we can send our children about the grace and love of God being available to them than to allow Christ's truths to permeate our hearts so we can reflect His truths in our words and actions. It's this commitment that helps solidify the legacy of faith for generations to come.

"Train up a child in the way he should go, teaching him to seek God's wisdom and will for his abilities and talents. Even when he is old, he will not depart from it."[21]

The routines my family has developed are the result of doing my best to follow God's call to train my kids in the way they should go. And when I mess up, there's no guilt, only grace and forgiveness. I rely on my internal compass to lead me back in the right direction.

INTERNAL COMPASS

The monarch butterfly would not survive without instincts. Without divinely created characteristics embedded into its nature, the butterfly would never be able to make the miraculous 3,000–mile migration from Mexico to Canada. It's the monarch's internal compass incorporating the time of day and the sun's position that directs each generation of monarch on its path home.[22] Just like monarchs, we, too, have inherent greatness and power through the internal compass of the Holy Spirit to lead us on the path toward home—a path that's continually refining us into the image of Christ and directing us to our eternal home with Him.

Furthermore, depending on the weather, obstacles, or hardships in its path, the monarch can get off course. How true is that for us? How quickly can we get pushed off course by the storms, struggles, distractions, and challenges of life with kids? How easy is it to get trapped in our rebellion and act out of anger and frustration?

When monarchs are blown off course, their internal compass is alerted and activated. They reset their direction and are back on track, heading home in the right direction. The same is true for us. When our rebellion knocks us off our desired intentions as a mom and when we are in tune with the Holy Spirit's presence in our lives, our internal compass alerts us. For me, when I react in ways that aren't congruent with my heart's intentions, I get a nasty feeling in my gut that awakens a deep sense of awareness and remorse. I'm then reminded and inspired to reset my heart, mind, and emotions that place me back on track with my divine purpose and intentions.

I'm not always able to reset immediately, but what's so humbling is when my *sons* recognize my rebellion and lovingly and respectfully invite me to reset—to get back to being my best self. Those moments take my breath away. They leave me speechless because I see the internal compass of the Holy Spirit working in their hearts, inspiring them to give me grace and nurture me back to greatness. I'm so grateful God opened my eyes to the most honest, raw, beautiful way to live life with my kids. I pray you'll be inspired to embrace these actions and implement them into your heart and home so that you can experience the same.

Making it Matter

Getting our family of six ready for a five-day winter vacation is no easy task, and if you're anything like me, you're the one in charge of making sure everyone has what they need. I couldn't seem to do what my husband suggested. "Tell the kids to pack their own bags."

Now, I'm all about empowering responsibility and independence. They can easily pack their own bags for a quick overnight at their grandparents' or cousins' houses. But a trip like this—when there were so many necessary items—I couldn't risk it. So, to prevent any crazy wardrobe mishaps, I helped them pack. I was down to the last kid. Stressed and exhausted with a lot on my mind, I entered my oldest son's room. It took everything in me not to lose it right then and there. His room was a disaster. In his defense, it had been a long, busy week. Plus, he's a teenage boy, for goodness sake, give him a little grace. Right?

I felt my body tense and my steps get quicker and more direct as we searched for clothes to pack. My heart rate increased the more mess I uncovered. Then, I tugged on his socks and undies drawer. It wouldn't open. I tugged again. Hard. Socks and undies popped out. It's as if all sensibility were wiped from my mind, and I had been injected with a freak-out serum that took me from zero to one hundred in less than a second. Today, I'm embarrassed to admit such childish behavior. But that's what I did: I freaked out. Over socks and undies, I lost it.

Completely out of line, I raised my voice and asked him ridiculous, demeaning questions, like, "Don't you know how to match socks?" "Don't you know how to fold?" "This drawer is a mess. How do you ever find anything?"

Oh, it gets worse.

I dumped the entire drawer into the middle of the floor and proceeded to have an all-out, adult hissy fit. Ridiculous, right? Meanwhile, my son's tone now escalated to match mine, and my other son who happened to walk in at the wrong moment received a rude little response from me. Mother of the year, right here, my friend. Mother … of … the … year. By the way, his room wasn't really *that* bad. At least there wasn't food rotting under the bed.

And then, as quickly as I had snapped out of control, I snapped back in. I left the room to reset, saw with clear vision how crazy I acted, and instantly felt remorse. The Spirit convicted me of my craziness and softened my heart toward compassion.

I took a deep breath, calmed down, said a little prayer, and realized it was my responsibility to make things right. First, I went to my younger son whom I had scolded when he innocently entered the room and explained to him how I had lost control. I told him I wasn't perfect, and I make mistakes. I reminded him we all need God's love and grace to cover our imperfection and flaws—even moms and dads. I apologized for my actions and behavior and then said,

"Will you please forgive me, buddy?"

He knew this was coming, for it wasn't the first time I'd apologized for my behavior. With a gentle look in his eye and an understanding smile on his face, he embraced me while he muttered, "Always, Mom, always." I whispered in response, "Thank you, sweet boy, for showing grace and being Jesus to me."

A little nervous to talk to my older son fearing I had hurt his heart, I cautiously knocked on his door asking if I could come in. He whispered a hesitant, "Sure." Could I blame him for hesitating? I'd be upset if I were him, and I certainly wouldn't want to hang out with me either. When I opened the door and entered his room, I found him already in bed and clothes put away exactly like I had asked. I paused, looking at him in adoration and amazement, and thought, *He's so responsible, independent, patient, and obedient. He's a remarkable young man.*

My heart ached to talk to him because I felt so badly for the way I had acted. I sat on his bed, and before I could even speak an apology, he could sense my remorse and so kindly said, "I forgive you, Mom."

What? He wasn't mad? Disgusted? Frustrated? Before I had even asked for forgiveness, my teenage son was ready to give it. That's grace coming from the mouths of babes—grace that comes through the power of Christ growing in them. Those sweet boys chose to be Christ's hands and feet to me in that moment. What a precious gift! I squeezed him tightly and thanked him, too, for giving me grace.

I share this story not to brag about my boys. Please know that. I don't take credit for their awesome choices, anyway. Those are all God. I share this story so you can see how embodying a Christ-centered mindset not only produces a rich harvest, but it also activates the deepest kind of joy and delight in motherhood.

This is all within your grasp. You have the inherent love you need to do the work God is calling you to do—to point your kids to Christ and pass the baton of faith. Take some time right now to reflect on and write about your current condition. What type of culture have you created in your home? Is it one of stress, fear, and inconsistency? Do you feel you're living in chaos? If this is you, then journal about the areas in which you struggle the most. Is it follow-through and consistency? Is it losing your temper or not being present enough? Are you struggling to feel the presence of God and tap into His power—the power that fuels your ability to love with grace? If so, what's holding you back? And what steps can you take today to create a Christ-centered culture in your home? (Check out the back of the book for the Grace-Giving Quick Guide to help get you started and for more opportunities I offer to dive deeper into developing a Christ-centered heart and culture in your home.)

Or is the culture you've created one of grace, understanding, forgiveness, and acceptance? Do you have godly intentions in the way you act and respond to your kids? Are you sensing the Spirit's presence? If so, journal what that has been like for you and your kids and praise God for His goodness. No matter where you are on your journey of transformation, the migration will eventually come. Trust in God's timing, surrender to His goodness, and He will do the work He desires to do in and through you so you can experience true joy and freedom for yourself and be the reflection of God's love and grace to your children.

_____

_____

_____

_____

_____

_____

_____

_____

_____

A Momma's Prayer

Awesome God, we are overwhelmed by Your love—how You love us no matter what. It's a love that permeates our hearts, giving us everything we need to love like You—to be the mother we want to be to our kids. But this mothering gig is not easy. It's the hardest work we've ever done yet also the most significant. Give us, Lord, the courage, confidence, and wisdom to create a culture in our home that reflects Your love and grace. You know the condition of our hearts, so help us recognize the rebellion in our own hearts so we can help our children understand and manage the rebellion in their own. Humble us and help us admit when we are wrong. Help us purposefully connect with our children in ways that will deepen our relationship with them. Grant us wisdom as we seek to infuse you into the center of our homes. Help us establish routines in our homes that create loving structure and boundaries for our children—routines that communicate love and grace instead of fear and shame. Give us words to ignite their souls and nurture their hearts so they know the truth of their worth and belonging. Help us to be emotionally and spiritually present in our homes. Help us see our children the way You see them, Lord, as always deserving of love. And protect our children. Keep them safe from temptation and harm. Build them up, Lord, when we fail. Strengthen their reliance and trust in You as we continue to point them Your way. In Jesus' name we pray, amen.

 Meaningful Truth

The Lord is compassionate and gracious, slow to anger, abounding in love. He will not always accuse, nor will he harbor his anger forever; He does not treat us as our sins deserve or repay us according to our iniquities. For as high as the heavens are above the earth, so great is his love for those who fear Him; as far as the east is from the west, so far has he removed our transgressions from us.

—Psalm 103:8–12 (NIV)

We can rejoice, too, when we run into problems and trials, for we know that they help us develop endurance. And endurance develops strength of character, and character strengthens our confident hope of salvation. And this hope will not lead to disappointment. For we know how dearly God loves us, because he has given us the Holy Spirit to fill our hearts with his love.

—Romans 5:3–5 (NLT)

~ CHAPTER 12 ~

The Personal, Yet Connected, Race

GOD MADE YOU TO RUN YOUR ROUTE AND LIVE UNITED

The marathon. You've heard a lot about it. But there are some pieces of the story I've waited to tell until now. As you know, I didn't run the marathon alone. I had a team. Four women committed to conquering 26.2 miles together, yet each ran her own individual race—one that held a unique purpose for each of us.

Marathon day. It was time. We'd had a good night's sleep. We had fueled our bodies, gotten dressed, pulled our hair back in ponies, gone to the bathroom, tied our shoelaces, and grabbed our drop bags. We were ready to head out of the hotel room door and make it to the race with plenty of time to warm up and mentally prepare.

And then my friend, Lori, got a phone call.

The expression on her face conveyed what we had feared. Waiting in silence for her to share the news, I prayed for her. Slowly dropping the phone from her ear, she looked up through tears in her eyes and softly spoke:

"My dad died this morning."

Her dad had been sick for some time, and she knew the end was drawing near. But nothing can prepare you for that call. And never had she imagined the timing—for his last day to be the day of the marathon, a day for which we'd been preparing for half a year.

Sara, Jen, and I immediately surrounded Lori to console and support her in this heavy moment of grief. Silence, heartache, and love held the space among us for some time as we ached for our dear friend. I don't even recall who spoke first, but we saw the time and realized we had a decision to make. Are we still running the marathon?

This is the moment the race became more than a race. It was about friendship, support, encouragement, love, sacrifice, loyalty, and sisterhood. You see, I'm certain each of us—in a heartbeat—would have sacrificed our marathon experience for Lori. I was already entertaining the idea in my mind, but Lori wouldn't have it. Lori, in her selflessness, thought about us—how hard we had worked and how much we had sacrificed for this moment. She wasn't about to let us give up on this goal.

Having recently lost my dad, I'm in awe of her ability to think of others at such a difficult moment. Talk about strength. Before we knew it, we were no longer jogging but sprinting to the starting line, worried we weren't going to make it in time. (I think it's fair to say we ran two miles before we even began the marathon.) But we made it—right in time to catch our breath and acknowledge the significance of the moment.

Our plan had always been to run together. We had trained to run the same pace and had similar goals. Most importantly, we wanted to enjoy the run and not kill ourselves doing it. But now more than ever, it was all about supporting Lori and helping her through what was sure to be an intense emotional battle.

If you've ever ran a race, you know the chaos I'm about to describe. It's like running in a pack of wildebeests being chased by hungry hyenas. You're constantly looking forward and glancing back to make sure you don't trip over anyone. To maintain a pace, you must weave in and out of runners, always thinking a second ahead to your next spot. Meanwhile, adrenaline fires strong within your veins as you concentrate to control your breathing and steady your strides.

In most races, the pack breaks apart. Not this race. We were in a pack nearly the whole time, constantly maneuvering for position. Imagine the difficulty of this while trying to run with a team of four. Our heads were on a constant swivel, not only to watch out for other runners but to also keep track of one another. One of us would weave ahead first. When another opportunity to pass came, another would make her strategic move. And so on. That's how we ran the first seventeen miles.

I'm not sure how it happened, but around mile eighteen, Sara, Jen, and I couldn't spot Lori. We slowed down and called out her name, taking turns looking back. When that failed, the three of us looked at one another and knew what to do. We shimmied our way to the edge of the road, stopped running—dead in our tracks—and began scouring the crowd of runners for our beloved friend.

There is something you need to know about these women. Like me, they don't stop in the middle of a race. Ever. We don't even stop when we're training. They are driven, competitive, strong women who inspire me to push myself to greater depths than I ever thought possible. But like our friend had sacrificed for us to run the race, it was our time to sacrifice for her. That's what friends do. We laid to rest our personal goals for the marathon because it no longer mattered. What mattered was Lori—finding her and making sure she was okay.

I'm not certain how long we stood on the side, watching runner after runner go by, frantically searching for our friend. Several spectators tried to encourage us to keep running, obviously having no clue why we had stopped.

And then, there she was, in the middle of the pack. So relieved and excited to see her, we immediately started cheering and calling her name as we made our way to surround her, as if subconsciously trying to create some shield of protection … of comfort … of support … and of love. The look on her face spoke a hundred words. She was giving this race everything she had, and I've never been more inspired.

We did not finish together. Lori insisted we run ahead, and respecting her sincere encouragement, we did. Later, like I mentioned in an earlier chapter, as I was feeling unexpected strength and energy, Sara and Jen insisted I run ahead. So, I did. Although we ran this race as a team, we also each ran our very own unique race with meaning far greater than we had ever expected.

For Lori, it was the belief her dad was finally getting to see her run for the first time from front row seats in the stadium of heaven. For another of us, it was an opportunity to be a part of something positive and inspiring—something greater than herself. And yet for the third, it was the joy of the comradery and the sacrificial love and support of friendship. For me? Well, this is the experience that pulled me out of a pit, jump-started radical change in my life, and gave me gifts I will treasure for a lifetime.

Even though we each ran our own race, we also ran together. Our race was not only an exemplary display of friendship—an unbreakable bond rooted in authenticity, love, and support—but the race was also an expression of personal acceptance and commitment. We were a beautiful illustration of the way God desires for us to live as individuals and in our relationships with others. As women growing in faith and wisdom, we have the privilege and responsibility to model a lifestyle where we accept one another for who we uniquely are, embrace the race God designed us to run, and then confidently live it out in ways that nurture loving unity.

And this message comes directly from the mouth of Jesus where He emphasizes the importance of running our own race while at the same time standing united as a family of believers.

RUN YOUR RACE

Remember Jesus' disciple, Peter? The fisherman who accepted Jesus' invitation to follow Him? And the one who walked on water toward Jesus? They spent a great deal of time together during Jesus' ministry and grew to be dear friends. There are countless stories I love about them.

However, the last message Jesus gave Peter is one we need to take to heart. This encounter took place after Jesus' resurrection, before He ascended into heaven. Prior to this—on the night of Jesus' crucifixion—Peter had denied knowing Him. Not once, but three times. Therefore, this conversation was Jesus' way of reconciling their friendship and confirming Peter's love and commitment to spreading the message of salvation and to being a leader in establishing the church. But that wasn't all.

While they were talking, Peter noticed John (another beloved friend and disciple of Jesus) was following them. A bit curious about what role John was going to play, Peter asked, "Lord, what about him?"[1]

Jesus quickly responded, "What is that to you? You must follow me."[2]

In other words, Jesus was saying, "Don't worry about what role John will play. You play *your* role. You be who I've created *you* to be. Don't look at anyone else but yourself because I need you to be you."

This truth is one I must be reminded of often because it can be so easy to get caught up in comparing our lives to others. It's human to desire to be like that mom who seems to have it all together on Facebook, Pinterest, or Instagram. The mom who seems to be successful at everything she does. Even when our hearts have been set right, we can get wrapped up in comparisons. And then we begin to doubt our significance. We fool ourselves into believing we are less than these other women, which causes us to miss out on the roles we were designed to play.

Have you ever compared yourself to another woman? Another mom? I have. Many times. I've envied women who have successful careers outside the home. When I see moms who rock healthy meal planning, I instantly feel guilty for not always doing the same for my family. (Confession time: Yes, on occasion, I serve chicken nuggets, corn dogs, and frozen pizza.) Running one marathon in a lifetime I thought was awesome, but I know moms who run five marathons a year. (What? That's rock-star status, if you ask me.) I could go on and on about the comparisons we get trapped in. What I've also recognized is this comparison thing we do goes beyond one another and filters down to our kids. In other words, I'm also influenced to compare because my kids compare. I hear comments like, "So-and-so has a phone. Why can't I?" Or "How come I can't have Snap Chat? Everyone has it." We moms are constantly bombarded with messages meant to tempt us into questioning who we are and what we stand for.

I've been caught in the trap of wondering why some women move so quickly forward in their career of writing and speaking while I seem to be moving at a much slower pace with a much smaller audience. I wonder how these women are doing what they are doing and how I can do the same. I could wish to be more like them, and I have. But the truth is, I'm not equipped to run their race. And that's okay because I've been equipped to run my own—just like you've been equipped to run your own. Our end purpose might be the same, but the race we each run is different. And the races are different for a reason.

We've all been given different gifts and passions so we can have our own unique impact on the world. Everything you've been through in your life has prepared you for this moment—for the roles you play. Even though there are times we doubt our abilities to play these roles and wish we had more of what someone else has, God consistently equips us to play these roles in our own special way. Therefore, the only way we will experience genuine contentment is when we don't try to be anyone else but ourselves. It's in choosing to be ourselves—trusting fully in God's design and accepting who we are and the race we are called to run—where we gain the confidence to live it out.

Tragedy happens when we try to be either someone we aren't or neglect to be the person we are. In other words, we will always feel like something isn't quite right if we try to run someone else's race or avoid to run the race we've been uniquely created to run. The fullness of who we are won't ever be experienced. On top of that, the kingdom of God will miss out on your contribution because no one can make the impact only you can make. No one else can play the role you were uniquely designed to play. If you don't make the contribution, it won't be made.

Tragedy happens when we try to be either someone we aren't or neglect to be the person we are.

So, I'm here to tell you. Run your race. Because when you do—when you align your gifts, passion, personality, and experiences and discover your race—life will feel so right. So intuitive. So good. You will experience fulfillment, satisfaction, and fruitfulness like never before. You'll experience the joy God created you to experience.

Jesus *needed* Peter to accept his role and not worry about what others would be doing because he was chosen to play a critical part only he could play. The early church depended on Peter's leadership. One can only speculate if the church would have grown like it did without Peter's influence and commitment to the role Jesus called him to play.

Jesus calls us to do the same—play our part, run our race.

But like my marathon experience, just because we have our own unique race to run doesn't mean we were meant to run it alone. In fact, quite the opposite is true.

CHOOSE TO RUN UNITED

God created us in such a way that life is better when we live in unity with Him and others. In the book of Acts—after Jesus ascended into heaven—we find Peter not only embraced his role as a leader in establishing the church, but he also did it in community with others—in ways that ignited growth and togetherness.

> The community continually committed themselves to learning what the apostles taught them, gathering for fellowship, breaking bread, and praying. Everyone felt a sense of awe because the apostles were doing many signs and wonders among them. There was an intense sense of togetherness among all who believed…They were unified as they worshiped.[3]

As daughters of God, it's our individual responsibility and privilege to accept who we are—the part we've been given to play—and live it out in ways that bring glory to God and make His name known. In addition, as sisters in Christ, it's our humble honor and mission to stand unified—supporting and encouraging one another—in those divine purposes. Although we run on the same road, we are called to run different races. And although we run different races, we are called to run united. The apostle Paul, in his letter to the Ephesians, reinforces this message, beautifully.

> I want you to get out there and walk—better yet, run!—on the road God called you to travel. I don't want any of you sitting around on your hands. I don't want anyone strolling off, down some path that goes nowhere. And mark that you do this with humility and discipline—not in fits and starts, but steadily, pouring yourselves out for each other in acts of love, alert at noticing differences and quick at mending fences.
>
> You were all called to travel on the same road and in the same direction, so stay together, both outwardly and inwardly. You have one Master, one faith, one baptism, one God and Father of all, who rules over all, works through all, and is present in all. Everything you are and think and do is permeated with Oneness.
>
> But that doesn't mean you should all look and speak and act the same. Out of the generosity of Christ, each of us is given his own gift.[4]

Although we run on the same road, we are called to run different races. And although we run different races, we are called to run united.

But as we know, running life's race cooperatively with others is easier said than done. It is difficult because we are sinners living with other sinners. This unity we're called to nurture encompasses the vast array of relationships we have—ones with our children, spouses, parents, siblings, friends, and even strangers.

I will never forget the time when a mom said to me, after I had led a Mothers of PreSchoolers (MOPS) meeting, "I just have to tell you, I had you all wrong."

At first I wasn't sure if it was meant to be a compliment or an insult. As she began to talk about how I always had my hair and makeup done and always dressed so nicely, I began to realize this was her way of apologizing for judging me on my appearance long before she got to know my heart. (Little did she know how most of my days were spent in yoga pants with no makeup and my hair in a ponytail.) Aren't we all guilt of this? Judgment. I know I am, even if I only think it in my mind. But judgment divides and builds walls between the very spirits God desires to unite.

Can you recall instances of conflict rooted in judgment within any of your relationships? Have you ever found yourself jealous of another woman? Or jumped to wrong assumptions about someone? Maybe you've experienced miscommunication or had a misunderstanding that drove a wedge between a relationship? Judgment, jealously, gossip, slander, betrayal, deceit all lead to one place—division. And division robs us of joy and peace. Division threatens to destroy relationships and God's design for unity.

And though we don't nurture togetherness perfectly, there is beauty and power in transformed hearts aligning with

God's. As women who are seeking God and desiring to be more like Christ, we are able to pave the way—to pour out our hearts in love to others, to be quick to resolve conflicts, to stand confidently in our convictions, to forgive when we have been wronged, and to love one another and one another's kids without judgment. The more confident we grow in realizing we have a combined divine purpose and in accepting our unique place in the race, the more certain we become in unfurling our wings to be the leaders in reconciliation and building unity in God's kingdom.

The truth is, my friend, we're more alike than we are different. We may run our own leg of the race, but we're all trying to do the best we can. And we need one another. What if instead of judging, we do what the Lord asks? What if we have compassion to listen, encourage, and help one another? What if instead of focusing on the differences that divide us, we focus on the similarities that unite us?

As Scripture says, "Let's discover the beauty in everyone."[5] Instead of noticing the part someone is not playing, how about we notice the parts they are? Instead of seeing our sisters through sinner's eyes, how about we see them through God's? Perhaps, then, we can realize we are on the same team. And when we are on the same team, there's no stopping us from reaching the finish line and having significant impact on our families, our communities, and God's kingdom.

I want to set an example for my children. I want them to see their mom and dad work respectfully and lovingly through any differences. I want them to see kids at school through the eyes of God. I want to show my boys how to build healthy, strong connections and relationships with others despite differences. I want my sons to embrace their gifts—stand true to who they are—and seek ways to engage with others as God has commanded so my sons can experience the joy that comes from living in positive, genuine relationships.

THE RELAY RACE OF THE MONARCH

Motherhood is a bond we share. It links us together and offers us an opportunity to develop a system of support—one similar to the migratory journey the monarch butterfly embarks on which is like none other in nature.

Their journey is often called the "Relay Race of the Monarch."[5] To survive the cold winter months of the north, the monarchs must migrate south. However, to make the one-way trip from Canada to Mexico, four generations of monarchs transform from caterpillar to butterfly during the migration. The northern generations of monarchs only live four to six weeks, but those flying the last leg south live up to eight months as they migrate and hibernate for the winter. And no monarch migrates alone. When the flock reaches Mexico for the winter, they huddle together to survive, often finding the same tree as their ancestors. Snuggled close together, they create a canopy to protect themselves from the cold winter weather.[6]

They work together not only to keep one another on track but also to survive. They rely on one another to complete their journey. They can't do it alone, yet they each must play their unique role, fly their own route, and run their own leg of the race. Otherwise, the chain would be broken.

I believe, like the monarchs, we are better off doing motherhood together than apart. We aren't isolated mothers. We're part of a community of faithful daughters—a blended legacy of multiple generations—each being uniquely molded and refined by the gracious hand of God for His glory and His purposes. All the heart work you've done has led us to this point. It has prepared us to step out in confidence to be who we are and to unite with others in authentic relationship.

We're part of a community of faithful daughters—a blended legacy of multiple generations—each being uniquely molded and refined by the gracious hand of God for His glory and His purposes.

Together, we can be mommas soaring united and freely on the breeze of the Spirit, faithfully beating our wings to fulfill our divine purpose as daughters of the King and to leave a legacy of faith for generations to come.

 Making it Matter

When my dad died unexpectedly, it rocked my world. All sense of normalcy was thrown out the window. I couldn't eat, sleep, or remember things. I wasn't sure I'd be able to continue writing because my grief was so heavy. Yet here I am, almost to the end. There's no doubt I am where I am because of the community of people who rose up—as one—and surrounded me and my family in our greatest time of need.

Before we could even wrap our brains around what had happened, people were already flooding us with love and support. My family and I witnessed the orchestration of God's magnificent power as people chose to be His faithful instruments—giving what they uniquely could give—which, when combined, produced the most beautiful symphony of God's enduring and faithful love.

What greater testimony to the power of unity in Christ than that—God's children acting as one, unwavering pillar of faith and goodness. Here I am, a writer, yet I struggle to find the words to express the indescribable beauty of the alliance of believers. I am moved to tears of joy and gratitude. God hopes for us to live this way—to use our unique gifts in combined efforts to be His love in the world. The world desperately needs us to stand united and strong as it's continually threatened by the enemy with a mission to divide and destroy community and relationships. The enemy wants nothing more than to crush the beautiful, natural instinct we have to be who we are and live united in peace and joy. But there's no need to worry because we have the greatest weapon of all. We have a mighty, faithful, loving God on our side and with Him, all things are possible.[7]

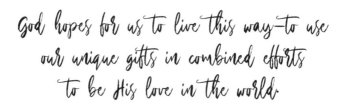

God hopes for us to live this way—to use our unique gifts in combined efforts to be His love in the world.

Finishing this book without my dad was not in my plan. There were many days I was so stricken with grief I couldn't write—days when my perseverance weakened and confidence wavered. Those were the days I wondered if I could press on to the end. But I did. And there's only one reason why.

I was never alone.

Not only did God walk with me through the high places, but He also proved Himself faithful in the valleys. And I was surrounded by a team of women—warriors of the faith. These were friends who chose to walk by my side every step of the way. They comforted me through the tears, encouraged me through the doubts, and picked me up when I was ready to throw in the towel. Their united, solid, steadfast presence—time and time again—inspired, strengthened, and renewed my purpose so I could press on and cross this finish line. I'm forever grateful for the gift they are to my life.

That's the power of the community of believers—relationship, friendship, faithfulness. These women gave me but a small glimpse of the glorious unity which awaits us in heaven.

Now it's your turn, my friend. Think about the relationships you have with other women and answer these questions in the space below. Remember, this is a time to peer honestly into your heart, for it's through our honest admittance of our own realities where growth and transformation happens. Have you experienced the beauty of authentic relationship with other women? If so, what is it like? Or, do you feel you're doing life on your own, without much understanding and support? How can you go about finding connection? Looking back, have you ever been the target of judgment or been caught in the comparison trap, insecure about who you are? How did you handle it? Were you able to seek unity and build friendship rather than allow your differences to create more division? As mommas, we are stronger together than apart, but we each play a special role in building that unity. What makes you, you? What special part do you play? And how can you contribute to building connection and unity with other women?

_____

_____

_____

_____

_____

_____

_____

_____

 A Momma's Prayer

Dear God, thank You for making each of us different and for giving each of us a unique part to play in Your world. Help us embrace who You've made us to be and give us the courage to live it out. Remind us we are on the same team. Take away our distorted lens of judgment. Instead of being intimidated by one another's differences and tempted to fall into the trap of comparison, help us see one another the way You see us. Help us be Your instruments of love and grace in the world, working together as a united sisterhood for Your good and Your glory. Help us model to our children how to accept our beautiful identity in You and nurture genuine relationships. Continue to fill us with Your power and wisdom so we can be leaders committed to building up Your kingdom and passing on faith to the next generation of believers. In Jesus' name we pray, amen.

Meaningful Truth

*We are like the various parts of the human body. Each part
gets its meaning from the body as a whole, not the other
way around. The body we're talking about is Christ's body
of chosen people. Each of us finds our meaning and function
as a part of his body. But as a chopped-off finger or cut-off
toe we wouldn't amount to much, would we? So since we
find ourselves fashioned into all these excellently formed and
marvelously functioning parts in Christ's body, let's just go
ahead and be what we were made to be, without enviously or
pridefully comparing ourselves with each other,
or trying to be something we aren't.*

—Romans 12:4–6 (MSG)

CHAPTER 13

The Baton of Faith

GOD INSPIRES OUR HANDOFF AND BEARS THE OUTCOME

For the first time in all these months of writing, I am not sitting in my office where I've written nearly every word of this book. I'm sitting with the same intention—to write the book scripted in my heart. But right now—all truth on the table—as we're approaching the finish line, I'm feeling the pressure to complete this book. Not only because school will soon be dismissed for the summer, which means life is about to get really hectic with all four boys at home running in all different directions, but I'm struggling to find the *right* story to share that will wrap this whole thing up and have lasting impact.

I've started and deleted and rewritten the opening of this chapter more times than I can count. It's one that's been waiting for weeks to be written, and although I know what I want to say, I haven't been able to find the words. Partly because it requires a tender, delicate place of my heart and partly because our time together is coming to an end. I so badly want these words to leave you feeling loved, empowered, and inspired to boldly soar to heights beyond your wildest imagination in the security and freedom of God's extravagant love and grace.

That's been my prayer for you our entire time together, but I know it's not my job to change your heart. That's God's business. I'm simply one messenger. Whatever impact is meant to happen will be directed by God, not me. I don't carry that responsibility. Therefore, I did what I always do—release this message into God's hands, trusting in His wisdom and His guidance to direct these last words.

And like always, God delivered. I woke up this morning with this assuring intuition compelling me to go to the place that embodies the message I want to share in this chapter and brings the essence of the book full circle. God's timing and presence never ceases to amaze me. I find it so remarkable how, although I had a plan and outline for this book, it has taken many unexpected turns. This particular turn led me directly back to the place where my journey of faith began.

So, here I sit in the sunroom of my parent's home—in the comfort of my daddy's brown, cloth-covered recliner with the sun glistening warmly through the windows. My mother, like always, is busying herself with something in the kitchen. A picture of Dad sits on the table in front of me—his lively, warm, loving presence so greatly missed. I find myself glancing up at his contagious smile often, imagining him shaking his head ever so slightly in humble adoration, saying with a tender tone of love in his voice and tears in his eyes:

"Keep going, honey. God's got this. He's given you everything you need. I believe in you. Just get 'er done."

Using the tips of my fingers to wipe the silent tears continuously streaming down my cheeks, I'm vividly reminded—as I'm awakened from my daydream by my mom's melodic humming—of where my faith journey began and of how fortunate I am to have been raised in a loving, Christian home.

Therefore, no other place seems more appropriate and fitting for me to write about legacy—the impact we want to leave on the people we love—than my parent's home. This is the place that represents the two people who not only gave me life but also introduced me to the giver of life. What better place to emphasize the incredible, unmatchable influence and impact we have on the lives of our children than to go to the very people who have had the most impact on mine. What better place to remind you that we have the humbling privilege and honor of passing on the baton of faith to our children than to go to the very ones who have passed it on to me.

THE GIFT OF FAITH

As I've mentioned before, I've known Jesus my whole life. Meaning, I have no memories of a time without knowing who Jesus is and what He did for me. I'm sure I was singing

"Jesus Loves Me" as soon as I could mumble the words. I don't recall a time where going to church wasn't an expectation and requirement on Sunday mornings—even throughout high school when all I wanted to do was sleep in. Not only that, but we were also the family who attended all the Lenten and Advent worships, even amid our busy school and athletic schedules. Attending church became ingrained; we grew up understanding church was not only important but also routine and necessary.

Some of my earliest memories include dressing in my Sunday best for church, then going out for lunch afterward. Many of my best memories from high school include the time spent with friends in youth group. This was the norm for me. I've always had faith, and I've never known life without it.

But as I've been writing and reflecting on my past, I've realized how, for years, I took having been raised in the faith for granted. Did my parents do it perfectly? Of course not. Would they have done some things differently? Probably. In fact, as my parents witnessed my transformation and maturity of faith that came out of my struggle in motherhood and naturally impacted the way I mother my boys, they began to express their desires to have raised me with more intention to faith.

My parents were raised in traditional Lutheran homes where faith was very personal and not talked about a great deal. The existence of faith was evident through traditional actions and rituals, but it wasn't openly discussed in everyday life. When they saw how my faith inspired me to openly, honestly, and intentionally weave faith into every aspect of my family's life, they began to express how they wished they had been more intentional in doing the same. And the same was true for my mother-in-law as my husband and I share very similar upbringings in the faith.

But here's the undeniable truth that makes me forever grateful. These parents all made a critical, intentional choice: They *chose* to plant the most important seeds in their children's hearts. The seeds of faith. At the root of their efforts was extravagant, unconditional love—a love that comes only from God—that permeated through everything they did and said. And so, these seeds, having years and years of tender, diligent cultivating—powered by the grace and love of God—began to grow and flourish. My husband and I are people of faith committed to raising our boys in the faith. My brothers and their wives are doing the same. The baton of faith was, indeed, successfully passed and received.

As a kid, I didn't realize the priceless gift I'd been given. And I'm overcome with a flood of emotions as I consider the fortitude, resolve, and discipline that generation upon generation of my family and my husband's family had in passing on the baton of faith—a baton exchange that should never be underestimated.

THE DIVINE RELAY

If you have ever run or watched a 4 x 100–meter track relay, then you know how critical the baton handoffs are in the outcome of the race. If they aren't absolutely precise—if the handoff is fumbled—the team risks losing precious milliseconds, which is often all that divides the winners from the losers. Even more disheartening than losing precious time is if the racers run out of the exchange zone. Or worse, if they drop the baton. In both cases, the teams are instantly disqualified. The race is lost.

Author Christine Caine, a champion and rock-star racer for Jesus, brilliantly describes in her book, *Unstoppable*, the epic journey of the USA Olympic Women's 4 x 100–meter relay teams. After years of heartache as three consecutive Olympic attempts at the gold ended because of failed baton handoffs, redemption finally came in the London 2012 games as fans watched four incredible athletes not only win the gold but also smash the world record. These women ran against the fastest female runners in the world. They knew winning would come down to perfectly precise baton handoffs.

In fact, the USA starter for that race said, "I just knew that if we had clean baton passes that we would challenge the world record. Smash it like we did? I had no idea. But I knew it was in us."[1]

"Clean baton passes." The passing of the baton is a critical moment in a relay race. The baton is passed within a 20–meter exchange zone, making the exchange zone the most important seconds of the race. One runner runs into the zone with the baton outstretched while the next runs ahead, reaching back for the baton. The outcome of the race hinges on the precision of the handoff occurring seamlessly within that short distance.

I can't help but connect to how true this handoff is in our own lives. Our exchange zone—the years we have at home raising our children—is our priceless opportunity to pass on the baton of faith. Therefore, the outcome of our children's races is impacted greatly by what occurs from the time they are born until the time they leave our homes. Because remember, we are the ones who have the most powerful and significant influence on our children's lives. The attitudes, morals, habits, and traditions we deem important will leave significant imprints on our children's hearts—even if our kids don't realize it at the time.

Our exchange zone—the years we have at home raising our children—is our priceless opportunity to pass on the baton of faith.

In other words, if we model what it's like to have an intimate relationship with Jesus, place high value on living by faith, and mother with the love and grace of Christ, I trust those truths will naturally seep into their internal belief system. Furthermore, I trust that the intentional, consistent efforts we make to impact the spiritual lives of our children from day one will be the foundational source of truth rooted into the core of their being and will naturally influence the trajectory of their lives. Instilling faith—passing the baton— will act as a safety net ready to catch them when they fall.

And fall, they will. I'm not naïve about what our kids are up against. Whether you've been raised in the faith or have come to faith on your own, the world—with its temptations, distractions, and hardships—seeks to threaten our exchange zone, disrupt a smooth handoff of the baton, and endanger our legacy of faith. This is a similar danger the monarch butterfly knows all too well.

THE THREATS TO THE HANDOFF

The existence and life cycle of the monarch butterfly is nothing short of miraculous. We've talked about the various, intricate transformation that must take place for the species to survive. We've learned that monarchs rely on their family—the generations of butterflies that have gone before them—to complete the migration and maintain their life cycle. If one generation fails to survive, the entire species is threatened.

However, external forces threaten the monarch's existence and their ability to make a clean handoff. The monarch population is at an ongoing risk of extinction as its numbers have dropped by more than 80 percent since the mid-1990s. The main reasons for the decline include climate change and severe weather, habitat loss due to illegal logging, and the increased use of pesticides on genetically engineered crops to control unwanted weeds—the very weeds (milkweed) the monarchs need to survive. These threats are constant and increasing.[2]

Like the monarch, *our* exchange zone is hampered by an enemy who lurks, seeking to destroy our handoff. When *our* personal defenses can't be broken, the enemy will strike our kids, knowing full well the exchange zone is a vulnerable, impressionable time of our children's lives. Worldly temptations and distractions will appeal to the rebellion in our children's hearts and threaten to tear them away from us and God's purposes.

Therefore, the handoff of faith is not always smooth. We might fumble the baton. The baton might drop. We might even run outside the exchange zone where hope of crossing the finish line victoriously will seem shattered. The enemy wants nothing more than for our relay race to be broken. Our handoff to be destroyed. Our legacy of running the race extinct.

We've talked about how our primary role as mom is to point our kids to Christ. But what happens when they fall away from the faith? When they walk into sin? When they rebel against you and God? Are we to blame?

I witnessed one of my dearest friends experience the real, raw heartache of watching her teenage son succumb to his heart's rebellion—fall into sinful temptation—as if suddenly forgetting the truths she'd consistently poured over him his entire life. I listened as she desperately wondered, *How did this happen? What did I do wrong? Have I failed him as a mother?*

Overcome with disbelief, anguish, and desperation, she instinctively reverted to blaming herself for his choices, resulting in her carrying a weight of guilt that was slowly sucking the joy of life right out of her. And this is a woman who lights up a room with her contagious smile and positive, joyful energy. The enemy's strikes were in full force, attempting not only to unravel this family and destroy the relationship my friend had with her son but also to weaken her faith and resolve.

Because of her vulnerability and transparency, she was able to reach out to trusted friends for support and to be reminded of this truth: It's not our fault. We aren't to blame for our children's rebellion. Our divine role of mom must be viewed in light of God's sovereignty, grace, and love so we don't take on the responsibility of carrying a burden that is not meant for us to carry. This truth realigned my dear friend's heart and freed her to trust her son's choices and life into God's loving care.

Our divine role of mom must be viewed in light of God's sovereignty, grace, and love so we don't take on the responsibility of carrying a burden that is not meant for us to carry.

GOD'S THE HEART CHANGER, NOT US

I'm just going to come out and say it. No matter how we choose to mother and no matter how hard we try to raise our kids in the faith, there is no guarantee. We can't make our kids love Jesus. We can't make them make godly choices. We can't make them see themselves the way God sees them. We can't make them accept God's love and grace. *We have power to influence*, but we do not have the power to transform their hearts. That job has always and will always be God's. What is true for us is true for our children. Only the power of the Holy Spirit can awaken our children to their need for Christ. We can't take the credit nor the blame for the outcome of our children's faith.

Only the power of the Holy Spirit can awaken our children to their need for Christ.

Would it be miserable to watch our kids walk away from a God who loves them and wants the best for them? Without a doubt. Would it rip out our hearts to watch them intentionally walk directly into sinful temptation? Few greater heartaches exist. When our children suffer, we suffer.

Many mysteries surround the whys of suffering and hardship, but suffering is part of being human. Like my parents couldn't shield me from my struggles and sufferings, we can't shield our kids. But I trust that just like God used my struggles and sufferings to draw me closer to Him, to reveal His extravagant plans for my life, to refine, mold, and sharpen me for His purposes, I trust God will do the same for my kids. Our children's struggles and sufferings are *their* personal journeys, which God will use to draw them closer to Him and into a relationship with Jesus.

So instead of being weighed down with guilt as if our children's sinful actions are somehow our fault, we must accept that the outcome of our children's faith does not rest on our ability nor our desire to instill, teach, and nurture faith perfectly. Like there is rebellion in our hearts we can't always control, there is rebellion in our children's hearts they can't control, nor can we control it for them. We need to stop the enemy in its tracks and rise with godly confidence and courage. Out of abundant faith, transformed hearts, and joyful souls, we must relinquish control—like we do with our own hearts—and acknowledge we aren't enough for our kids and trust that God is.

This truth remains—and it's a truth that brings me lasting comfort, peace, and hope. What's true for us is true for our children. God is constantly in pursuit of them. He's always walking with them, even when they don't realize it. God desires our children to know and love Him even more than we do. He wants their hearts. He wants them to realize the fullness of His love for them. He's out to save them, free them, and love them—each and every one of His beloved children.

God desires our children to know and love Him even more than we do.

But remember, the role of mom comes with incredible power to influence our children's hearts in profound ways by pouring Christlike love and grace upon them. And yes, we have the responsibility and privilege of passing the baton of faith, of leaving a legacy of faith for generations to come. We hold untouchable power to impact our children in lasting, meaningful ways. That truth is undeniable. It's why God places such value on the role of mother and of why it's a divine calling.

I want to encourage you to embrace your role as mom with the understanding and acceptance that you can't control your child's heart. Then and only then will you be freed from carrying unnecessary guilt and freed to accept what you *can* do, releasing the rest into the faithful arms of Jesus.

If your child walks away from the faith or if he or she is suffering or struggling from the realities of life, do not lose hope, my friend, for the divine compass in our hearts leading us home is the same one present in our children's hearts seeking to lead them home, whether they know it or not.

The divine compass in our hearts leading us home is the same one present in our children's hearts seeking to lead them home, whether they know it or not.

So instead of being discouraged and hopeless, be diligent in prayer—never underestimating its power over you and your children. Continue to be real and transparent about *your* need for Jesus. Even in their rebellion, commit to shepherding your children's hearts with God's love and grace. Admit your own weaknesses and imperfections, struggles and sufferings so your kids feel permission to do the same. Consistently feed them the Word of God—truths with power to penetrate the most delicate, hardened places of their hearts. Help them understand the rebellion in their hearts. Don't back down. Discipline with kindness and understanding. Continue to nurture an atmosphere in your home of forgiveness and acceptance. Persistently communicate that they are loved, accepted, and adored. And lastly, don't give up hoping that the foundation of faith you are building will be the truth to which they instinctively return.

I walked in the valley with my friend for several months as she chose to be faithful and trust her son to God's perfect care. Countless people prayed for this young man, never giving up hope that his heart would repent, and he'd recognize his sin and turn back to Jesus. I'll never forget the day she contacted me—overflowing with joy and gratitude—to tell me her son had apologized and turned away from his sin. Our prayers were answered. Although there was a great deal of restoration and healing yet to be done, he was now walking in the right direction. Praise God, for He is faithful!

Keeping in mind there is no guarantee, I know as long as we stay the course and continue to commit to protecting and strengthening our faith, the handoff will happen (although rarely within our timing), and there will be growth in the kingdom of God for generations to come—a resurgence of faithful followers of Jesus. Comparatively, the monarch butterfly has experienced a resurgence in population in recent months. Due to increased conservation efforts to protect the monarch in the last few years by the United States, Mexico, and Canada, the monarch butterfly population is finally beginning to slowly increase.[3] There's always hope. Always.

No matter what struggle or suffering your child may endure and no matter what heartache you may experience because of it, we can find strength, comfort, and hope through the faith and story of one mother who humbly surrendered her Son's future into the hands of God, trusting in His plans, purposes, and promises.

A MOMMA'S COURAGE AND TRUST

Imagine being told days after your child is born that many people will accept and love him, but many will hate and reject him. And then, imagine being warned the rejection your son will endure will cause you intense anguish and grief—like that of a sword piercing your soul.[4] The most famous mother in the Bible—Mary, the mother of Jesus—knows first-hand the agonizing heartache of relinquishing control to God's divine plan and watching her precious, first-born son suffer.

From the moment Jesus was conceived in Mary's womb, she'd known He was the Son of God and destined to reign over His kingdom. What she couldn't fully comprehend was what *exactly* that meant. All she knew for certain is she loved Him and God had important plans for His life. Therefore, she treasured all the prophesies she heard about her Son and pondered them in her heart.[5]

Regardless of the proclaimed plans for His life, He was her little boy. She raised Him, educated Him, and gave Him a home and family. Like any mother, she wanted the best for Him, and she loved Him with a mother's love.

Shortly into Jesus' ministry, He returned to His hometown of Nazareth to preach. Instead of being accepted, He was rejected and threatened with death. Scripture doesn't say Mary was there, but I can't imagine she'd miss seeing her Son speak. And I have no doubt she kept tabs on Him and learned of the growing hatred against Him. I wonder how many times Mary yearned to run to her Son's rescue ... to protect Him from the cruelty of others ... to shield Him from the enemy's attacks ... to prevent Him from enduring pain, rejection, and ridicule ... to pull Him off the cross. But she didn't.

Don't we all, instinctively, want to protect our kids from any and all harm? As mommas in love with our kids, we'll always do what we can for them. But we can't protect them from *every* temptation, hardship, or rejection. The sooner we accept our powerlessness, the sooner we will embrace a posture of peace and hope. Peace and hope will empower us to be courageous and trust in God's faithfulness, like Mary, and allow God to do His mighty work in the lives of our children—to turn their struggles and pain into great purpose and direction.

As moms, let's stand united, encouraging and supporting one another in this crazy adventure of motherhood. Together, let's remain faithful, praying and trusting that what we do within the exchange zone will inspire our children to unfurl and extend their own wings and to take flight and soar to the unimaginable heights God has planned for them. And let's continue to trust that with the baton of faith in their hands, the relay will not be broken, and our legacy of faith will live on.

A remarkable discovery I've recently had is that this passing of the baton of faith to our children is not only for their benefit, but it is also part of the refining process of *our* faith—a continual journey of becoming more and more like Christ. It is a process calling us back to a time of simplicity and innocence, a time of humility and sincerity. A process inspired by the belief that every choice we make and everything we do, matters. Not only for us, but for our children and families, and for generations to come.

Making it Matter

A few mornings a week for the past seven years—after sending my boys off to school—I'd belly-up to the kitchen counter at my parents' home with a hot cup of coffee in hand and countless things on my mind. I never imagined they would end up living so close and that we would have the daily privilege of sharing in even the most mundane and simple things in life. It's been one of the most treasured gifts of my life. Not only because I love hanging out with my parents and having them be an active part of our lives but also because I've had the priceless joy of witnessing their faith deepen and mature right before my eyes.

Every conversation, no matter the topic, some way or another always led us on some unexpected journey to heartfelt truth accompanied with tears of joy and hope. I can still picture Dad taking his white handkerchief from his back pocket and gently wiping the tears cascading from his eyes. My glistening eyes would meet my mom's with a glance that spoke a thousand words. We both saw what was happening. My dad didn't always feel this deeply, and he wasn't always this tender-hearted. He had never talked so vulnerably and honestly about his faith.

For years, my dad's physical body had been failing him, yet he endured and pushed through the pain and the struggle without complaint to make the most out of his life—to live whatever days he had left with purpose and love. My heart broke to witness a strong, confident, ambitious man grow physically weaker, year after year, week after week, day after day. But what I saw happen amid his physical struggle was nothing short of extraordinary. It's the last lesson Dad would ever teach me—a priceless lesson I'll cling to for the rest of my life. It wasn't a lesson he lectured. It was one he lived. And it's the one I want to leave you with as we end our time together.

Although my dad was physically growing older (like all of us), I had the precious gift of watching him *grow young*. That's right—grow young. And that's not all—my mom grew young right alongside him. I had a front-row seat to one of the greatest shows on earth—a show packed with love, hope, grace, joy, peace, and comfort. I witnessed first-hand my sweet parents grow closer and closer to Jesus together. My mom has always had a tender, sweet, gentle heart and demeanor, so the change happening in her was subtle. But the change happening in my dad was obvious to us. The closer he grew to Christ, the more childlike in awe of God he became, and he expressed this change with deep passion through countless conversations over coffee. He loved and trusted Christ with his whole heart. There was no reluctance, no hesitation, no fear of death. He had let go of the meaningless worry and stress that can so easily consume us. Courageously and humbly, he accepted the life he'd lived and the struggles that came with it.

The hearts of all believers are invited to release our adult tendencies to control and instead take on the innocence of a child. An innocence that strips us of our pride, independence, self-reliance and instead clothes us with the characteristics of Christ—humility, compassion, gentleness, and acceptance.

I saw the Lord open my dad's heart to a beautiful, eternal perspective that undoubtably brought him peace and comfort like never before. The more my dad came to realize and accept his mortality, the more intense his soul began to yearn for home—to be in the presence of his heavenly Father ... to, like a child, sit on his Father's lap and feel the comfort and security of God's love, peace, and joy.

By nature, children are trusting and eager, simple and sincere. They have an overwhelming capacity to love, accept, and forgive. They aren't yet preoccupied with the world and its distractions. This childlike demeanor I saw my dad grow into is the very heart posture Jesus emphasized to His disciples in Matthew 18:3–4 (TPT) and is the one He calls us to take as well.

> Learn this well: Unless you dramatically change your way of thinking and become teachable, and learn about heaven's kingdom realm with the wide-eyed wonder of a child, you will never be able to enter in. Whoever continually humbles himself to become like this gentle child is the greatest one in heaven's kingdom realm.

Death may not be knocking at our doors today, but our tomorrows on this earth are no guarantee. My dad's sudden death, my forty-one-year-old sister-in-law nearly dying of a heart attack, and her brother's wife—a young mom with two babies—being diagnosed with stage four colon cancer have all been recent reminders of how delicate and precious life is. Most of us rarely pause amid our crazy lives to consider the frailty of life. And although this life on earth is but a blink of an eye in comparison to what God promises us in eternity, what we do today and how we choose to live, grow, and share the faith matters. This truth moves me to share one last, very recent story.

Two weeks before I was ready to submit this book for publishing, I attended a conference where I experienced a profound encounter with God. I fought the urge to write about this because I thought my book was done. But I learned the Lord had one last message He wanted to emphasize and to ensure it was, indeed, received.

While visiting with a friend I had met at this same conference a year prior (one who has quickly become very dear) and sharing with her the premise of *this* book, she insisted I read a *different* book. To be honest, my first thought was, *Really? I don't have time to read a book right now because I'm working tirelessly to finish mine.* With a sweet, thoughtful yet somewhat intense demeanor, she kept insisting I buy this particular book. And then moments into our conversation I felt the urging I've talked about in previous chapters—the feeling in my gut telling me I should probably comply to her suggestion. It certainly helped when she told me it was a small, short picture book that could be read in one sitting. *Perfect*, I thought. Plus, we happened to be in a bookstore. It must have been my lucky day because there was one copy of the book left. But as you've come to know me by now, I didn't think this had anything to do with luck. I had a feeling God was behind this orchestration of events and stirrings.

I bought the book, put it in my bag, and forgot about it as the hustle of the conference took my full attention. That is until I was on my last flight home from the conference—a quick 45-minute trip—and I remembered this sweet, little book. Having no other work that seemed worth the hassle of getting out for this short flight, this moment was the *perfect* moment to read this book I was assured I could finish in one sitting.

The events leading up to this moment on the airplane are significant, and as I reflect on them now, they still take my breath away. If I had not gone to the conference—and there were many reasons why I was contemplating not going—not only would I have missed seeing amazing friends, meeting new, inspiring ones, and hearing valuable messages, but I also would have been robbed of some of the greatest words ever spoken to me, confirming the purpose and the vision God planted in my heart years ago.

The presence of God was undeniable as I experienced time and time again—over the course of those few days—God's truths declared over me, telling and reassuring me of His plans and purposes for my life—a purpose that had vividly flashed in my mind when I was researching the monarch butterfly for the first time years prior and one which had led me on this journey to speaking and writing. For years, my heart has wanted to share the messages of God's redeeming love and grace and the transformational work He's done in my life. I've been patient and obedient to every moment right in front of me, serving, teaching, seeking, and learning, yet often wondering when or if more would come. More impact. More influence. More speaking opportunities. More women. More moms.

The words God spoke to me through a few of His faithful sons and daughters confirmed that what I'm sharing with you in this book is crucial. Life-changing. They confirmed the readiness in my heart and God's call to me to continue to lead, encourage, equip, and empower a movement of moms willing and ready to rise up with unwavering faith, unshakable courage, and undeniable strength and band together to build up the *next generation* of Christ followers, *and the next, and the next*. I was told that before I got home, God would make it known to me, beyond a shadow of doubt, that this was indeed the role God needed me to play, the role He desperately needs us all to play.

So, here I was sitting on this little airplane reflecting on all that had occurred the past few days while sensing a warm closeness to heaven and holding *this* book.

The Butterfly Effect: How Your Life Matters by Andy Andrews.

The moment I started reading, I began to weep. Yes, a stranger was sitting next to me hearing my sniffles and sobs. But that didn't matter because what I was reading was the final message God promised He'd send me before I arrived home that had the power to shatter any lingering doubt or fear and to powerfully ignite a fire in my heart so mighty and confident—a fire that would propel and guide me on the mission He was calling me to lead.

While quickly turning page after page of this beautiful, profound little book, I discovered the butterfly effect is a proven principle that states the flap of a butterfly's wings can set into motion a rippling effect to be felt on the other side of the world. The same effect can be said for people. In other words, the simple, yet profound message is: Every single thing we do matters. The choices we make have a *butterfly* effect—a rippling effect—that has the power to have profound impact beyond our imaginations. And when I read the words scripted on page 107 only moments before I landed at home, the final shred of doubt to the role God needs me to play was destroyed and replaced with unwavering peace, purpose, and confidence.

> There are generations yet unborn whose very lives will be shifted and shaped by the moves you make and the actions you take today. And tomorrow. And the next day. And the next.[6]

Are you seeing what I'm seeing? Are you connecting the dots? Some would call this coincidental. But I operate in the belief system that this truly is God at work. I mean there I sat with an incomplete manuscript on my computer filled with God's word and truths about butterflies and *this* darling book with a butterfly on the cover whose message matches the one in this final chapter ends up in *my* hands? I had no choice but to listen and write these words in these pages. It's undeniable to me that God wanted me—wanted us—to hear this message loudly and clearly.

What we do with our life matters!

How we choose to mother matters!

God needs us to rise up and be leaders, daughters, princesses of the faith!

We hold incredible power as moms to build an army of believers!

We have the ability to impact generations upon generations and leave a lasting legacy of faith!

We get one life to live. How will you choose to live the rest of your days? For yourself or for God? Imprisoned or free in Jesus? I don't want to wait until life slows down or until certain things are in place or until I'm lying on my death bed to become more like Christ or to live empowered to use all that God has given me to make a difference in the world for Him. I don't want to sit on the sidelines watching everyone else live their lives, embrace their purpose, and make their dreams come true. I want to grow young daily—exactly like my mom and dad—and continue to embrace the wide-eyed wonder and humility of a child. I want to choose, today and every day, to become the woman God made me to be and live it out to the fullest for the sole purpose of glorifying God and building up His kingdom of believers.

So, join me, my dear friend, and choose to live freely and joyfully with divine purpose and intention. Unfurl your wings and soar with me—in your unique way—to heights known only to God. Let's not waste another moment of our lives being chained down by guilt, shame, inadequacies, failures, fears, or doubts. That's all been taken away by the blood of Christ and His extravagant, sacrificial love for us. God's eagerly waiting for us to let the chains fall so we can do what He made us to do—*soar*. It's time to rise as a sisterhood of believers who authentically and confidently live out and pass on faith to the next generation. Together we have the power to change the world. The time is now.

God's eagerly waiting for us to let the chains fall so we can do what He made us to do—soar.

Forever etched in my memory is the humble, peaceful, compassionate, childlike demeanor my Dad exemplified as I watched him run fiercely and confidently toward the finish line into the loving arms of His Savior. He played his part. He ran his race. He passed the baton. I have no doubt that when my dad stood at the entrance of those pearly gates, He heard the loving voice of God, "Welcome home, my son. Well done, my good and faithful servant. Well done."

What's astounding to me is how, even in his death, my dad's legacy of faith continues to empower and impact others. My dad was a beautiful example of a man who, in his weakness, found strength in Christ. His genuine, tender heart and depth of character and integrity propelled Him to deeply love and organically inspire and encourage many. The indisputable power and proof of the baton pass is still seen as my dad's spirit and heart live on through my mom, my brothers, me, his grandchildren, and the friends whose lives he touched. I will live the rest of my life inspired and empowered by my parent's example of faith to continue to pass on the legacy of faith. I pray you'll join me.

I hope you've found this journaling portion helpful. One last time, I invite you to share your heart in writing as you eagerly and confidently step out in faith and allow God to be your mighty transformer. How is your relay race going? Is the baton handoff to your children going smoothly? If so, make note below of why you think so. Or, are you fumbling the baton within the exchange zone? Has the baton been dropped? Have your children turned away from you? Fallen into temptation? If so, journal about the struggle and how you are coping. Are you holding on to guilt and blaming yourself?

If so, now is the time to release the burden to God. Share your heart with Him, and He will give you what you need to endure and continue the race. Are you ready to rise up to your calling as a mom and join the sisterhood of daughters ready to powerfully and positively impact the next generation? If so, write down how you will remain committed to doing so or the help you need to get there. No matter where you are in your journey of accepting grace, embracing your purpose, passing the baton of faith to your children, remain steadfast. Stay the course. And trust that God is yearning for each and every one of us to run fiercely across the finish line—like a child eager to see her father—into His tender, yet mighty, embrace.

_____

_____

_____

_____

_____

_____

_____

_____

_____

_____

_____

_____

_____

A Momma's Prayer

Dear God, thank You for the gift of motherhood and for opening our eyes to the significant responsibility, privilege, and joy we have of raising our kids in the faith and pointing them to You. Help us never underestimate the life-altering impact and influence we have on our children as we remain resilient and committed to passing the baton of faith to them. Thank You for our loved ones who have passed on the faith to us. Give us the strength and wisdom to continue the legacy and make a successful handoff. We're realistic and know the exchange is not always smooth. Our kids are facing ongoing threats that seek to turn them away from You. Although we so desperately want our kids to know and love You, Lord, we realize and accept we don't hold the power to transform their hearts. Only You do. Therefore, we pray for Your protection over our kids. We know You love them even more than we do, so we place our trust in You, Lord. And as we do, renew our hearts and release any burden or guilt we are tempted to carry. You are a trustworthy and faithful God, so we place our hearts and the hearts of our children into Your mighty, loving care. We pray, as we continue to be obedient to our divine calling, that You will ignite a spark of faith in the hearts of our children. A spark that will become a flame. And a flame that will grow and continue to ignite faith in others, passing on the legacy of faith for generations to come. In Jesus' name we pray, amen.

Meaningful Truth

Why would you ever complain, O Jacob, or, whine, Israel,
saying, "God has lost track of me. He doesn't care what
happens to me?" Don't you know anything? Haven't you been
listening? God doesn't come and go. God lasts. He's Creator
of all you can see or imagine. He doesn't get tired out, doesn't
pause to catch his breath. And he knows everything, inside
and out. He energizes those who get tired, gives fresh strength
to dropouts. For even young people tire and drop out, young
folk in their prime stumble and fall. But those who wait upon
God get fresh strength. They spread their wings and
soar like eagles, they run and don't get tired,
they walk and don't lag behind.

—Isaiah 40:27–31 (MSG)

Dear Friend,

YOU WERE MADE TO SOAR

*O*h, friend! I weep as I write knowing our time together, at least in this capacity, is coming to an end. If you haven't figured it out by now, I'm a bit of a crier. I feel deeply. These tears are a combination of my gratitude to you for choosing this book and taking the time to journey with me into God's truths, my awe of God's undeniable presence among us, and my gratefulness to God for being ever so faithful. These are also tears that deeply desire for you to claim and experience the freedom, joy, peace, and hope I've come to know and trust through our Lord and Savior, Jesus Christ.

Our time together has been spent learning who we are in Christ and how our identity in Him leads to deeper understanding of the divine nature of our role as mom. We've discovered that when we relinquish control to Him, walk in His truth, and accept the fullness of His grace, we are inspired and empowered to unfurl our wings, soar in the confidence of His love and grace, and pass on the legacy of faith to our children. This transformation of our hearts ignites a desire to embrace the divine responsibility given to us to extend Christ's extravagant love and grace to our children in ways that inspire them to take their own flight with Christ.

I don't know the current condition of your heart. Where are you in the process of accepting grace, releasing motherhood into the hands of God, and finding freedom and newfound purpose in His presence? Wherever you are in the journey toward transformation, I want to make sure you hear a few last things. If you are experiencing transformation like never before where God's truth is setting you free to live in the wonder and fullness of His grace, then I am praising God with you because only God can do that work in your heart. Take flight and soar, my friend.

On the other hand, I want you to know that if you are struggling to understand or grasp any of the truths I've shared, you're not alone, and the struggle doesn't mean you're destined for failure or your kids will be ruined. If you're unsure or doubtful about how precious you are to God and about how much He desires a relationship with you, the doubt you feel doesn't make you a bad mom. If you have anxiety about where you are as a mom or if you're not ready to let Him in, your uncertainty and anxiousness doesn't mean you love your kids any less than the next mom, and it certainly doesn't mean you are exempt from God's love.

Struggles, doubts, and fears mean you could use someone to talk with you. That's what friends are for—it's why God created community. Therefore, I encourage you to reach out to a Christian friend for support or reach out to our amazing and growing online sisterhood or to me, personally. By now,

I hope I feel like a friend to you. I'd love to hear from you and have the privilege of supporting you (see the back pages for ways we can connect). Above all, continue to seek Him and trust your transformation will come because God will never give up on you—He will be after your heart forever.

Because like me, God doesn't want you—any longer—to feel less-than. He doesn't want you to feel inadequate, alone, or discouraged. He doesn't want you to feel guilty, afraid, or anxious. He wants you to feel joy, peace, and freedom. But it's only through Him that you'll experience the fullness of the love and grace He offers.

Regardless of where you are in your walk with God, this truth remains.

You are the most powerful influencer in your child's life. *You.*

Therefore, you are the one with the ultimate opportunity to impact your children, including their faith life. Have no doubt your kids will reap the fruits produced from a momma's heart that's been changed and nurtured by the grace and love of God. However, in light of that truth, remember the outcome of their faith is not your burden to carry—a burden that's been taken away from you by the death and resurrection of Christ. We've been set free to lay our burdens down. God's after your children's hearts just like He's after yours. Trust that where you fail, God triumphs. He promises to use our weaknesses to display His power and presence.

God's in the business of transforming lives. He knows what He's created you to be. Will you let Him do His mighty work in you? When you surrender, like a caterpillar, into the protection and comfort of God's chrysalis, He will transform you into the beautiful butterfly He made you to be from the moment of your conception. And you will be empowered with the freedom and confidence to unfurl your wings, take flight, soar with joy into the beauty of your divine purpose, and pass the baton of faith to your children.

In the Gospel of John, Jesus spoke these simple yet precious words, "And you will know the truth, and the truth will set you free."[1]

Please know I'm praying for you. I am praying that the truth of God has set you free to soar in the wonder, joy, and peace of God's abundant, unconditional grace and love. I am praying God surrounds you with a community of faithful, courageous women seeking to live authentic lives anchored in Christ—women you can be real and honest with about the ups and downs of being a woman, wife, and mother. I'm praying you are inspired to extend love and grace to others, especially your children, and to be an example to other women of what it looks like to live centered in Christ and covered in His grace. I'm praying you'll join me so together we can rise as a sisterhood of believers empowered by God to impact generations and generations to come.

So, before we say good-bye, I'd love to pray one last time with you.

Gracious God,

You are magnificent. You are the source of our heart's longings. In You, we find everything we need to live our lives freely, joyfully, and purposefully. You are compassionate, forgiving, kind, and faithful. Thank You, Lord, for my friend and for the precious time we got to spend together. I pray she feels Your mighty presence and is moved to seek You and accept Your love and grace. We are grateful to be Your daughters and to call You our God. We are grateful to be mothers and to nurture Your children. Continue to transform our hearts so we progressively grow into the women You've conceived us to be and so that we remain steadfast and faithful to You and to the roles You've called us to play, especially the role of mother. Help us release any guilt tempting to tear us down and remember we don't have to be enough for our kids because You are. There's no need for perfection because the perfection of Christ has covered us. Help us trust that Your power is made perfect in our weakness. Help us to make You known to our children and establish Your grace and love as the foundation upon which our homes are built. Make us Your instruments of extravagant love and grace as we rely on the power of Your Holy Spirit to produce the fruits of the spirit in our own lives and the lives of our children. Help us mother with joy instead of anger, peace instead of chaos, humility instead of pride, faith instead of fear, connection instead of control. In everything we do, help us point our kids to You, the author and perfecter of our faith. Help us pass the baton of faith and nurture in the hearts of our children a love for You—one anchored in Your love for them. Thank You for Your love, Your grace, and Your never-ending presence in our lives. We love You. In Jesus' precious and powerful name, amen.

In closing, I'd like to leave you with the words my seven-year-old son, Parker, so boldly proclaimed to me the other day, in a moment of my human weakness.

"Mom, it's okay. We all need Jesus."

Oh, how right he is. There's nothing quite like truths spoken from the hearts of our kids to wake us up and get us back on track.

If anything, I pray, despite all the words and stories you've read here, the message you tuck away in your heart is this: "We all need Jesus."

Because that message alone is all you need to get started on your journey to transforming your heart, unfurling your wings, and soaring to the heights God's uniquely planned, especially for you. Thank you for allowing me to be a small part of the story God's writing in your life. I'll see you in the sky, my friend.

Breathe peace,

Natalie

Acknowledgments

Reflecting on the steps—both the expected and the unexpected—that have led me to this moment, my heart is flooded with humble gratitude to those who have walked along side me in this journey. Your love, encouragement, and support have helped make this book—my dream—a reality.

To my husband. It's my life's joy and privilege to be your wife, Darin Hanson, and to be raising our boys together. Your gentle faith, compassion, selflessness, sense of humor, integrity, kindness, courage, humility, tender hugs, and fatherly heart overwhelms me with joy and gratitude. Our boys are so fortunate to have you as such an extraordinary example of a loving man of God. This book is possible because of you. Your unwavering belief in me and my dreams wows me. We both know there were times when you believed in this book for the both of us. I have no doubt God used you—your faith in me and in what you witnessed Him do in my heart—to be His instrument of ceaseless support and encouragement to me as I followed this calling. You saw, first-hand, the ups and downs of this journey and loved me through it all, never once questioning the dream on my heart. When doubt or fear tempted to pull me off course, your matter-of-fact sensibility confidently renewed my focus. I know how much you have sacrificed for me and continue to sacrifice for me so that I can passionately follow this calling to write and speak. You are a huge piece to this work God has called me to do. We are in this together. I'm forever grateful, my love. I love you with my whole heart.

To my precious boys, Peyton, Samuel, Cooper, and Parker. Your patience as I poured my heart into this book day after day and your excitement for me to finish it, amazes me. I have no doubt God was working in your hearts to help make this book a reality. I'm forever grateful for your unconditional support and love. The greatest delight and honor of my life is being your mom. I love nothing more than doing life with you and your dad—I love the big moments and the little moments. I love playing dodgeball in the basement; bean bag toss in the foyer; boating and tubing on the lake; snuggling on the couch for movie night; playing baseball, basketball, and football in the yard; cheering you on in your activities; having deep conversations at bedtime; and praying and blessing you each and every day and night. Being the mom I dreamed of being for you turned out to be so much harder than I ever thought. As you know, I don't do this mothering thing perfectly and am daily in need of forgiveness and grace. But I'm so grateful God is at the center of our lives together. That He, alone, is using our imperfections to show us and teach us more and more about His magnificent grace for us all. I adore the young men you are and absolutely love the ones you are becoming—the ones God created you to be. I love having front row seats to the beautiful script God is writing in each of your lives. My sweet boys, always know how much I love you and how much I treasure the incredible gift of being your mom.

To my parents, Royal and Pam Lyson. So much of who I am today is because of you. Not only did you provide me an extraordinary example of what it means to have a loving, Christ-centered marriage, but also as an extension of that love gave me the most priceless gift by raising me in a loving home where faith was central. Your joy and belief in the work God has called me to do and your endless support and encouragement inspires me to trust and pursue this dream. Dad, you believed in this book before I did. As much as it aches my heart you aren't here in person to see this dream fulfilled, I feel you in spirit and know it brings you overwhelming joy and delight to watch me be obedient to God's calling. And Mom, my dear mom—you are my best friend. You are a pillar of strength and faith. Your love for Christ and the peace He brings you is seen in everything you do. Your faith inspires me. No one understands my heart quite like you. I can't thank you enough for supporting me through the tears and triumphs of this journey and for encouraging me every step of the way. It's my heart's joy to share this moment with you. I love you both so much.

To my mother-in-law, Darla Hanson. You have supported me and the work God has called me to do in more ways than I can describe. From watching the boys to running errands, from running kids to activities to bringing us food, you blessed us and helped us get through this long writing journey. You are thoughtful and selfless, gracious and considerate. Thank you for believing in me and for being so supportive and loving. And thank you for raising such a remarkable son and for bringing him up in the faith. It's truly the greatest gift. I love you dearly.

To my faithful, steadfast friend, Leanne Elmer. No doubt our friendship was God-ordained. I'm forever grateful our hubbies brought us together. I don't think they had any clue how we'd so quickly become family. In my heart, I call you sister. From the first moment I shared with you my aches and pains of motherhood to my dreams of speaking and writing, you loved on me and believed in me. Thank you for your countless, faithful prayers and for your ceaseless support and belief in what God has called me to do. Thank you for always reminding me that we have an audience of One. You are humble and hilarious, witty and wise, thoughtful and loyal, and gracious and kind. You bring my life so much sweet joy. I love you for who you are and for always inspiring me to spread my wings and soar.

To my dear friend, Chelsey Anderson. Your friendship blesses me daily. What a beautiful surprise God had in store for us when He moved you to the neighborhood forging a sweet friendship between our families. Thank you for the many times you offered to take my boys so I could write. Thank you for always, always asking about the book and for understanding and valuing its importance to me. You know how difficult this year has been on me, and your encouragement, support, and humor has lifted my spirits on countless occasions. You have one of the most selfless, giving, gracious hearts, and I am so blessed to be a recipient of your friendship. You know how dear you are to me. I love you, Chels.

To my amazing friends, Nicole Kjesbo, Shelli Allen, Stacy Swenson, and Mindy Beyer. Your vulnerability, authenticity, and endearing spirits inspire me to write—to share the messages God's scripting in my heart. You challenge me to keep seeking God's wisdom. You are the definition of friends. You show up when I need you. You never judge, only love. And you support me with your whole hearts. Thank you for being you and for loving me through the toughest year of my life. I love you girls.

To my dear friends Jen Heydt, Sara Oldenkamp, and Lori Hochhalter. When we met twelve years ago, who would have thought you'd play such a pivotal role in directing me to the purpose and path God was calling me to pursue? Our marathon will forever be one of the top experiences of my life because it was through the marathon God took hold of my heart in a whole new way. Thank you, from the bottom of my heart, for the laughter and the tears, for the runs and the wine nights, and for allowing me to share our story. I cherish our friendship and love you dearly.

To my besties from high school, Sarah Jordan, Mandi Green, and Melissa MacPhail. You are home to me. You are the rare few who have known me for most of my life—really known me. Although life doesn't allow us to be together much, I know in my heart I can always count on you and that you are always, always rooting for me. No matter what. Thank you for always loving me for who I am and for believing in the work God has called me to do. I love you, girls.

To my dear friend, Julie Loken. You believed in me from the moment I began sharing with you the incredible work God was doing in my heart. God has gifted you with the unique ability to exude positivity, joy, and enthusiasm into the world in a way that makes everyone who knows you feel so loved and so special. I'm so blessed to be a recipient of your love, support, and encouragement. The way you go to work for me on behalf of what you see God doing in my life amazes and humbles me. You are one of my biggest cheerleaders, and I'm so grateful for you. Thank you for your faithful prayers and for trusting me with your prayer requests. I treasure our sweet friendship. I love you.

To my beta readers, proofreaders, prayer team, editors, endorsers, and countless friends. To Kaare Risbrudt, Chelsey Anderson, Stacy Swenson, Pam Lyson, Darla Hanson, Stephanie Sutton, Mareen Biss, Charlene Blume, Chelsie Tatge, Shelli Allen, Niccie Kleigl, Daphne V. Smith, Katie Christensen, Heather Godfrey, Renee Vidor, Pastor Jean Ohman, Lanelle Vasicheck, and Lisa Moser. You have each contributed to this book in profound, lasting ways that has most certainly enhanced its content. I can't thank you enough for graciously offering your time, commitment, wisdom, prayers, and encouragement. You are so special to me. I love you.

To the lovely and generous, Miss Susan Snyder. What a remarkable gift you have been to me and to this book. After graduating from your English class as a senior in high school twenty plus years ago, I'm amazed at how God so sweetly allowed us to cross paths once again. The wisdom, knowledge, insight, and feedback you so willingly provided was invaluable. The sensitivity, love, and respect you gave this message means the world to me. Thank you for believing in me then and for believing in me now. You are so dear to my heart, and I'm so grateful to be reconnected.

To my readers, my friends. You've been on my heart for years, and are in my constant prayers. Is it weird I feel like I know you? We are sisters, after all. I hope you sense the same sweet connection I do as we walk together as daughters of the King. I can't thank you enough for journeying with me through the pages of this book. It's been my heart's delight to share my story with you and to invite you into the story God is so beautifully writing in yours. May you be daily inspired by Him to continually move closer and closer to the purpose He needs you to fulfill. And perhaps one day, we will meet in person. Wouldn't that be something. Until then, breathe peace, my dear friends.

And lastly, to Jesus. My sweet Jesus. I'm eternally grateful to know You. I would be nothing without You. You are my anchor and my hope. You are constant and everlasting. I'm so grateful for the wonder of your indescribable love and grace and the miracle You have done in my life. May I never lose the awe of who You are. May I never stop soaring for You. May this book be my heart's love song to you, Lord, and may it be a vessel to lead other mommas to the joy, peace, freedom, and purpose You so freely give. You are my everything, and I love you with my whole heart.

About the Author

Natalie Dawn Hanson has a heart for mommas, especially those whose joy, delight, and wonder in this most important role have been overshadowed by the unexpected and surmounting demands and challenges that come with motherhood. She aches for them because she was one of them. Now, as a speaker, author, and coach who by the magnificent grace of God reclaimed motherhood and it's joy, Natalie vulnerably shares her story of transformation in hopes to encourage, equip, and empower other women to passionately seek God so they can claim freedom, embrace unshakable joy, and renew their divine purpose as a precious daughter of the Most High God.

In addition, through the wisdom of great mentors and Jesus, the greatest teacher who ever lived, Natalie has a passion to equip moms with Christ-centered, practical, and applicable skills and strategies not only to confidently connect with and correct their children but also to passionately and organically pass on the baton of faith. As an advanced trainer in the Nurtured Heart Approach® and owner of Breathe Peace

Consulting, Natalie trains and coaches parents, counselors, teachers, and anyone who does life with kids on how to love them with big, bold, Christ-like love.

Natalie loves connecting with people. She leads a community of women in online Bible studies, speaks at schools, churches, women's retreats and conferences, and has been known to guest preach on Sunday mornings. Apart from being wife and mom, sharing the messages on her heart with others is when she feels most alive and most in tune with who God created her to be. Natalie is committed to her calling to lead a movement of moms so in love with Jesus they can't help but pass the faith on to the next generation of believers. It is truly her life's joy and humble privilege to share Him with others.

To those who do life with her, Natalie is simply a chauffeuring mom who loves and relies on Jesus (and coffee, nutritional food, and exercise) to get her through the crazy adventure of motherhood. Natalie adores friends and good conversation, is committed to her family, involved in church and school, and struggles like we all do to manage a household daily requiring cooking, cleaning, and oh so much laundry. But at the end of a long day, she is no longer crying herself to sleep, but instead, she's hopeful and grateful for this beautiful, yet messy thing we call life.

Natalie lives on one of Minnesota's beautiful lakes and is a wife to a farmer—her hubby, Darin, who she's still wildly in love with—and momma to four lively, lovely boys who teach her more about extravagant love and grace every day. It's in the loud, crazy and quiet, calm moments at home where her most important ministry happens.

Natalie would love to connect with you and hear your story. In a perfect world, you'd be sitting together on her front porch—one of her most favorite places—drinking coffee (or sipping on a glass of wine) and chatting the day away. Because that's not possible, at least for today, Natalie's grateful for the opportunities and means to connect no matter where you live. Feel free to reach out to her today.

Website: www.NatalieDawnHanson.com
Email: natalie@nataliedawnhanson.com
Facebook: @nataliedawnhanson
Instagram: nataliedawnhanson

Grace-Giving Quick Guide

*G*iving and exemplifying grace to our children and being transparent in our own imperfections, which allows them to offer grace in return are the most organic ways we can live the faith and pass it on to our children. Once we embrace that our newfound purpose and role as mom is to lead our kids to Christ and have the Holy Spirit as our compass guiding us in truth, we naturally begin to embody grace which enables us to execute our purpose of passing on the faith and responding to life, our kids, our husbands, and others in ways that express extravagant love, ignite their hearts, build them up, and expose their innate greatness and worth.

To help you in those high-intense moments when the rebellion in your heart wants to take charge and you don't have time to page through the book but simply need a quick reminder, I've created the *Grace-Giving Quick-Guide* as your go-to tool for those tough moments.

But let me remind you, when you mess up and do or say something you wish you hadn't (because you will), it's okay. You are human too. The grace of God covers you and forgives you, so give yourself grace and don't hold on to any guilt threatening to tear you down. Remember, those not-so-great moments of ours are also valuable opportunities to demonstrate faith—*our* desperate need for Christ.

TO GIVE GRACE, YOU NEED TO RESET FIRST. HERE'S HOW:

✦ PAUSE YOUR ANGER. When you feel you're about to explode, STOP. Don't say anything or do anything. Take a break. If you have to, walk away.

✦ BREATHE—Take several deep breaths. In through the nose, out through the mouth.

✦ PRAY—While you're taking deep breaths, pray for the Holy Spirit to fill you with patience and self-control and give you the confidence and courage to give grace.

✦ VISUALIZE THE CROSS BETWEEN YOU AND YOUR CHILD—Imagine how Jesus would respond and focus on the following:

- We are both sinners in need of a Savior.

- I am the boss of the narrative.

- My child's behavior is not a result of my parenting. He/she has rebellion in his/her heart.

- This behavior is a gift—my opportunity to love like Christ.

WHEN RESET, CONNECT AND ACTIVATE GREATNESS
BEFORE CORRECTING
HERE'S HOW:

✦ DO NOT ENERGIZE NEGATIVITY. Do not focus on or criticize the negative behavior that just occurred or is still occurring. Don't ignore. Instead, be actively patient.

✦ INVITE THEM TO RESET/COOL DOWN. Do not engage until they are at a more neutral emotional level. For example, say:

- "Reset."

- "I need you to cool down."

- "I'm going to give you time to reset."

✦ ENERGIZE SUCCESS. When your child is calm enough for you to talk, acknowledge, appreciate, and recognize the success you see in the current moment. Remember, there is always something going right, even if everything seems like it's going wrong. For example, say:

- "I love how you are no longer screaming. That shows so much self-control and power."

- "Even though you are mad about doing your chores, I see you are doing them anyway. You are showing outstanding maturity and responsibility. You could choose not to do them. But by choosing to do them, you are showing me so much respect. Thank you. Your ability to do something you don't want to do but you know you should do, shows grit, resilience, and incredible consideration and kindness. I'm so proud of you."

- "I know how hard it is for you to get up in the morning to make the bus, especially because you don't like riding the bus. But I notice you are no longer crying or yelling. You got up and ready and are now getting on the bus. You have amazing courage."

✦ CORRECT AND RESTORE. Once you have recognized your child for the success he/she has displayed by choosing to no longer engage in negative behavior, you are now ready to offer more guidance and teaching and invite restoration, if necessary. For example:

- "Now that you're reset, is there anything you feel you want to say to your brother?" (Never force kids to apologize. The Holy Spirit will be working on their heart and they will feel remorse on their own, even if they don't communicate it right away. It's good to invite them to mend hurt when they are ready.)

- "How do you feel now? How were you feeling earlier? Why do you think you were feeling that way? What are some things you could do to help calm down when you get angry?"

✦ ENGAGE FAITH. Acknowledge how you see the fruits of the Holy Spirit working in your child's heart—self-control, patience, kindness, gentleness, etc. Help your child build a solid foundation of faith by opening Scripture and discovering what God says about their behavior and choices. For example:

- If there are recurring behaviors, choices, or feelings your kids are struggling with, such as anger, go to Scripture and find out what God says about it. For a scripture reference guide, go to madetosoarbook. com and download this helpful resource today. It's best to read Scripture and have these discussions when the behaviors aren't occurring so that in moments of conflict you have wisdom to reference.

- Pray with and for your child.

Download your convenient, printable *Grace-Giving Quick Guide* at MadeToSoarBook.com.

Building a Deep Relationship with God

Knowing God and *knowing God* are very different things. I knew God my whole life and was certainly impacted by Him in amazing ways growing up. However, I didn't really get to *know God* and experience His abundant, transforming grace until I made the choice to really get to *know Him*. If you are eager to build a deeper relationship with God—one rooted in grace, love, peace, and hope—it's absolutely within your reach. Getting to *know God* requires awareness, desire, daily commitment, discipline, and intention. If this idea is new to you, I've provided you some tips below on how you can get started. It's sure to be an exciting journey, my friend, one that will inspire you to soar to heights beyond your wildest dreams.

Mindset Shift

✦ Know and trust God is constantly speaking to you. He doesn't choose a select few to communicate with and make His presence known. He attempts, every day, to connect with every single one of His beloved children. The difference is … who is paying attention.

✦ Be attentive. Actively look for God working in your life. Silence the distractions. Open your eyes and ears and expect God to speak. He communicates in more ways than we can imagine—through His Word, others, nature, prayer, to name a few.

Dedicate Time

✦ Decide when you want to spend intentional time with God. For me, I love waking up with God, so I spend my early mornings with Him before the rest of my family awakes. But for you, it may be different. Maybe it's during your lunch hour or before bed. It doesn't matter when; it simply matters that you make time.

✦ Change your habits.

- Instead of spending time on Facebook or iPhone apps and games, spend that time with God.

- If you watch TV every night before bed, commit to having alone time with God before you sit on the couch.

+ If it's difficult to carve dedicated time, start by defining the habits you already have and adding God-time to them. For example:

  • If you brew coffee every morning, have your Bible by the coffee maker and read some Scripture while your coffee brews.

  • Have a Bible in the bathroom—it's a given you'll be in there a time or two throughout the day.

  • Carry a Bible in your purse or have one in your car that you can read when you're waiting for your child to get done with practice.

  • Listen to an audio version of the Bible while driving.

Open Your Bible

+ If you don't have a Bible, you need to get one. There are several translations, but I'd recommend starting with a translation containing modern, easy-to-understand language or one containing helpful commentary and devotions throughout the pages, such as *The Message* or *The New International Version* Life Application Study Bible, or *The New Living Translation*. However, it's really a personal preference.

Begin Reading

+ This is the part which often intimidates new readers of the Bible. I suggest beginning with the Gospels in the New Testament—Matthew, Mark, Luke, and John. I'd wait to start in Genesis with, "In the beginning…" The Old Testament books are rich with incredible wisdom and stories of faith; however, they can be difficult to get through as a new studier of Scripture.

✦ Or I suggest to begin your reading with a few of the shorter books of the New Testament filled with God's messages of grace and love such as Galations, Ephesians, Philippians, and Colossians. (These books are fully highlighted in my personal Bible.)

✦ Don't overwhelm yourself. The Bible is jam-packed with amazing truths, so I suggest reading small sections at a time.

✦ If the Bible intimidates you, seek the wisdom of experienced authors and teachers of the faith to help you get started. The first book that jump-started my faith was Lysa Terkeurst's, *Becoming More Than a Good Bible Study Girl*. Lysa shows readers how to dive into the Word of God and teaches them to search God's truths for answers to their soul's longings. With her guidance, I did. And eventually, I found the confidence to read and study the Word of God on my own.

HOW TO READ AND STUDY SCRIPTURE

✦ Every book of the Bible is divided into sections. Choose a book of the Bible to study and then work through that book section by section.

✦ Buy a journal you specifically write in for your Bible studies. Date each study, write the Scripture you're studying, and then do the following.

✦ Once you read a section, I encourage you to do the following in an effort to bring Scripture alive and see how it applies to your life:

- **Read it again.** This time read with a heart eager to understand what the Lord is trying to tell you in this moment.

- **Write the Scripture.** In your journal, write the section of Scripture you are studying that day, word for word. There is something powerful about writing Scripture that helps connect the mind and the heart.

- **Define the key message.** In your own words, journal what you think this Scripture means. Read the commentary available in many Bibles to help guide your understanding.

- **Investigate the message**: Spend time determining what this Scripture is trying to teach you. Is there a promise God wants you to accept? Is there a sin God highlights and encourages you to avoid? Is there a command God desires for you to follow? Is there something completely new God has taught you about Him, His ways, and His love?

- **Recognize which verse spoke to you the most.** In your journal, copy your favorite verse from this section of Scripture and explain why this verse touched you this day.

- **Articulate what this verse means to you.** In your own words, journal what this one verse means to you.

- **Apply this message to your life.** Answer these questions honestly in your journal. How does this truth impact you today? Does it inspire you to change the way you live your life? If you were to embody this truth right now, what would be the benefits? How would practicing this truth make a difference in your life?

SHARE YOUR HEART WITH GOD

✦ Pray to God and listen for His response. Invite the Holy Spirit to speak to you and guide your prayers.

✦ The most helpful habit for me was journaling my prayers. I'd read my Scripture for the day, and then I'd write my heart to God. I would communicate what I thought His Word was telling me through the whispered promptings I'd hear in my mind, ask for His guidance to apply those truths to my life, share my heart cries and struggles, thank Him, and then ask for Him to open my eyes to His presence and glorious goodness around me.

FIND A SISTER OF THE FAITH—AN ACCOUNTABILITY PARTNER

✦ Invite a supportive, encouraging friend to be your accountability partner in this journey to growing deeper in faith. Someone who you can text, email, or call every day or week to share stories on what God is teaching you and how your faith is changing and growing. (If you're interested, I'd love to be for you to join my online Bible study as we, together, dive deeper into God's Word utilizing all of these steps. To learn more, go to www.MadeToSoarBook.com.)

✦ Join a Bible study in your local church.

✦ Connect with me via Facebook, @nataliedawnhanson or via email at natalie@nataliedawnhanson.com

✦ Join our online sisterhood of women on Facebook devoted to seeking God, living our lives for Him, and soaring with amazing purpose.

If you have the desire to *know God* and you remain committed, intentional, and disciplined in building a relationship with Him, you will reap the fruit of a heart nurtured by God.

THE REWARDS OF SPENDING TIME WITH GOD—THE 6 Ps

1) **Peace**—unexplainable peace, which exceeds anything we can understand. It will overwhelm your heart as you get to know God and you will experience less worry, stress, and anxiety. (Philippians 4:6–7)

2) **Power**—the Holy Spirit's power that lives in us through faith in Christ. It will fan the flame of your heart and inspire you to live your life for Him. (Ephesians 1:17–20)

3) **Purpose**—the why of your life. You will discover the divine race God has uniquely created you to run. (Ephesians 2:10)

4) **Perspective**—how you see life. You will begin to see life and others through the gracious, loving eyes of God. (Ephesians 5:1–2)

5) **Progress**—the act of moving forward. You will begin to recognize God's will for your life and how you are no longer standing still, but making progress forward for God's glory. (Romans 12:2)

6) **imPact**—a direct and positive effect. You will be empowered to have meaningful, intentional influence on others and make a remarkable difference in the world for the sake of God's kingdom. (Philippians 2:1–4)

Download your convenient, printable *Building a Deep Relationship with God* resource at MadeToSoarBook.com.

Truths I Want You to Remember

Chapter 1: The Unexpected Dream

+ Amid our murky, presumably failed dream, God is working to clarify and fulfill His dream for our lives.
+ God will transform our heartache and confusion into purposefully lighted pathways, guiding us toward our divine purpose.

Chapter 2: The Rise of Self-Reliance

+ The deceit we cling to today becomes the lies we drown in tomorrow.
+ The pressure to be perfect can be transformed from a debilitating stronghold into a life-giving spring of hope and purpose that can propel us from striving and surviving to thriving and living.

✦ Seeking perfection in the world robs our joy, but seeking our potential through Christ produces joy.

Chapter 3: The Hushed Fall of Joy

✦ God makes His presence known. We simply need to open our eyes and be attentive to Him so we don't miss out on the magnificent displays of His love.

✦ Jesus is the remedy to our heart condition—the cure that mends our weary, wounded souls.

✦ The void you're feeling was meant to be and can only be filled by God.

Chapter 4: The Battle with Identity

✦ What the enemy wants to use to destroy us, God uses as a compass to lead us to Him—the only place we'll discover our true identity.

✦ Our worth does not balance on what we've done nor on what others think but on who Jesus is, what He's done, and who we are through Him.

✦ Our identity in Christ inspires us to mother in a way that brings glory to God and points our kids directly to Him.

✦ Jesus sees you in the beauty and perfection in which you were first created.

Chapter 5: The Invitation of a Lifetime

✦ Saying "yes" to Jesus means we are ready to strip me from me and replace me with Him.

✦ It's in our selfless surrender to God where the metamorphosis of our souls begins to take place.

✦ God can finally do the work He so desperately wants to do in you when you say, "Yes, Jesus. Yes."

Chapter 6: The Conversion of the Heart

✦ All of my attempts at being the perfect Christian mom and at raising good, godly kids left me feeling overwhelmed, discouraged, frustrated, and lost because I hadn't fully received the gift of grace for myself.

✦ To extend grace to others, we must first give grace to ourselves by accepting the grace God fully offers.

✦ The only way to an intimate relationship with Jesus— one rooted in His grace—and to discover your divine purpose is through His Word and prayer.

✦ To fully emerge as the beautiful butterflies God created us to be, we need to release the insecurities that limit our potential and take intentional action to know Him so we can grow in the knowledge and wisdom of who He is and who He says we are.

✦ God's faithful Word and the power for life-change it carries becomes the antidote to our aching hearts.

✦ God is waiting in the chambers of your heart for you to notice Him, seek Him, and get to know Him. There is no perfect time, no special formula, no detailed instructions on how it goes. There is simply your moment etched in His perfect timing.

CHAPTER 7: THE LIES AND STRUGGLES THAT HOLD YOU HOSTAGE

✦ Wrestling with God—drawing near to Him with the doubts, frustrations, shame, fears—is our best weapon against the enemy.

✦ God's Word is like a sword that can penetrate our thoughts, helping us discern the lies from His truths.

✦ The struggles we endure are imperative to our survival and are necessary in guiding us to recognize our true identity and rely fully on God.

✦ Struggle and suffering are powerful vehicles with the capability to move us toward reaching the potential God sees in us.

CHAPTER 8: THE POWER OF HIS PRESENCE

✦ There will be times in life when we break, but that doesn't mean we are broken.

✦ I am an imperfect human in dire need of God's perfect grace that gives strength to my every weakness.

✦ God will take our hearts that break and our aches that paralyze—He will take our falls, our stumbles, our moments of sinking in the waves—and He will nurture growth and wisdom within our souls.

Chapter 9: The Courageous Take-off

+ The role of mom is a divine, God-ordained calling whose primary purpose is to point her children to God.

+ The ability to love—without conditions—is a divine gift inserted into the masterful design of our DNA.

+ Instilling faith in our children becomes a dance of doing our part and trusting and allowing God to do His part in capturing and molding their hearts.

+ When we have ready hearts that absorb the redeeming truths of God's love and grace, we are prepared to take flight with newfound purpose.

Chapter 10: The Unselfish Choice

+ The gift of being a mother was never meant to be at the expense of robbing us of vital necessities that help us reach the wholeness God has for us.

+ It's not two commands but three Jesus gives. Love God. Love others. Love ourselves. That's right … love ourselves.

+ It's at the intersection of our attentive surrender and God's presence where growth happens.

+ Distractions interfere in our relationship with Jesus and stunt our growth to a more complete life.

✦ When we choose to focus on ourselves and what we need to be our best selves, our precious loved ones reap the benefits.

Chapter 11: The Innate Gift

✦ Love is woven into the foundational chains of our DNA, and it's the very thing which inspires us to parent our kids the way God desires and which feels right with our souls.

✦ The certainty of God's love does not rest on the ability of what we can do but on the reality of whose we are.

✦ It's not a question if love is enough. It's a question of whether we know how to tap into our source of love that combats our rebellion and empowers our ability to love.

✦ A Christ-centered mindset is the overflow of Christ's love from your heart into the hearts of others.

✦ The burdens of your past require healing.

✦ You and your children are both sinners in need of a savior.

✦ You are boss of the narrative.

✦ Blame is not ours to bear.

✦ Behavior is a gift—a priceless opportunity to instill faith-centered values.

✦ Building desires in the heart of your children is God's job.

+ Aim to connect before you correct.

+ Admit your own flaws.

+ Apply grace instead of shame.

+ Activate greatness.

+ Adhere to prayer.

+ Affirm routines and traditions.

Chapter 12: The Personal, Yet Connected Race

+ Tragedy happens when we try to be either someone we aren't or neglect to be the person we are.

+ Although we run on the same road, we are called to run different races. And although we run different races, we are called to run united.

+ We're part of a community of faithful daughters—a blended legacy of multiple generations—each being uniquely molded and refined by the gracious hand of God for His glory and His purposes.

+ God hopes for us to live this way—to use our unique gifts in combined efforts to be His love in the world.

Chapter 13: The Baton of Faith

+ Our exchange zone—the years we have at home raising our children—is our priceless opportunity to pass on the baton of faith.

+ Our divine role of mom must be viewed in light of God's sovereignty, grace, and love so we don't take on the responsibility of carrying a burden that is not meant for us to carry.

✦ Only the power of the Holy Spirit can awaken our children to their need for Christ.

✦ God desires our children to know and love Him even more than we do.

✦ The divine compass in our hearts leading us home is the same one present in our children's hearts seeking to lead them home, whether they know it or not.

✦ God's eagerly waiting for us to let the chains fall so we can do what He made us to do—soar.

Download your convenient, printable *Truths I Want You to Remember* at MadeToSoarBook.com.

Blessings to Pray Over Your Children

W e all need reminders of who we are in Christ and of how much we are dearly loved. Blessing our children daily not only reminds them of how precious, loved, and known they are by God, but the intention of beginning and ending our days focused on Christ—the giver of life—demonstrates to them where to place their hope, their trust, their faith, especially as they grow and discover hard realities of life.

Simply place your hand upon your child's head, shoulder, or back and pray one of these blessings over him or her. It doesn't matter how old your children are or if you've never done this before. Once you begin, the blessings will become special moments your children will look forward to sharing with you. These moments will become gifts you both cherish. My heart jumps for joy every night when my teenage son says goodnight and leans his head into my hand, signaling he's ready for the blessing. Or when another son says, "Mom, don't forget to bless me." Or when one of my sweet boys is moved to bless me in return. Blessing our kids is simple. Quick. Yet priceless. Don't miss this precious opportunity to connect and share the faith. Below are some blessings taken directly from Scripture to pray over your children.

✦ May the Lord bless you and keep you, [insert child's name]. May the Lord's face shine upon you and be gracious to you. May the Lord look upon you with favor and grant you peace. In the name of the Father and of the Son and of the Holy Spirit. (Numbers 6:24–26)

✦ [Insert child's name], I pray that Christ may live in your heart by faith. I pray that you will be filled with love. I pray that you will be able to understand how wide and how long and how high and how deep His love is. I pray that you will know the love of Christ. His love goes beyond anything we can understand. I pray that you will be filled with God Himself. (Ephesians 3:17–19, NLV)

✦ I have never stopped thanking God for you, [insert child's name]. I pray for you constantly, asking God, the glorious Father of our Lord Jesus Christ, to give you, [insert child's name], wisdom to see clearly and really understand who Christ is and all that he has done for you. I pray that your heart will be flooded with light so that you can see something of the future he has called you to share. I want you to realize that God has been made rich because we who are Christ's have been given to Him! I pray that you will begin to understand how incredibly great his power is to help those who believe Him. (Ephesians 1:16–19, TLB)

✦ Every time I think of you, [insert child's name], I give thanks to my God. And I am certain that God, who began the good work within you, will continue his work until it is finally finished on the day when Christ Jesus returns. I pray that your love, [insert child's name], will overflow more and more, and that you will keep on growing in knowledge and understanding. For I want you to understand what really matters, so that you may live pure and blameless lives until the day of Christ's return. May you always be filled with the fruit of your salvation—the righteous character produced in your life by Jesus Christ—for this will bring much glory and praise to God. (Philippians 1:3, 6, 9–11, NLT)

✦ For it is by grace you, [insert child's name], have been saved through faith—and this is not from yourselves, it is the gift of God—not by works, so that no one can boast. For you, [insert child's name], are God's workmanship, created in Christ Jesus to do good works, which God prepared in advance for us to do. (Ephesians 2:8–10, NIV)

✦ May the God of hope fill you, [insert child's name], with all joy and peace as you trust in Him, so that you may overflow with hope by the power of the Holy Spirit. (Romans 15:13, NIV)

✦ I ask God that you, [insert child's name], may know what He wants you to do. I ask God to fill you with the wisdom and understanding the Holy Spirit gives. Then your lives will please the Lord. You will do every kind of good work, and you will know more about God. [Insert child's name], I pray that God's great power will make you strong, and that you will have joy as you wait and do not give up. I pray that you will be giving thanks to the Father. He has made it so you could share the good things given to those who belong to Christ who are in the light. God took us out of a life of darkness. He has put us in the holy nation of His much-loved Son. We have been bought by His blood and made free. Our sins are forgiven through Him. (Colossians 1:9b–14, NLV)

✦ The temptations in your life are no different from what others experience. And God is faithful. He will not allow the temptation to be more than you can stand. When you are tempted, [insert child's name], he will show you a way out so that you can endure. (1 Corinthians 10:13 New, NLT)

✦ It is God who enables you, [insert child's name], to stand firm for Christ. He has commissioned you, and he has identified you as his own by placing the Holy Spirit in your heart as the first installment that guarantees everything he has promised to us. (2 Corinthians 1:21–22, NLT)

✦ The Holy Spirit produces this kind of fruit in your life, [insert child's name]: love, joy, peace, patience, kindness, goodness, faithfulness, gentleness, and self-control. (Galations 5:22, NLT)

✦ May the God of peace make you holy, [insert child's name], in every way, and may your whole spirit and soul and body be kept blameless until our Lord Jesus Christ comes again. God will make this happen, for he who calls you is faithful. (1 Thessalonians 5:23–24, NLT)

✦ May our Lord Jesus Christ Himself and God our Father, who loved us and by his grace gave us eternal comfort and a wonderful hope, comfort you, [insert child's name], and strengthen you in every good thing you do and say. (2 Thessalonians 2:16–17, NLT)

Download your convenient, printable *Blessings to Pray Over Your Children* at MadeToSoarBook.com.

SPEAKER. AUTHOR. COACH

Bring Natalie to Your Church, Conference, or Organization

Natalie knows the importance of choosing the best speaker for your event and audience.

The speaker has the power and responsibility to set the tone and atmosphere for rich, authentic growth and engagement, which can either be transforming or disappointing.

With a vibrant, sincere delivery, she speaks from the heart powered by her intense desire to encourage and love on each and every individual in the room.

Natalie customizes each message or training to meet and exceed her client's expectations with intention to have a positive, lasting impact on your audience.

Contact Natalie today
to begin the conversation!

NatalieDawnHanson.com

You, my friend, were...

Made to Soar!

Don't wait! Take your next step toward transformation, today!

You've read the book, worked through the chapters, and hopefully believe you were, indeed, *Made to Soar*. It can be hard to know how or where to take that first step toward becoming more and more the woman, wife, and mom God created you to be. Especially if you're doing it alone or if faith is new to you. As a gift to you, I've created a *FREE Reference Guide*, based on the chapters of this book, to help lead you on your continued journey toward divine transformation.

Access your *FREE Reference Guide* at

MadeToSoarBook.com

What's the cost of having wings that never unfurl and never soar in the beauty in which they've been designed?

Are You Ready to
Soar,
but could use some help?

If you're ready to soar in the wonder and beauty of your divine purpose ... if you're ready to dive deeper, dream bigger, and become the best version of *you* God created you to be ... if you're ready to live your best life but need someone to help you get there, Natalie would be delighted to work with you.

It's her passion and mission is to encourage, equip, and empower women to rise up in their callings with courage, strength, and confidence so they can live out their purposes with powerful impact and pass on the legacy of faith to the next generation.

Natalie will help you renew and define your purpose, develop goals, work toward dreams, and stay intentional, disciplined, and focused?

To learn more about personal coaching, visit:

MadeToSoarBook.com

And to be Daily Encouraged
Join our Soaring Souls Sisterhood!

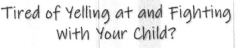

Notes

DEAR FRIENDS, I WANT YOU TO KNOW

1) Hebrews 12:2

INTRODUCTION

1) Al Haskvitz, "The Ultimate Relay Race: The Monarch Butterfly Story" AwesomeStories.com. Nov 10, 2016. Nov 03, 2018. <http://www.awesomestories.com/asset/view/The-Ultimate-Relay-Race-The-Monarch-Butterfly-Story>.

2) Ephesians 2:10

CHAPTER 1

1) Psalm 139:16 (The Message)

2) Genesis 2:16–17b

3) Romans 8:28

CHAPTER 2

1) Amos (The Message)

2) Genesis 2:25

3) Genesis 1:31

4) Genesis 3:7

5) Hebrews 10:17b (The Message)

CHAPTER 3

1) Psalm 139:13–16 (The Message)

2) Luke 10:38–42

CHAPTER 4

1) Romans 8:39b (GNT)

2) John 4:7–10 (The Message)

3) John 4:13–14 (The Message)

4) John 4:25–26

5) 2 Corinthians 5:17

6) Psalm 139:14

7) Genesis 1:27

8) Psalm 139:2–3

9) Galations 5:1

CHAPTER 5

1) Mark 1:17

2) Mark 1:18

3) Matthew 4:21b-22

4) Luke 9:59–62

5) Romans 8:31b

CHAPTER 6

1) Acts 9:3b-4

2) Acts 9:5

3) Acts 9:15

4) Romans 7:25; 8:1–2 (The Message)
5) Proverbs 4:20–22 (The Message)
6) Isaiah 55:3b (The Message)
7) Isaiah 55:8–12 (The Message)
8) Ephesians 3:20
9) Romans 8:28

CHAPTER 7

1) 1 Peter 5:8b
2) Genesis 32:26b
3) James 4:7–10
4) Ephesians 6:14–17
5) Debbie Hadley, "What Do Monarch Butterflies Eat?" February 4, 2019. https://www.thoughtco.com/what-do-monarch-butterflies-eat-1968211
6) SK Films, "The Life Cycle of the Monarch Butterfly." 2012. http://www.flightofthebutterflies.com/life-cycle/.
7) James 1:2–4 (VOICE)
8) Romans 5:3–5
9) John 16:33b

CHAPTER 8

1) Matthew 14:27b
2) Matthew 14:28
3) Matthew 14:29
4) Matthew 14:30b
5) Matthew 14:31a
6) 2 Corinthians 12:7–10 (The Message)
7) 2 Corinthians 12:9b
8) John 10:11
9) Psalm 37:23–24

CHAPTER 9

1) 1 John 4:19
2) Genesis 1:26a, 27–28 (The Message)
3) Malachi 2:15a (The Voice)
4) Deuteronomy 6:1–7 (The Message)
5) Deuteronomy 32:45–47a (The Message)
6) The Center for Youth Ministry Training. *The National Study of Youth and Religion in a Nutshell Making Sense of Teens and "Fake" Christianity.* http://assets.ngin.com/attachments/document/0042/5177/NationalStudyYout_Religion.pdf. 2011
7) The Center for Youth Ministry Training. *The National Study of Youth and Religion in a Nutshell Making Sense of Teens and "Fake" Christianity.* http://assets.ngin.com/attachments/document/0042/5177/NationalStudyYout_Religion.pdf. 2011
8) The Center for Youth Ministry Training. *The National Study of Youth and Religion in a Nutshell Making Sense of Teens and "Fake" Christianity.* http://assets.ngin.com/attachments/document/0042/5177/NationalStudyYout_Religion.pdf. 2011
9) The Center for Youth Ministry Training. *The National Study of Youth and Religion in a Nutshell Making Sense of Teens and "Fake" Christianity.* http://assets.ngin.com/attachments/document/0042/5177/NationalStudyYout_Religion.pdf. 2011
10) Matthew 13:10–13 (The Message)
11) Romans 12:2a
12) Romans 12:2b

CHAPTER 10

1) 1 Corinthians 6:19–20
2) Mark 12:29–31
3) 1 Thessalonians 5:23–24 (The Message)

CHAPTER 11

1) John 14:16 (NLT)
2) Ephesians 3:16 (The Message)
3) Ephesians 1:17b
4) Ephesians 1:19a
5) Ephesians 1:19b-20
6) John 8:2–5 (TPT)
7) John 8:6b (TPT)
8) John 8:7b (TPT)
9) John 8:10–11 (TPT)
10) Romans 8:1
11) Psalm 147:3
12) Romans 3:23–24
13) 1 Peter 2:9 (The Message)
14) 1 Corinthians 15:58
15) Hebrews 10:22–24 (The Voice)
16) Ephesians 2:8–10 (The Message)
17) 2 Corinthians 9:6
18) Awakin.org. Interview call with Howard Glasser. March 19, 2016. http://www.awakin.org/calls/249/howard-glasser/.
19) Romans 2:4 (TLB)
20) Galations 5:22
21) Proverbs 22:6 (AMP)
22) James Urton, "Scientists Crack Secrets of the Monarch Butterfly's Internal Compass."

April 14, 2016. http://www.washington.edu/
news/2016/04/14/scientists-crack-secrets-of-the-monarc
h-butterflys-internal-compass/.

CHAPTER 12

1) John 21:21
2) John 21:22b
3) Acts 2:42–44a & 46a (The Voice)
4) Ephesians 4:1–7 (The Message)
5) https://www.awesomestories.com/asset/
   view/The-Ultimate-Relay-Race-The-Monarc
   h-Butterfly-Story.
6) Jules Poirier, "The Magnificent Migrating
   Monarch." December 1, 1997. https://
   answersingenesis.org/animal-behavior/migration/
   the-magnificent-migrating-monarch/.
7) Mark 10:27b (NIV)

CHAPTER 13

1) Christine Caine, *Unstoppable* (Grand Rapids:
   Zondervan, 2014), p.18.
2) Christine Peterson, "The Four Biggest Hazards Facing
   Monarch Butterflies, and How You Can Help." April
   5, 2016. https://blog.nature.org/science/2016/04/05/
   the-four-biggest-hazards-facing-monarc
   h-butterflies-and-how-you-can-help/.
3) World Wildlife Fund, "Monarch Butterfly Populations
   are on the Rise." 2019. https://www.worldwildlife.org/
   stories/monarch-butterfly-populations-are-on-the-rise.
4) Luke 2:35b (NIV)
5) Luke 2:19 & Luke 2:51b

6) Andy Stanley, *The Butterfly Effect: How Your Life Matters* (Illinois, Simple Truths, LLC, 2009), 107.

DEAR FRIEND, YOU WERE MADE TO SOAR

1) John 8:32 (NLT)

CPSIA information can be obtained
at www.ICGtesting.com
Printed in the USA
JSHW011513011219
2721JS00002B/4